JIM BOB FROM CARTER

In the Shadow of my Former Self

By Jim Bob

First published in Great Britain in 2019 by Cherry Red
Books (a division of Cherry Red Records), Power Road
Studios, 114 Power Road, London W4 5PY
© James Morrison 2019

ISBN: 978-1-909454-71-2

Layout by Nathan Eighty (nathan.eighty@gmail.com)
Cover designed by Nathan Eighty and Mark Reynolds from
a Jim Bob idea. Illustrations by Mark Reynolds. Back cover
photograph of Jim Bob by Paul Heneker.

Lyrics for 'The Ballad of Rancid Mortimer' written by Ward
and White and printed courtesy of Danielle Ward and
Martin White. Lyrics for 'The Only Living Boy in New Cross'
and 'Sheriff Fatman' printed courtesy of Universal Music.
Lyrics for 'The Queen Visits Stereoworld', 'Rock 'n' roll
Relay Race' and 'Victim' printed courtesy of Cherry Red
Songs.

BY THE SAME AUTHOR:

Biography/memoir:
'Goodnight Jim Bob – On the Road with Carter The
Unstoppable Sex Machine'

Fiction:
'Storage Stories' and 'Driving Jarvis Ham'

As J.B. Morrison:
'The Extra Ordinary Life of Frank Derrick, Age 81' and
'Frank Derrick's Holiday Of A Lifetime'

Dedicated to Les

Just in case

CHANGING LANES

So, this happened on Twitter:

Jim Bob *@mrjimbob . 5m Apologies for my recent Twitter silence but I have been incredibly busy. The great news is that I am now absolutely delighted to be able to announce that I have just discovered the cure for cancer.*

Dennis *@Snafflebold_Den69 . 3m Lol. Love Carter USM. Never forget you beating Schofield up at the Brit Awards! #YouFatBastard*

I'm joking of course. I haven't even been working on a cure for cancer. I've not put in the necessary laboratory hours or had sufficient training if I'm honest. Quite frankly my fake tweet is a massive insult to all the hardworking oncologists and scientists who have. Besides, @Snafflebold_Den69 doesn't exist, and last year when I made him up, my announcement contained too many characters for a tweet. It is however, an exaggerated version of something that happens to me almost every time I announce a solo record or a new novel. If I were to cure cancer or win the London Marathon or be the first man to walk on Mars *@Snafflebold_Den69*'s reaction would probably be the same. I must admit it could be a little frustrating at first. I felt like *@Snafflebold_Den69* wouldn't allow me to move on. He was constantly telling me *hey girlfriend, stay in your lane*. But now it's a reaction that's so expected, that I'm disappointed when it doesn't happen.

In the twenty-one years since Carter The Unstoppable Sex Machine first broke up, I've released eleven solo albums, I've performed on my own, in a disco-pop-punk band and with an orchestra. I've written songs for Ian Dury and for a West End pantomime and I've had four novels published. I've even appeared in a musical. But if at any time, I was ever to forget I was Jim Bob from Carter, Dennis, or someone like him, was always there to remind me. Look at this poster:

Okay, it says Jim Bob *of* Carter rather than *from*, and in my memory of the poster, the Carter logo was a lot bigger. Proportionately though, as in, compared to the Jim Bob logo, it *is* bigger. Still, at least they've included my name. In 1999, my disco-pop-punk band Jim's Super Stereoworld turned up at a gig in York to find the entirety of the publicity for the gig consisted of a blackboard on the pavement outside the venue with just the words written in chalk: 'Tonight: Carter The Unstoppable Sex Machine'.

I hope this doesn't make me sound bitter or ungrateful. I promise you I'm not. I'm guilty of the same poster clickbait myself. Surely the title of this book is intended to make more people buy it. Incidentally,[1] I recently watched a television news item about Paul McCartney's new solo album and the presenter referred to him as Paul McCartney from The Beatles, just in case Paul or anyone else had forgotten.

At least me and Paul from The Beatles can be proud of our heritage. We aren't **Insert band member here** from **Insert band name here**. Imagine that indignity. Every time I'm reminded by *@Snafflebold_Den69* or on a gig poster that I've strayed out of my lane, even when I pull over to sit on the hard shoulder and do nothing for a while, at least – to paraphrase Oasis, who in turn were misquoting French philosopher Bernard De Chartres – at least I'm sitting on the hard shoulder of giants. *Boom-tish*. That right there is the quality of the jokes you can expect if you continue to read this book. Shit puns, ladies and gentlemen. Jim Bob from Carter, doing exactly what I say on my tin.

Before I started writing this book I dug out my old pocket diaries and compiled a list of gig dates and places I'd been to in the years following the break-up of Carter. It was the same way I began work on my first book *Goodnight Jim Bob - On the Road With Carter The Unstoppable Sex Machine*. There were no insights in the diaries. No clues as to how I was feeling at the time, no thoughts or opinions, just the name of the town and maybe the venue or the recording studio where I needed to be on that particular day. The diaries didn't even tell me what it was I was doing in the studio or how that day's gig had gone. So I'm afraid I've had to rely a lot on my memory. I say 'afraid' because my memory is not what it used to be. This memory lapse may lead to errors in the story but with a bit of luck, your memory will be as unreliable as mine and so you'll have no choice but to take my word for whatever it is I'm suggesting happened at any given point – like that time, about halfway through the book, when Fruitbat is abducted by aliens.

I did do a bit of research. I looked under the bed and emailed Les twice for a start and I found some reviews and news stories to help jog my memory when I was really stuck. The period immediately following

---

1 The first of many incidentallys. And the first footnote as well. I thought we would have at least made it past the prologue.

the break-up of Carter, for instance, was a time I particularly struggled to recall for some reason. And then I found ten fat folders under the bed. They contained pages and pages of faxes from my manager and from various record companies, sent in the years I was having particular trouble remembering. I opened the folders, expecting the Dead Sea Scrolls to spill out before me, but instead I found sheet after sheet of near blank thermal fax paper. Oh well, you know me. I'm not one to let the fax get in the way of a good story.

I played fewer gigs in the years following Carter and consequently there are more blank pages in my old diaries. 1998's is so blank that it looks like I couldn't find a pen. And in 2003 I lost my diary when I was mugged. I had to ask my friends what they remembered from that year. They remembered so little that I started to wonder if being mugged might be the most exciting thing to have happened to me in 2003. I began to rethink this whole project. Was it possible that I'd used up all my good show business anecdotes in my first book? What if I didn't have enough material to justify a sequel? I'd already written about what it was like to be in a band on tour: all the stuff about riders and service stations, hotel rooms and tour bus toilet etiquette. And even if in the unlikelihood that while I was writing this I was invited on to a music awards show on live television, I was far too nice to wrestle the presenter to the floor.

I shared my doubts and concerns about the book with my manager Marc. He reassured me that the book would be like *Bouncing Back*, Alan Partridge's autobiographical account of how he bounced back after losing his job at the BBC, leading him to a breakdown and an addiction to Toblerone. I too, Marc said, could write about my attempts to revive my flagging career with various records and bands, books, film scripts and other projects. The difference would be that Alan Partridge doesn't actually bounce back and the many unsold copies of his book are pulped. I on the other hand *would* bounce back – as an award-winning author, prolific solo artist and eventually with the (spoiler alert) successful reformation of Carter. Needless to say, I really would have had the last laugh.

DISCLAIMERS, DENIALS AND GET OUT CLAUSES

Any mistakes you find are deliberate. If I say something happened in December when it actually happened in January, or if I use the number five when it should be four, any such errors have been placed there on purpose, to give the pedants something to do, keeping them busy and stopping them from revolting. That was a pun. There will be puns. If like me you don't like puns, now is probably a good time to put the book down and walk away. I really do hate puns by the way. At one point in this story

I'll go as far as to say that I feel the same way about puns now as Albert Einstein came to feel about his part in the invention of the atom bomb. I had at first said that it was J. Robert Oppenheimer not Einstein who lived to regret the bomb. But I looked it up and found out that was a popular misconception and Oppenheimer's regret was a bit more complex and nuanced than that. There will be other moments in this book where I'll either not bother checking if other such facts are correct or not. I might even leave them in after I've found out they're wrong, because it's better for the story or for the joke. Don't take anything for granted. Think of this as a very long Wikipedia page in need of a hell of lot of citation.

Expect contradictions. For example, when I started writing I was certain that I didn't like the Carter album *I Blame the Government*. A few months later I had to listen to it because it was being included in a box set of Carter records. I realised that it wasn't half as bad as I'd remembered it. I thought about going back and rewriting my earlier opinion but decided not to. Even if it's not how I feel right now, it's how I felt at the time. It makes this whole experience more of a journey. Yes, I one hundred and ten percent just said journey.

RECURRING CHARACTERS

There are a few people who will appear in this story almost as much as me. These include: Fruitbat from Carter obviously. Sometimes I'll refer to him as Les. Marc Ollington is mentioned far too much for my liking. Especially as I know he's really going to love that. Even though he will suggest that I remove some of his mentions, his modesty will be bullshit. Marc Ollington is my manager. He became Carter's manager in 2007. Mister Spoons (real name Neil Witherow) is my sort of roadie. I'll explain a bit more about Neil in a footnote later on. Chris T-T (Christopher Thorpe-Tracey) is/was a wonderful singer and songwriter. He also plays on most of my recent records and we've toured together loads. Marc, Neil and Chris have been collectively known as Team Jim Bob for a number of years now. I can't imagine my life without any of them, and not just because I can't drive while they all can. Right. I think that's it. In the words of Ian Dury on the *Live Stiffs Live* album version of 'Sex & Drugs & Rock & Roll': "better start the fucking thing".

JIMTY McJIMFACE

Goodnight Jim Bob - On the Road With Carter The Unstoppable Sex Machine ends on a sunny August 4 in 1997 at the Rookery café on Streatham Common, where I meet with Fruitbat and we agree to break up the band. We sit at a wooden bench table outside the cafe and have a coffee and a Kit Kat and then we walk through the Rookery, looking at the flowers and the trees, passing under leaf-covered arches and through sun-dappled walkways and around the ornamental pond and the massive goldfish in the murky water. We stroll past the sundial that I mistook for a drinking fountain when I was six-years old, jumping up to get a drink and cutting my lip open on the thick brass shadow caster at the sundial's centre. We carry on through the rookery to the adjacent gardens and walk past the tennis courts and head up the hill to the woods where I let off bangers and genies when I was fourteen. By the time we return to the café for a Cornetto, Fruitbat is called Les, I'm just Jim and Carter The Unstoppable Sex Machine are no more.

I don't know exactly when I'd decided I didn't want to be in the band anymore, maybe at one of the low points on the final UK tour, in Kidderminster for instance, when we had to argue with the promoter because we didn't want to play inside a cage on the stage like in the *Blues Brothers*. Or maybe it was as we walked offstage at the London Astoria (currently a building site for the Crossrail development) because somebody threw a full can of beer at my head. Or it could have been at any of the nights on that same tour when I hid in my tour bus bunk between soundcheck and stage time, pretending to be asleep to avoid conversation with my fellow band members. Or perhaps I'd given up on Carter on that final tour of America when I frequently wished I'd been in the support band Thin Lizard Dawn because I thought they were better than us. I became so desperate on that American tour to tell everyone how I was feeling but was such a coward that I'd drop hints about it on stage instead, singing the opening lines of 'My Way' at the end of 'Sheriff Fatman' and introducing songs with 'this is the last time you'll ever hear this' and so on.

Bands don't bother splitting up these days, do they? They have long breaks and indefinite hiatuses instead. They go on sabbaticals and take time out for side projects or to spend more time with their families like disgraced MPs. They leave things open-ended. The chickens.

I was dreading telling everyone else what we'd decided on Streatham Common. I felt like I had to inform relatives of a death in the family or sack a loyal employee who'd been at the company for forty years. It isn't as easy as Alan Sugar would have you believe. We had to tell the rest of the band first and our manager Adrian. We had to inform our still quite new record label Cooking Vinyl. They must have lost any hope of recouping the advance they'd just given us. And then we had to break the news to our live agent and our publisher and our accountant and our lawyer. And of course we had to tell @Snafflebold_Den69 and all the other Carter fans. At least there were fewer of those than there would have been in previous years. Every cloud.

In spite of the dreaded prospect of having to tell everyone Carter were no more, I left Streatham Common feeling liberated, thinking about what lay ahead and what I was going to do next and how exciting it was that it could literally be anything at all. The world was an oyster. I was already making mental lists of what my new name was going to be. Thinking about what would look good on all the gold and platinum discs and Grammy Awards I was going to be presented with. I wasn't going to be Jim Bob anymore, I was sure of that, let alone Jim Bob from Carter. I was going to shake the Carter Etch-a-Sketch and start again.

I've always enjoyed thinking of names for bands. The first one I remember was Prairie Dog. I was fourteen. We sounded a bit like Bad Company. I was the lead singer. I had a leather Stetson. All the other band members were imaginary and I got on with all of them. Our logo was great. It was hand-drawn, coloured-in with felt tip pens and surrounded by desert and cactuses. I think a snake was involved. A few years later, my band was called The Ballpoints. We would eventually rehearse and play gigs and make demo tapes but at first The Ballpoints was just me and my stepbrother Derek and only existed inside our heads. We gatecrashed sixth-form discos and told girls we were in a band. "We're called The Ballpoints," we'd say. "We sound like The Monkees." I was the singer and Derek played bass. He always wore sunglasses and called himself Mister X. He carried a toy gun. I had pink shoes and a small brown suitcase. Poly Styrene from X-Ray Spex once cycled past me and said "cool shoes". It's still one of the greatest moments of my life. The Ballpoints had a neat logo of course. This time created with Letraset I stole from my job at an advertising firm. We had badges as well. Not hundreds of them. Just two. One for me and one for Derek. I don't think the real Ballpoints ever lived up to their mythological potential. To be honest, once a band is named it's pretty much downhill from there. In an ideal world I'd like to come up with a name, design the logo and split up.

I feel a bit sorry for bands formed on television talent shows. The closest they get to take part in choosing their name is to select their least hated option from a very short list of three: the year they were born, the postcode where they pretend to share a house or the number of members in the band. Even then, the name is still not their final decision. It has to first be put to a focus group and then signed off by Gary Barlow and David Walliams. The solo artists are all called Martin, Susan or Alison.

When I got home from my meeting with Les on Streatham Common, I turned my mental list of potential band names into a physical one. Unfortunately I haven't kept the physical list. Or if I have I must have faxed it to myself. I do remember starting by writing down variations on my birth name that I hadn't already used. I'd been Jim and Jamie and Jim Bob so far and I wasn't keen on Jimmy. I didn't want to be James because I associated it with being bullied at school. And that was just by the teachers. They loved reciting A.A. Milne's 'Disobedience' poem to me when I did anything the slightest bit wrong – *James James Morrison Morrison, Weatherby George Dupree*. Also, James Morrison was my indoors name. It was the name I used in music shops and banks to avoid having to constantly explain that yes, my name was actually Jim Morrison and no, I didn't used to be in The Doors. Nine years later of course, just as bank clerks and music shopkeepers were starting to be too young to have heard of The Doors, along came UK pop-soul sensation James Morrison. I suppose I should have been flattered when I was well into my forties and an HSBC cashier genuinely believed I could be my twenty-nine year old namesake. A mistake once repeated – and keep this to yourself – by the Performing Rights Society, when they paid me £24 in royalties for writing his worldwide smash hit single 'You Give Me Something'[2].

There was another pop James I was once mistaken for. It was in 2008 at an all day charity gig in the back room of a London pub. I'd just come off stage after playing half an hour of solo acoustic Carter and Jim Bob songs and I got into a conversation with a bloke who told me at great length how much he loved my band. He was particularly fond of our appearance at Reading Festival in 1991 and his favourite moment was when we got the whole audience to sit down.

Other famous people I've been mistaken for include Jake Shillingford from My Life Story. It was in the bar after one of their reunion shows in 2006. Five different people spoke to me that night thinking I was Jake, including My Life Story's keyboard player, who'd just spent almost two hours onstage with him. Another time, I was upstairs at the Kentish Town Forum and a woman started talking to me, really bigging me up and telling me how much she admired my words. After about ten minutes I realised she thought I was the poet Murray Lachlan Young. It wasn't a massive problem until she asked me for my autograph. I hope I spelled it right.

---

2 Twenty-four pounds.

My new stage name would come to me eventually one night – not in a dream, I'm not Sting. It was when I was watching a video of *Boogie Nights*. In the film, Don Cheadle, who plays porn star and stereo salesman Buck Swope, was talking about his dream of opening a hi-fi shop called Buck's Super Stereo World. Immediately everything fell into place. Not just my band's name but the style of music we were going to make, the disco beats and the light show and how it would be a band rather than a solo act, the entire concept. The clothes, the haircuts, the prosthetic penis…

WELCOME TO JIM'S SUPER STEREOWORLD

Carter briefly reformed in the latter part of 1997 and then again at the beginning of 1998, first to finish recording and then to promote our posthumous final album *I Blame the Government*. If telling people about the break-up of the band was informing them of a death, then mixing and mastering the record was like selecting the coffin and the flowers. The reviews when it was released were the autopsy. The interviews were the inquest. And so on.

We started recording the album in December 1996 at the House in the Woods, the same residential studio where we'd recorded the previous album *A World Without Dave*. What I remember most about the House in the Woods was playing bar billiards in the evenings and somebody rescuing an injured bat. I also remember watching the cook open the oven one morning and being engulfed in a ball of backdraft flames. I remember sitting silently in the dark every night, waiting for the badgers to appear on the grass outside and I remember when we left, that Fruitbat forgot his favourite hat. I remember very little about what we were actually supposed to be in the studio for.

I mention the hat because, as we were leaving the House in the Woods at the end of our recording session, we passed the next band arriving at the start of theirs. We didn't know The Bluetones and we exchanged moody British indie band nods as we passed each other on the threshold. More than twenty years later, when I finally got to meet Mark Morriss from The Bluetones, he told me how he'd found Fruitbat's hat in one of the bedrooms at the House in the Woods and had worn it for the next four years.

After a few gigs and a long Christmas break we went into Simon Painter's new studio to finish the album. There was no cook, no kitchen, no bar billiards and no bats or badgers. There wasn't even running water at Simon's studio. To get to the toilet we had to sneak past some terrifying dogs at the house next door and then cross a muddy road to the neighbouring farm, where there was a portable toilet in a field. I always tried to make sure I went in the morning before leaving home.

We were in and out of Simon's studio for a while, interrupting the album's recording to play the live shows where it would all start to go tits up for Carter. In between tour bus fights and airport arguments we returned to Simon's studio to try and finish the record. And then we had to go to America and by the time we came back Carter had split up. We still needed to finish mixing *I Blame the Government* though. I imagine we didn't care too much about the album by that point and just wanted to get it over and done with.

All things considered, it's perhaps not surprising *I Blame the Government* is my least favourite Carter record. I think it would have worked better as a collection of unreleased rarities rather than as a proper Carter album, especially as it was the last one. No band wants a *Greatest Hits* collection to come out one day with all the songs placed in chronological order, knowing that nobody would ever quite make it to the end of the CD.

Apart from 'Girls Can Keep a Secret' I couldn't really tell you what any of the songs on *I Blame the Government* are about. Some of the lyrics are actually a bit embarrassing. They read like they've been written for a biopic about Carter but the filmmakers couldn't get permission to use any of our actual songs and had to employ someone to write some in a similar style. For example, 'The Man Who Bought the World' is supposed to be about Rupert Murdoch but there's none of the lyrical attention to detail of say, 'Sheriff Fatman' or 'The Only Living Boy in New Cross'.

Whenever Carter played at The Loft club in Berlin, we'd always walk around the corner to the Irish Bar afterwards. We'd drink Paddy Irish whiskey and eat cheese toasties served in little baskets (great band) into the wee small hours (another great band). We went to the Irish Bar after signing our record deal with Chrysalis Records. One time I met this bloke there who told me about a long essay he'd written, annotating and deconstructing the lyrics to 'The Only Living Boy in New Cross' for a German audience. I really wish I'd asked him for a copy of his essay so that I could reproduce it here. I remember it being a more detailed version of this sort of thing:

THE ONLY LIVING BOY IN NEW CROSS
The title is a pun on the Simon & Garfunkel song, 'The Only Living Boy in New York'

Hello, good evening and welcome to nothing much
Hello, good evening and welcome was the catchphrase of British television host David Frost. It was how he opened his shows in the 1960s and '70s.
A no holds barred half nelson and the loving touch
These are wrestling terms. No holds barred means that all wrestling moves are allowed. The half nelson is one of those wrestling moves
The comfort and the joy of feeling lost with the only living boy in New Cross

Fill another suitcase with another haul

'Another Suitcase in Another Hall' is a song from the Tim Rice and Andrew Lloyd Webber musical 'Evita'

Of hotel towels and toothpaste and the bathroom wall

Then wipe the lipstuck heart and flowers from the glass and chrome

To write on a mirror with lipstick. Lipstuck – past tense of lipstick application. A Jim Bob made up word

Take five or six hot baths and showers and come on home

To the comfort and the joy of feeling lost with the only living boy in New Cross

I've teamed up with the hippies now I've got my fringe unfurled

Like the hippies letting their hair down, the singer is allowing his famous, award winning spaghetti fringe to flow free. Unfurling it like a flag

I want to give peace, love and kisses out to this whole stinking world

The gypsies, the travellers and the thieves

From the song 'Gypsies, Tramps & Thieves' by Cher

The good, the bad, the average and unique

A nod to the Sergio Leone Spaghetti western 'The Good, the Bad and the Ugly'

The grebos, the crusties, the goths and the only living boy in New Cross

Grebos were the fans of a late 1980s, early 1990s subgenre of alternative rock. Influenced by punk rock, electronic dance music, hip hop and psychedelia, played by grebo bands such as Pop Will Eat Itself and Gaye Bykers on Acid. Crusty was a term used in the UK to refer to members of another subculture in the early 1990s. Related to the New Age travellers movement. Goths are the darkly-dressed followers of goth music. Beginning in the UK in the 1980s, goth is a punk influenced style of music, often with dark or mystical overtones.

Eyes down and I'll keep you up to date. Two fat ladies in 1988

Bingo caller references. Eyes-down is said by the bingo caller at the start of a game (Eyes down for a full house). Two fat ladies is the bingo nickname for the number 88, because it looks like two fat ladies standing next to each other

The safe sixteen lovers who lied

A reference to a debate at the time the song was written, about whether the age of consent for same sex relationships should be lowered to sixteen. Under age lovers would lie about their age to avoid prosecution

Purley's queen and mother makes five
Pearly queens are part of a cockney tradition, wearing clothes decorated with mother-of-pearl buttons. Purley is a southern part of Croydon. 'And Mother Makes Five' was a British ITV sitcom starring Wendy Craig

Butchered bakers and deaf and dumb waiters
From the nursery rhyme 'Rub-A-Dub-Dub' (Three men in a tub. And who do you think they be? The butcher, the baker, the candlestick maker…) A dumb waiter is a small lift, usually used to transport food from the kitchen up to the restaurant

Marble Arch criminals and clause 28'ers
Play on words. An arch criminal is a particularly skilled criminal. Marble Arch is an area of London at the West end of Oxford Street. Clause 28, AKA Section 28 was a 1988 amendment to a local government act, stating that local authorities "shall not intentionally promote homosexuality or publish material with the intention of promoting homosexuality" or "promote the teaching in any maintained school of the acceptability of homosexuality as a pretended family relationship".

Authors, authors, plastered outcasts
Theatre audiences would shout Author! Author! at the end of a play, in praise of the writer and to encourage them to come onstage, take a bow and receive the applause and plaudits and shit. 'Author! Author!' is also the title of a film starring Al Pacino. Plastered outcasts is a play on 'plaster cast'. Plastered is slang for drunk.

Locked up daughters, rock 'n' roll stars
More wordplay. 'Lock up your Daughters' was the name of an old musical and also something twats would say when arriving in a town, implying that they would be so irresistible to all the young females who lived there that the girls' parents should probably lock them up until the twats had left.

Goodbye Rudy, David and Rosie
A cheeky reference to Carter being sued by the publishers of The Rolling Stones for using the words 'Goodbye Ruby Tuesday' in the chorus of the single 'After the Watershed', the single released not long before 'The Only Living Boy in New Cross'

Abraham and Julianne and anyone that knows me
The gypsies, the travellers and the thieves
The good, the bad, the average and unique
The grebos, the crusties and you and I
Hello, good evening, welcome and goodbye
David Frost would close his shows by saying 'Hello, good evening and farewell'.

Nowadays there are hundreds of lyric websites that do a similar job with just a few clicks of a mouse but back in the dark ages before Britpop and Deliveroo, you had to travel to an Irish bar in Berlin. It was flattering that someone should take the time and effort to do such a thing and I wonder how well it would have worked for some of the other Carter songs. I'm not suggesting I'd like to sit in a German bar drinking Irish whiskey listening to a line-by-line exposition of every Carter song ever written[3]. But if such a thing was to happen, I imagine the experience would peter out towards the end. Just like that chronological Greatest Hits album.

Another fun thing to do with my puns would be to correct them all. This happened with the title of the Japanese collection of Carter cover versions *This is the Sound of an Eclectic Guitar*, which was corrected and released as *This is the Sound of an Electric Guitar*. And I remember when the first edited proof of *Goodnight Jim Bob* came back from the editor, the chapter *The Loneliness of the Long Distance Punner* had been changed to *The Loneliness of the Long Distance Runner*. In a way puns could be viewed as mistakes or typos I suppose. Somebody really should correct all the Carter puns. But who in their right mind, would take on such a pointless and soulless task?

Dennis *@Snafflebold_Den69 . 2m. It should be Twenty Four *Hours* From *Tulsa*, and it's The Taking of *Pelham* 123. And it isn't Billy's Smart Circus, it's Billy *Smart's. Plus, Surfin' U.S.A. not USM. #Youfatbastard*

---

3 I would

ENOUGH OF THE POLITICS

After the release of *I Blame the Government*, I had the first of many meetings with the record label Cooking Vinyl to discuss my potential solo career. I had a new band name – Jim's Super Stereoworld – and the meetings usually began with me playing the label my latest demo version of what would one day be the first Jim's Super Stereoworld single 'Bonkers in the Nut'. Every time I returned to Cooking Vinyl with a new version of the song, the arrangement would have become slightly more ridiculous than before. By the time I'd finished and released the song as a single with Fierce Panda (Cooking Vinyl must have had enough of me) it featured whistling, military snares and timpani drums, 'Leader of the Pack' style call-and-response backing vocals, scratchy vinyl record sounds, a bicycle bell, a harp, explosions, more whistling, an opera singer, at least one key change and a chorus of 'When the Saints Go Marching in'.

There are no guitars on the record though. Apart from some light acoustic strumming on the slow songs, there'd be no guitars on the first Jim's Super Stereoworld album either. I presume I was trying to distance myself from my old band. A shaking of the Carter Etch-a-Sketch that was also evident in the Jim's Super Stereoworld lyrics. Apart from ditching the puns I also clearly wasn't in the mood for politics and social commentary anymore. This new direction led somebody in the audience at our first ever Glasgow show, to shout out halfway though the gig, with pinpoint sarcasm, after yet another upbeat disco pop song: 'Enough of the politics. *Play some more pop!*'

'Bonkers in the Nut' was the first music I'd recorded without Fruitbat since 1979. I wished I'd paid just a little more attention during those eighteen years in the studio. For the first few weeks after the break-up of Carter I had to keep phoning Les to ask him how to plug things in and make sounds come out of them. To the best of my knowledge he didn't feel the need, either then, or at any time since, to phone me for any of my technical advice.

Les gave me a small mixing desk and the two Carter live Adat tape machines (I'm sorry if this is getting a bit technical) and the same Atari computer that we'd previously used for the Club Carter mailing list database. I bought the Korg M1 synth keyboard from Carter's producer Simon Painter. It was the keyboard we'd used on the first three albums. Even when we'd stopped using the sounds inside the keyboard we still used it as the master keyboard, which if I understand it correctly is something to do with *Doctor Who*. I've still got the Korg M1. It weighs a ton and doesn't work anymore and I'm always stubbing my toe on it. I would get rid of it but it's too full of history. The bass line on 'Sheriff Fatman' came out of that big old keyboard. It's like John Lennon's white piano that he wrote 'Imagine' on, or that two-string guitar made out of beer cans and a mop that Seasick Steve pretends to have written all those Seasick Steve songs on.

By the time 'Bonkers in the Nut' was finally released, my bedroom studio had fully evolved into 'Stereoworld'. It was now a vast space, way too big to realistically fit in my house. Luckily my imagination had room to spare and Stereoworld quickly became a hub of activity and creativity, always full of interesting people doing interesting things. Leon Knight opened a Stereoworld record shop called Leon Knight's Record Shack and invested huge sums of imaginary money into me and my band. DJ Feltpen and Bubblegum were Stereoworld's resident DJs and graffiti artists, and star-crossed lovers Evelyn and John let me write a song about them for the first album: 'My Name is John (And I Want You Back)'. I also wrote songs about Stereoworld's most loveable guy Ray of Light, The George Dong Singers and a man called Kenny who worked in the Stereoworld office. The George Dong Singers were a back-up vocal group who'd all met when they were working in the porn movie industry. They sing the backing vocals on 'Bonkers in the Nut' and also on the first album. Any suggestion that George Dong, Lucky Maguire, Suki Iksander and Bam Bam were in fact my girlfriend, Fruitbat, Fruitbat's girlfriend and Fruitbat's brother Brian is bullshit.

When I wasn't writing songs about my new imaginary friends I wrote about some of the crazy shit that went on at Stereoworld, such as the 'Miss Stereoworld' beauty pageant and the time the Queen and Prince Charles came to visit the studio. A bit of the old Carter politics managed to find its way into the last line.

THE QUEEN VISITS STEREOWORLD

There's a black limo outside the studio
And I've had to change my shirt
For the Queen has come and she's brought her son
And they want to see us work
So we scrubbed and cleaned
For our lovely Queen
And we put some fish in the pond
We had to get the desk fixed so she could help us mix
Our new song then the Queen sang along
Sha la la la la
Then she bid farewell

To the familiar smell
Of the freshly painted paint
I would have bent my knee to her majesty
But I cannot be what I ain't

I also wrote a song about the Stereoworld sports day. An annual event when pop stars would take part in three-legged races, egg and spoon races and so on. I recorded a song about the 'Rock 'n' Roll Relay Race', for the CD version of 'Bonkers in the Nut'.

ROCK 'N' ROLL RELAY RACE

Bowie takes the baton and he hands it to the King
Who passes it to Beck who hands it on to Fatboy Slim
Fatboy takes the corner with athletic grace and poise
And passes on the baton to a waiting Beastie Boys
The Beasties take a flyer and the finish is in sight
Via Nicky Wire, Elton John and Barry White
Barry sees a young Louise and passes it to her
Then David Essex, Björk and Blur
Jacko takes the baton and he passes it to me
And I run straight on through the tape
And home to victory.

A rock and pop sports day is on my list of *Dragons' Den* pitches, along with *Indie Aqua Aerobics* and *Jim Bob's Annual Hootenanny*, a New Year's Eve TV show hosted by me and featuring guest vocalists and musicians. Instead of the usual Tom Joneses and Beverley Knights the singers will be Niall from the Sultans of Ping, Paul from The Frank & Walters and James from EMF. They'll be accompanied by me on a boogie-woogie piano, which I have no idea how to play. We'll film it in July. I'm looking for a £500,000 investment for a twenty per cent stake in the company

It was pointed out to me recently how many of the competitors in the 'Rock 'n' Roll Relay Race' have died since I wrote the song. I certainly hadn't planned on it being quite so prophetic. I'd hate to be thought of as some sort of musical Nostradamus. At the end of 2016, a year that so many beloved and famous people died – David Bowie and my mum went on the same day – I was on tour and every night I would talk onstage about all the deaths. It's nice to have a theme. At a gig in Darwen I suggested having a live Twitter feed projected behind me, so that we could keep up to date with whoever went during the gig. I then 'joked' about which popular celebrity or national treasure that might be. When

I came offstage, I looked at my phone and saw that Andrew Sachs from *Fawlty Towers* had died. I felt terrible.

I often say things on stage that I regret. Back in 1990, I famously called the manager of a polytechnic in a city that shall remain nameless, the biggest cunt in Leicester. He sued us for slander and defamation of character. More recent examples have been more embarrassing than slanderous. Like in 2003 when I was onstage in Wigan and couldn't think of anything to say and resorted to taking the piss out of popular or famous locals. The only people I knew of who came from Wigan were The Verve and Starsailor. The groans from the audience were louder than I would have expected and there was a definite sharp intake of collective breath when I was rude about the singer from Starsailor. It turned out I was the only person in the venue who didn't know that Carolyn from The Atomic Hound Dog, the band who'd been on just before me, was James from Starsailor's sister.

I will say pretty much anything on stage for comic effect or entertainment value. It doesn't even need to be entertaining for the audience. I'm not just my own worst critic, I'm also my own best audience. I've got all my records. Even *I Blame the Government*. And putting my foot in my mouth isn't something I've grown (up) out of. I toured Australia with Pop Will Eat Itself in 2018. In Sydney, the venue was very close to the airport and before the show I was having an outdoors drink and planes kept flying very low and loud overhead. I remarked on this during my set. Saying how awful it would be if a plane crashed into the venue during the gig. The audience's uncomfortable groans only encouraged me. I said that if a plane did hit the building, I hoped it was during the last chorus of 'Sheriff Fatman', because that would look spectacular and would be a great way to end my set. Early the next morning as our latest domestic flight across Australia taxied down the runway, I remembered what I'd said on stage the night before.

There's one other thing I always regret saying onstage but still repeat over and over again. It's practically my catchphrase. When I'm in the middle of a gig and someone shouts out "Where's Fruitbat?" I often say that he's ill, or more often, that he's dead. This happened in Perth on the same 2018 Australian tour. After I'd said it, I felt terrible and guilty as usual and I told everyone that obviously I was only joking. I should have left it at that but instead I said: "Unless he's passed away since I've been on stage of course. In which case, this evening is dedicated to the memory of Fruitbat."

By writing this down in a book I realise I'm taking a huge risk. Allowing for the time it takes for editing and proofreading and for the puns to be corrected and then changed back again and for printing and delivery to the shops, by the time you read this, there's a danger I could come across as the world's most sick idiot. So if in the meantime, God forbid, the unthinkable has happened, I've dedicated this book to Les.

MIKA AYUKAWA FROM TEFLON MOHAIR

The final Stereoworld sports day took place in 2002. Sophie Ellis Bextor won pretty much every event that year. The final letter on the Leon Knight neon light popped not long after and Leon Knight's Record Shack closed down, just missing out on the resurgence in vinyl and cassette sales that might have saved it. Evelyn and John had split up again, this time perhaps for good, Ray of Light found God and moved to Los Angeles and I believe that DJ Feltpen and Bubblegum are now Banksy. Inevitably, The George Dong Singers returned to porn.

Two years after the final JSSW record, I'd start calling myself Jim Bob again and Stereoworld would revert to being just the spare bedroom in my house. I'm writing this there now. But I still worked with a few imaginary people from time to time. Kenny who used to deal with the Stereoworld admin sometimes writes my press releases and replies to enquiries from fans when I want to pretend that I'm too famous to do it myself. And the drumming on the 2005 Jim Bob *Angelstrike!* album is credited to somebody called Mika Ayukawa. Mika appears 'courtesy of Teflon Mohair'. Giving my drum machine a human name was enough to fool one *Angelstrike!* reviewer into commenting on what an improvement a real drummer had made to the sound of my solo records.

Mika Ayukawa didn't exist and neither did his band Teflon Mohair. They were both Marc Ollington fabrications. Marc became my 'manager' (his inverted commas) around 2003. Since then he's entertained and horrified me in equal measures, with his pseudonyms and prank calls to venues that I was just about to play, asking them whether I still had the long fringe and would I be playing 'Sheriff Fatman'. Some of Marc's other sock puppets may crop up later. Doug Hedges for example, who once persistently rang a free but sold out ticket-only gig in Portsmouth, to ask if there was any way he could get a ticket. The venue said unfortunately it was impossible as it was only a small room. Doug Hedges persisted, ringing quite a few times, pleading for a ticket. He eventually offered to pay the venue a thousand pounds if they could get him in. The venue agreed but promised to give the money to charity. On the night of the gig the promoter and the bar staff told us about a peculiar man who kept ringing up, declaring himself to be my biggest fan. They wondered if he would turn up and what he'd look like. Would he turn out to be dangerous? They seemed quite excited by Doug's imminent arrival.

We didn't tell them Doug Hedges was already there and they were talking to him right now.

On the first night of my 2016 'Jim Bob Sings Again' tour I was in the dressing room in Leeds. Chris T-T was playing piano with me and also opening with his own set. He was getting ready to go on when I received an email from Miles Hunt from The Wonder Stuff. Miles put forward the idea that he could play a surprise set at my upcoming Birmingham show and then join me for an encore. He'd already spoken to the promoter, who was up for it, as long as cutting the length of Chris T-T's set wasn't an issue. I made the mistake of telling Chris about the email. It was the first night of the tour and he was about to go onstage and I'd made him feel belittled, convinced that he was going to be bumped down the Birmingham running order. I assured him that I wasn't even considering Miles's offer. As I consoled Chris and desperately tried to think of a tactful and diplomatic way of replying to Miles, Mister Spoons couldn't bear it any longer. He told us that Marc Ollington, bored and alone out on the merch stall at the front of the venue, had set up a fake Miles Hunt Hotmail address and the email was from him.

Two days later in Manchester Chris got an email from the promoter of the following night's show in Devizes. The promoter, who was a friend of Chris's, told him he'd added an opening local support act to the show. Chris was furious. The tour was mostly sold out and it was all working so well and running smoothly, with just me and Chris T-T on the bill. Chris wrote a reply to the promoter, saying that under no circumstances was it okay and that he should cancel the local band immediately. It was only later in the evening, when Chris was telling a friend about Marc's hilarious Miles Hunt prank and then also about the Devizes email he'd received, that Chris's friend suggested he check the authenticity of the Devizes email. That was also from Marc, bored again on the merch stall.

Marc was the only real member of Teflon Mohair. Like all truly great bands, once they had a name and a logo, they chose not to ruin everything by making any music. The original name of the band was Mohair. The word Teflon had to be added later after Marc heard of another band with the same name. He first contacted them to request they change their name. The manager of the other Mohair pointed out that as his Mohair had been around for a long time and had records out and had been played on the radio, if anyone should change their name it shouldn't be them. At the time Marc wrote reviews for Teletext (television faxes) and wrote a five-star rave live review of his version of Mohair's sold out show at Brixton Academy. Marc took a photo of the review on his TV and sent it to the manager of the other Mohair, to prove how famous his version of the band were. At this point the manager of the other Mohair suggested the two bands' respective lawyers should deal with the matter. Short of inventing a fake lawyer, Marc decided to give in and change his band's name to Teflon Mohair. I'm sure that if he had invented an imaginary lawyer, he would have won the case.

Fake people in pop is a tradition that dates back to the nineteen fifties. There was a time when half the people in the music business were fictitious. Colonel Tom Parker, Phil Spector, ABBA, U2's manager. They're all fake. Brian Epstein was just Ringo Starr in a different wig. For those of us without big record labels and fat marketing budgets, fakery can be a necessity. Radio stations are less likely to play your records if you have to deliver them yourself or if it's your name at the bottom of the accompanying letter. Press releases written in the first person go straight in the bin. You'll stand less chance of getting your record reviewed if you admit that it's on your own label. Better to improve your chances by making a record label up and pretending it's staffed by a team of fifty people. The music industry likes go-betweens. If they have to be fake ones then so be it.

And fakery may be the only way left to retain a bit of mystery. Everyone knows the mechanics of pop these days. It's no secret that no one makes any money from record sales and the charts are a farce and Lady Gaga was paid £108 for one million Spotify streams of 'Poker Face'. No one is fooled by miming anymore. You can't get away with singing into thin air on *Top of the Pops* and not just because there's no *Top of the Pops*. Which in itself is another nail in pop's mystery coffin. Half the pop stars now look exactly like their parents. They might as well work in a bank. With David Bowie and Prince both gone, everything is a bit ready-salted crisps. All these pop stars using their real names and going to the toilet and dressing like the rest of us. It's not that there's anything wrong with Martin, Susan and Alison being approachable and down-to-earth but it's nice to think there's still a patch of middle ground left between Liberace and Ed Sheeran. I want to be told to fuck off for asking for a selfie every once in a while. More insincerity and fakery I say. A bit of pretense can even lead to romance. Cue Simon Bates *Our Tune* music.

Chris T-T used to have a live booking agent named Toby Jarvis. Once, during the course of his business, Toby got into an email conversation with Jake Shillingford from My Life Story's representative Helen. Helen and Toby got on well and through their emails they started to flirt a little with each other. All the time Toby didn't know that Helen was in fact Jake and Jake had no idea that he was chatting up Chris T-T.

Incidentally, Toby Jarvis also wrote for *Drowned in Sound* magazine. He wrote the first ever UK review of Decemberists and he reviewed my *Goodnight Jim Bob* book. I've just found the book review online. It's a really nice complimentary review but Toby only gave the book eight

JIM BOB FROM CARTER

out of ten. FFS. I can only presume he docked those two points from the perfect score to maintain the secret of his true identity as one of the author's friends.

In spite of everything I've just said, at the beginning of 1999, with the recording of the debut Jim's Super Stereoworld album almost complete and the first single about to be released, I decided to get some real people involved in the line-up. On one of the rare occasions I left my house, I thought I'd found them.

I was at a West End theatre watching *Slava's Snow Show*. I don't know if you've ever seen it. Google it, buy a ticket, it's amazing. I was spellbound by the troupe of clowns and the strange and funny, poignant otherworld they created on stage. They performed mimes with giant telephones, danced with hat stands, turned beds into boats and filled the theatre with a billion bubbles and with dry ice and enormous balloons. At one point a vast cobweb passed over the heads of the audience like a Mexican wave. And in the middle of the show's dramatic climax — a full on blizzard, accompanied by Carl Orff's 'O Fortuna' at deafening volume – I had an epiphany. It was similar to the one I'd had when I was watching *Boogie Nights*. *This* was what the Jim's Super Stereoworld live show was going to be like. The sad-faced clowns with their red noses, huge floppy-eared hats and big coats were *exactly* the people who I wanted to be in my band.

SEND IN THE CLOWNS

I've heard a lot of stories about how bands formed. Johnny Rotten from the Sex Pistols was apparently asked to join the band because he went into Malcolm McLaren's clothes shop wearing an 'I Hate Pink Floyd' T-shirt. For his audition he sang along to an Alice Cooper song playing on the jukebox. And I remember reading that Terry Hall from Fun Boy Three asked Bananarama to sing on the Fun Boy Three record because he liked the shoes they were wearing in an article in *The Face* magazine. Johnny Marr from the Smiths knocked on Morrissey's front door and asked him if he wanted to form a band with him, as though he was inviting him to come out and play football. Mick Jagger and Keith Richards from The Rolling Stones bonded on a platform at Dartford train station over the Chuck Berry and Muddy Waters records that Mick was carrying. I needed one of those anecdotes.

I bought a copy of *The Face* magazine but Robbie Williams from Take That was on the cover and Mrs Jim Bob immediately set fire to it, so I went down to Crystal Palace station and hung around on the platform, hoping in vain that somebody wearing clown shoes would see me with my armful of Sex Pistols and Kool & the Gang records. I would have gone back to the Piccadilly Theatre and knocked on the stage door to ask if Slava was busy and if he or any of the other clowns knew how to play keyboards or the bass guitar, but the circus had left town. A new play was on at the theatre, and as much as I love Judi Dench, I didn't think she would be right for the band.

So how was I supposed to find new band members? It wasn't as if there was an app for it. If apps even existed in 1999. I couldn't browse thousands of pictures of bass players, swiping left or right until I found the right one[4]. It was too late for me to meet likeminded people at school or college, like Genesis, Queen or Pink Floyd had done and I couldn't start a band with my relatives. It worked for the Partridge Family, the Walker Brothers and The Ramones, but neither of my sisters could play a musical instrument. My mum used to be a singer but I already had a singer.[5]

---

4 I'm looking for £450,000 for a 15% stake in the business.
5 Me, in case you weren't sure.

I found this ad that me and Les took out in the back of either the *NME* or *Melody Maker* when we were looking for band members to join our previous band Jamie Wednesday. It's the one that lists Orange Juice, Frank Sinatra and Donovan, along with G*** G******. I presume we added 'sausages' because we had one word left in the allocated amount of words and we wanted to get our money's worth:

I would have put an ad in the back pages of the music press for Jim's Super Stereoworld band members but if anyone answered the ad, I'd have to meet people I didn't know. I thought about the old music business saying: a stranger is just a Bono who you haven't met yet.[6] And what if I auditioned musicians who seemed great but then turned out to be unsuitable later on? I'd end up having to keep them in the band because I didn't want to hurt their feelings. I would never have the nerve to tell them they weren't suitable. Fruitbat had dealt with any hiring and firing of band members in the past. He was the Sir Alan Sugar of the band, or if you're reading this in America: the Donald Trump.

Every band I'd been in since I'd left school had consisted of me and one or more members of the band that had preceded it, each group morphing into the next one, begatting like Bible characters. Jeepster became The Ballpoints, who then turned into Peter Pan's Playground, who would be the starting point for Jamie Wednesday, who in turn decanted into Carter. I had no other choice. *Snafflebold_Den69* wasn't going to like it, but Carter would have to begat Jim's Super Stereoworld.

Dennis @Snafflebold_Den69 . 9m. 1/2 I thought you said you were going to shake up the Carter etch-a-sketch.
Dennis @Snafflebold_Den69 . 8m 2/2 There were more members of Carter in Jim's Super Stereoworld than there were in the original Carter line-up.
Jim Bob @mrjimbob . 7m You're correct. But the etch-a-sketch thing was how I felt at the time. I suppose I changed my mind.
Dennis @Snafflebold_Den69 . 6m. 2/2 Lol. Like all the times you changed your mind when Carter played their *last ever* gig and then

---

6 I've got nothing against Bono and I'm sure there are worse people to be in a band with. But easy targets are funnier.

announced another one? #justsaying
Jim Bob *@mrjimbob . 5m We only said that it would be our last ever gig one of those times. And stop trying to jump ahead in this story. We haven't got to that bit yet.*
Dennis *@Snafflebold_Den69 . 4m That's the part everyone is interested in though. The book is called Jim Bob of Carter.*
Jim Bob *@mrjimbob . 3m It's actually Jim Bob FROM Carter.*
Dennis *@Snafflebold_Den69 . 2m You were shit after Sheriff Fatman anyway.*
Jim Bob *@mrjimbob . 2m Fuck off Dennis.*
Dennis *@Snafflebold_Den69 . 2m Your making all this up.*
Jim Bob *@mrjimbob . 1m *you're**

Ben Lambert was the first member of Carter to join Jim's Super Stereoworld. Ben played keyboards with Carter during the Polyphonic Spree years. He knew all about synths and samplers and how to plug things in and make sounds come out of them. Ben's Stereoworld stage name was Doctor Ben Lambert, even though he was no more a qualified doctor than I would be when I later discovered the cure for cancer. Ben had, though, taken on the role of my therapist on a number of occasions during the last troubled Carter tour of America. He listened to me drunkenly pour my heart out night after night as I told him just how unhappy I was with everything. Ben, who had to pin me against the wall in a toilet at Dublin Airport a few weeks before the US tour after I'd made one too many drunken idiotic jokes about how posh he was. But still, in spite of knowing what to expect from me when I was at my worst, he agreed to join another band with me.

Salv from S*M*A*S*H* (and also from the Polyphonic Carter) played bass in Jim's Super Stereoworld. We called him DJ Salvatore, presumably because he was working as a DJ at the time. He also compèred a regular Battle of Bands competition at the Mean Fiddler in Harlesden and I went along one night to watch. After one of the bands that sounded exactly like The Jam left the stage, Salv put a Jam record on. That probably tells you everything you need to know about Salv. That and the time in Pizza Hut he asked the waitress for some olive oil. A few minutes later she returned with a small bowl. Salv dipped his fingers into the oil, slicked his hair back, thanked the waitress and gave her the bowl back. And then there was that time he shoplifted eggs from a German service station to throw at some posh looking cars. I've just realised, Salv is nearly an anagram of Slava.

I was a judge at a Battle of the Bands contest once. It was during Carter's later and less popular years. I only remember that because when I was introduced to the audience a lot of people booed. It's the bad reviews you tend to remember. The competition took place at Subterania, a club under the Westway in Ladbroke Grove. It's a venue that features a few times in my *Goodnight Jim Bob* book. Carter performed at the NME staff party at Subterania in 1990. It was the night Joe Strummer from The Clash told me he thought Carter were great and then I got into a drunken argument with Fruitbat and tried to decapitate him with a 12-string acoustic guitar. *Twelve strings* Seasick Steve. We survived that falling-out of course and three months later we were back at Subterania for an Indie Subbuteo competition.[7] We were disqualified for stealing the other teams' players and because Jon Beast dropped his football shorts and sat on the pitch.

At the Battle of the Bands final, the other judges were Bob Geldof from the Boomtown Rats and Glenn Tilbrook from Squeeze. When I'd had enough free booze I plucked up the courage to ask Glenn Tilbrook what the chords to 'Up the Junction' were. I genuinely wanted to know but I think he thought I was somehow taking the piss. He gave me a look but not the chords. I saw Marc Almond that night too but I wasn't bold and not yet drunk enough to ask him what he thought of Carter's cover of 'Bedsitter'. The cast of *The Bill* were at Subterania. They were behind a rope in the upstairs VIP section. I remember Reg Hollis was very drunk. This is starting to sound like a dream isn't it. When it came to picking the winning battle of the bands band I disagreed with Bob Geldof about which band it should be. We debated about it for a while until eventually Bob Geldof said that as he was getting paid more money than me, his word was final. He got quite angry. It wasn't even a Monday.

Pete Allinson was the final member of JSSW and the only one not to have previously been in Carter. He was a friend of Ben's and I went with Ben to meet Pete in a pub in Soho. I instantly liked him and felt as though I'd known him for years. He was a cross between TV detective Columbo and a member of the Bad Seeds. He was incredibly laid back. He had a sort of ruffled coolness. Like a charity shop James Bond. At that first pub meeting I watched Pete walk into the ladies toilet. When he came out I told him of his mistake and he seemed completely unfazed by it. Although Pete, who I'd rename Pete Allinson the Third for some reason, hadn't been a member of Carter, he was once in Radiohead. Pete Allinson from Radiohead. This isn't strictly true but he did go to school with at least one member of Radiohead and he played in some sort of school band with them and that's good enough for me. I have always said, and I see no reason to stop now, that Pete used to be in Radiohead.

Pete played keyboards and piano in JSSW — he could fit 'Dancing Queen' style piano stabs into pretty much any song — although we often

---

7 £300,000 wanted for a 40% stake in the company.

joked that Pete's main roles in the band were smoking and drinking. He always seemed to have a fag on. At our final gig in 2002 at a cinema in Welwyn Garden City, there was a strict no smoking policy and a member of staff had to keep asking Pete to put his cigarette out. During the gig a hilarious farce developed, with the same venue staff member repeatedly walking over to Pete during a song, taking the cigarette out of his mouth and walking away, only for Pete to light another. The gig ended with Salv launching his bass into the air of what was an incredibly high room. It hasn't come down yet. I remember seeing Pete a few years later. He was smoking an e-cigarette. I was happy that he was looking after his health but I couldn't help feeling a little more magic had gone from the world.

The day after meeting Pete in Soho, the neo-Nazi nail bomber David Copeland blew up the Admiral Duncan, just three minutes walk away. But let's not let that monster ruin the story. I had a new band and our debut gig was booked to coincide with the release of the single 'Bonkers in the Nut'. We also had shows at Reading and Leeds festivals. I just hoped I was ready for them. I hope I wasn't crippled by stage fright. I tried not to think about the previous summer when I'd had an anxiety attack at a Pulp concert.

SORTED FOR LES AND WEZ[8]

It was an all day gig in Finsbury Park. The sun was shining and I was watching Ultrasound, one of Pulp's afternoon support acts, when I started to feel nauseous and lightheaded. I was sweating and I had a dry mouth. I had pins and needles and palpitations.[9] I thought I was going to faint. Above all, I had a pressing need to escape. My anxiety had nothing to do with anything Ultrasound were doing and it had nothing to do with Pulp. I wasn't worried that Jarvis might lose his glasses or that they wouldn't play *Common People*. It was something else.

It wasn't the first time I'd been ill at a festival. But it was usually because I'd drunk too much or I hadn't eaten enough, or I'd stood for too long in the sun without a hat or any factor fifty on. Any of which might have explained my nausea and lightheadedness in Finsbury Park but not my desire to run away. What was I so scared of? I'd witnessed a lot of my mum's panic attacks in the past and I wondered if they were hereditary and if this was my first one. Perhaps it was stage fright by proxy. Maybe I was nervous on behalf of Pulp, pacing the floor backstage in their 'portable building'.[10]

---

8   This title doesn't really work. But we haven't had a pun for a while.

9   I was tempted to call this chapter 'Pulpitations' and I'd never forgive myself or live it down at the next Punmasters general meeting, if I didn't at least acknowledge that fact in a footnote.

10   When my first novel was published I received this email from a portable buildings manufacturer. *Hello there, I have recently been made aware of the book Storage Stories by Jim Bob. In particular, that it contains a page which refers to our name and how it should be used. (please see attached scanned pages), a misspelling of our Trade Mark is then used on a number of occasions elsewhere in the book. Firstly, I should say that we are surprised, pleased, even flattered that the status of our Trade Mark and how it should be used is considered sufficiently important to warrant so much copy in a book about a completely different subject. It's even flattering and very encouraging that our Trade Mark defence activities are so well known. So thank you! In order to maintain the correct perception of our activities that appears to be held by the author, I should just point out a factual discrepancy in the information given: the "c" spelling of our name, in trade mark terms, is simply a confusingly similar misspelling of the actual Trade Mark and falls within the scope of our obligations as trade mark owner to discourage or prevent such misuse. In other words, spelling our name incorrectly doesn't side-step the rules. In order to fulfill this obligation we have to ask you to bear this in mind for any future publications where our name has been considered worthy of inclusion. Thank you in anticipation! Regards*
**** ******** *Intellectual Property Manager*
*P********n Limited*

My daughter used to get anxious on my behalf before my gigs. She sometimes seemed more nervous than I was myself and I've had stage fright enough times to make me seriously question my choice of career. My mum used to say I was two different people: the quiet introverted offstage Jim and the one she announced every time I entered a shop in the village where she lived. "My son!" she'd say, with her arm held out before me like a red carpet. "He's a famous singer!" I was a regular disappointment to shopkeepers and customers who thought that Robbie Williams or Elton John had come to visit their village.

Was I born timid or did I grow into it? Was it nature or nurture? When I was researching this book, in among the faded faxes, I found my old junior school reports. In my first year, the report says, 'James is usually quiet and shy'. That's the first official record of my shyness that I'm aware of. At school I was shy enough to wet myself rather than dare ask if I could be excused. It was embarrassing enough for me but imagine how my daughter felt. She was mortified, as were most of the teachers at her parents evening.

That was a joke. I didn't really wet myself at my daughter's parents evening. I did wet myself when I was at school though. This was the nineteen seventies when things were different. I'll never forget being sent to the school 'nurse' and her saying "Number ones or number twos?" before she cleaned me up and smacked the backs of my bare legs.

There's a story that I left out of my *Goodnight Jim Bob* book, because it was 'too soon' and 'too much information'. But as this book is likely to be shorter on anecdotes – just wait until we get to the chapters when I'm writing a novel, there's a reason why there isn't a prime time Saturday night TV show called *Britain's Got Authors* – and as we're in the middle of a section about me being ill at festivals and going to the toilet in my trousers, now seems like the time to share it. You might want to skip a paragraph. I know I'm going to.

In 1994 Carter played the Phoenix Festival. After we came offstage I think somebody must have put something in my drink, because the next day, when we had to return to the festival site to sign autographs in a signing tent, I felt awful. I was too sick to eat or drink anything. I was dehydrated. I wished our signing would hurry up so I could go back to the hotel and sleep. When our time in the signing tent came, we sat behind a table and started autographing T-shirts and record sleeves. In spite of feeling terrible I was as consummately professional as ever, smiling for the occasional pre-selfie camera picture and cracking brilliant one-liners for a seemingly never ending queue of people, none of whom knew that just before the signing I'd had a little accident. I'm sorry. I was so dehydrated that I'm going to say number one and a halves. A bum wee. I'll probably edit this bit out.

I'd been to the Phoenix festival the year before as a punter. I didn't poo myself that year but I did get so drunk that I seriously contemplated stealing a car from the car park to get back to our manager Adrian's hotel where I didn't have a room. I can't drive by the way. I had to climb out of Adrian's hotel window in the morning.

Quickly changing the subject. I found another school report, this time from my fourth year at secondary school. My grades are pretty appalling. I don't think I was there a lot of the time. I can certainly remember the time spent in the lofts of derelict houses and being chased away from the railway lines by police more vividly than any of my lessons. My favourite line on the report is: *He must pull himself together and realise that an easy-going attitude will not earn him a living.*

Pos	LW		Title, Artist		Peak Pos
1	New		**1992 - THE LOVE ALBUM** CARTER - THE UNSTOPPABLE SEX MACHINE	CHRYSALIS	1
2	1 ↓		**STARS** SIMPLY RED	EAST WEST	1
3	4 ↑		**UP** RIGHT SAID FRED	TUG	1
4	2 ↓		**DIVA** ANNIE LENNOX	RCA	1
5	8 ↑		**GREATEST HITS** ZZ TOP	WARNER BROTHERS	5

Over the years I've found ways to deal with my social inhibition, or rather to avoid situations where it might be an issue, like not going for job interviews and not going to the doctors or the dentists. I've avoided hairdressers and suit fittings, massages and most clothes shops, apart from Marks and Spencer where the old ladies behind the counter are less intimidating or judgmental. That's why my clothes were such a poor fit in the nineteen nineties. I never had the nerve to go into a clothes shop changing room and try them on.

I've never been to a gym and I don't ask for directions. I'd rather get lost. I've never had a driving lesson or a tattoo. This is sounding like Carter's first single, 'A Sheltered Life'. No part of my body is pierced. I've never had my back, sack or crack waxed. A simple phone call to my bank or British Gas involves the kind of nervous build up that I'm pretty sure I didn't experience just before I went onstage and headlined Glastonbury.[11] I have to rehearse what I'm going to say on the phone before I start dialling. When I go into shops I work out what I'm going to say. I've been doing it for years. I have an early memory from secondary school. I was standing in the queue for the dinner hall. I was preparing myself to tell the woman sat at a table with a register, "free dinners". Two simple words, that was all I had to say. I repeated them in my head, over and over until I was at the front of the queue, when I said "Ten Number Six", which must have been something else I'd rehearsed saying and I'd got the two mixed up.

I drink the majority of my cappuccinos in branches of Caffè Nero — I'm writing this sentence in one of them now — and not just because they serve 'the best espresso this side of Milan' or because I admire their casual attitude to tax and really enjoy that one CD they play every single fucking time I go in there. But because I know what they sell and in what made-up language they size their cups in. The only question they're going to ask me is, "Chocolate on top?" I once flew to Los Angeles and back and made it all the way to Tokyo, without once using the airplane toilet, because I couldn't be sure how the lock worked. If I'm going to a restaurant I look at the menu online first.

I swim every week at the same pool, even though the showers are usually broken and it's further from my house and more expensive than the fabulous Olympic size pool at Crystal Palace Sports Centre. Because I know the system at my regular pool. I know where to pay and where the lockers and the changing rooms are. I know that the changing rooms are unisex but there are lockable cubicles, so I don't have to show all the other swimmers my balls like in the open plan Crystal Palace changing rooms. The pool at Crystal Palace is so difficult to find as well. Going for a swim there involves a series of secret transactions and handshakes. There's a passing of receipts to lifeguards and so on that I don't fully understand. It's just too intimidating for me. The one time I did go for a swim there, I was with somebody else. He paid and I followed him. But I didn't pay attention as usual. I was a passenger. I forget everything. I'm fine if there's someone there to accompany me and usually after I've been through an experience and know how it all works, I'm no longer intimidated by it.

Apart from the time Jim's Super Stereoworld were being interviewed in a barber's shop for a Welsh TV show that was never broadcast, I haven't sat in a hairdresser's chair since I was eighteen. Mrs Jim Bob has always cut my hair: from my Ballpoints mod do, via my Jamie Wednesday psychobilly fringe, to my award winning spaghetti bangs

---

11   Yes. I've headlined Glastonbury. And I doubt it will be the last time I mention it.

and the Barry Manilow mullet I had in Jim's Super Stereoworld, I have never had to pay for my haircuts. There's no awkwardness over the tip and Mrs Jim Bob knows where I'm going on my holidays because she's going with me.

That's how I've managed I suppose. Especially being in a band, where I've been able to surround myself with butlers, babysitters, hand-holders, hairdressers and designated drivers.

Here's a picture of my brain:

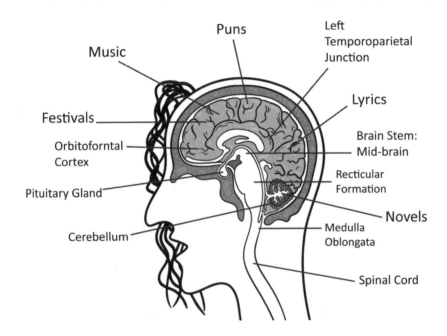

When researchers showed video clips of potentially threatening facial and bodily expressions to research subjects with high rates of social inhibition, they discovered an overactive orbitofrontal cortex, left temporoparietal junction and right extrastriate body area of their brains. Presumably these video clips included potentially threatening doctors and dentists, dinner ladies, tobacconists, hairdressers and shop assistants waiting in clothes shop doorways, ready to ask if they can be of any assistance. Social inhibition may be increased depending on the personality of an individual. Those who are dependent on and seek reassurance are more likely to display a greater level of social inhibition. There can't be many people more dependent on reassurance than pop singers, and seeing as how social inhibition can be reduced by the use of drugs and alcohol, maybe my choice of job wasn't as misguided as I'd thought.

I don't know if I have an overactive orbitofrontal cortex. I'd go and ask an analyst if I was suffering from social inhibition but I haven't got the nerve to phone one to book an appointment. Doctors Wikipedia and Google will have to do. They've both just informed me of another thing: social facilitation. It's also known as the 'audience effect'. It's the tendency for people to perform differently in the presence of others than they would when alone. That's what is says at the top of my CV.

I presume I must have been at least a bit nervous before I went onstage with Carter when playing the bigger gigs like Glastonbury and Reading festivals and at Brixton Academy and Wembley Arena. But it was when our popularity was dwindling and the venues shrinking to accommodate our smaller audience, that I really started to shit myself before a gig. If I'd ever had a fear of crowds it was nothing compared to my fear of empty spaces. And an empty venue on the way up is nothing like an empty venue on the way down, especially if it's the same venue.

Pulp didn't have any such problem in 1998 of course. They could fill a whole London park. Perhaps I wasn't really nervous but sick with jealousy, because I couldn't do that anymore. I retreated to the backstage guest area to breathe into a paper bag. The change of environment didn't seem to help with my nerves. If anything it made them worse. I now had the feeling that everyone was staring at me. Which was ridiculous because without my fringe and because I wasn't standing to the right of Fruitbat, I was as invisible as Ant without Dec (two men who had to live next door to each other to maintain their celebrity). But I was convinced that everyone in the guest bar was looking at me. All the journalists and bands and friends and families of bands. All the competition winners, the St John's Ambulance and the security staff: Showsec, Top Guard, Specialized (I'm naming security companies). I felt all their eyes were on me. The radio presenters and the television camera crews, the Workers Beer Company and the men pumping the shit out of the chemical toilets. I was convinced they were all looking at me. But it wasn't arrogance, far from it. I was embarrassed. I was, in the words of Moss from *The IT Crowd*, 'yesterday's jam'.

It was a feeling so distant from the one I'd had arriving backstage at Reading Festival in August of 1991, or when I'd been chased by fans through the streets of Tokyo or Tipperary (the only two places it's ever happened). I wanted to be stared at, but for the right reasons. I wanted to be cheered when I was announced at battle of the bands contests instead of booed and I wanted to get paid more money for being there than Bob Geldof, which I'd of course then give straight to his charity. I didn't want to be yesterday's jam. I wanted to be tomorrow's Marmite. I wanted to be loved and hated in equal yeasty extracts. What proper pop star craves ambivalence? I wanted to be loved enough for an enormous statue to be erected in my image and hated so much that people in Lewes would set fire to it on November 5th.

I sat on the Finsbury Park grass. I tried lying down, hoping physics would help calm my stomach but I still felt awful. I wanted to hide. I started to gag. I was drawing more attention to myself. To avoid throwing up or crying I had no choice but to leave. The simple act of walking through the exit gate and into the park outside was miraculous. On the other side of the gate it was just a park. I felt fine.

I didn't get to see Pulp in Finsbury Park but I did see Jarvis Cocker playing in Brighton eight years later. It was when his first solo album came out. I stood near the front of the venue, just behind a small group of blokes who shouted "Common People!" between each solo song and then they started shouting it *during* the songs as well. For them, the man on stage was Jarvis Cocker from Pulp and they couldn't understand what the hell he was playing at. It was only when he sung the chorus of 'Cunts are Still Running The World' that they stopped calling out for 'Common People'. *"This is a Pulp song. This is a Pulp song!"* they excitedly said to each other and jumped up and down until it was over, when they immediately started calling out for 'Common People' again. I found this Twitter exchange from around that time:

Jarvis Cocker @mrjarviscocker_. 9m I'm delighted to announce my first solo record 'Jarvis' by Jarvis Cocker is released on Monday. Exactly one year after I discovered the cure for cancer.
Dennis @Snafflebold_Den69 . 3m Lol. Never forget you showing your bum to Michael Jackson at the Smash Hits Poll Winners Party. #commonpeople

SLAVA'S NO SHOW

One year and one day later, just two point four Google miles away from Finsbury Park, Jim's Super Stereoworld played their first gig at the Kentish Town Bull and Gate (now a gastropub). In spite of all the malfunctioning samplers and synths, I remember the gig as a great success. The venue was packed. They even had to open the doors between the gig room and the bar so everyone could see the band. The live show wasn't quite as close to *Slava's Snow Show* as I'd hoped, although the Melody Maker's review did say that there was 'enough wackiness for a small circus-worth of clown shoes.'

Because of lack of budget and space in the transit van we had to ditch the snow and wind machines and the bed that turns into a boat. The venue wasn't big enough for the giant balloons, even with the doors between the gig room and the bar open. Pete forgot to bring the hat stand. But the spirit of Slava was very much with us onstage that night in Kentish Town. I wore a red nose until I realised it made me sing like Punch and I frantically hand pumped up balloons in the instrumental breaks of songs and produced confetti from my jacket pockets and fired bubbles from an Early Learning Centre bubble machine. Throughout our short time as a band JSSW would get through a ton of batteries and I'd spend a lot of time getting weird looks from the staff at the Early Learning Centre and Poundland, where I browsed the shelves for cheap kids toys. Onstage, I'd sing songs through plastic megaphones and robot voice-changers and the whole band would blow whistles. Every night was Mardi Gras in Jim's Super Stereoworld. We'd clap our hands like a Queen concert and I'd honk a bicycle horn and hand out sweets to the audience. You should have been there. Why weren't you there? That first night and at almost every Stereoworld gig that followed, we came onstage to the theme tune to *Jim'll Fix It*. But let's not let that monster ruin the story.

In spite of our fairly simple set up we still managed to annoy other bands and sound engineers with what they saw as our diva like onstage demands. Salv had these two old fashioned light boxes. They were quite big and very heavy. Inside the boxes there were different coloured light bulbs. There were a few settings to choose from to create patterns of light, and the speed and frequency of the patterns changed. We put the two light boxes at the back centre of the stage, where a drum kit would normally go. Ben and Pete would have their keyboards on stands behind the light boxes, like they were holding a disco press conference. Like half of Kraftwerk. Every night sound engineers would ask if we could put the light boxes and the keyboards at the sides of the stage instead, so that they could leave the support band's drums set up. Every night we refused. To make matters worse, we had our own drum kit too but we put that at the side where the keyboards should have been. What was especially annoying for sound engineers was that Ben only played the drums for the ninety second 'Part Two' of one song, 'When You're Gone (Parts 1 & 2)'.

In the early days of Carter, our gear was just two small practice guitar amps and a cassette machine that we'd put on a couple of beer crates. Sound engineers sometimes saw us as more of a novelty act than a band. A distraction for the audience while the other proper bands' equipment was moved into place behind us, sometimes during our set. Drums were even banged when we were in the middle of a song a couple of times. I would say that we were treated more like a DJ than a band but we were never treated as well as a DJ. At my most recent solo shows, I frequently had to leave the venue and take the whole heavily-drinking-money-spending-sold-out audience with me so that the following club night DJ could set up his laptop and play Spotify to an empty venue. Both as a solo performer and with Jim's Super Stereoworld I've arrived at venues where I was headlining to find the support band already set up on stage playing a song. This happened once at a JSSW London show. We turned up for our soundcheck and found a band with a hell of a lot of equipment already set up onstage and playing a song. They asked if they could leave everything set up and would we mind soundchecking in front of it. They would of course move it all after they'd played their gig. We said no and they got a bit arsey. They said the gig was important for them and they had record companies coming to see them. Things got heated. There aren't many rock 'n' roll rules that I adhere to. Just two really: no solids in the tour bus toilet and the main band soundchecks first. After they'd reluctantly moved everything, we did our soundcheck and they put everything back. In the dressing room before the gig they made an attempt at an apology and one of the band called Salv 'mate'.

"I'm not your mate," Salv said. "If you wanted to be my mate you should have been a bit friendlier earlier."

There are people in life you'd like to have on your side in a fight. Not necessarily the biggest people or anyone who you've ever seen throw a punch or even lose their temper. Salv was one of those people. In that dressing room he spoke with such menacing calm, it was difficult to not be impressed. I don't know whether all the record companies turned up to see the support band that night or not. But I've certainly never heard of anyone called Kasabian.[12]

Often at my solo gigs promoters liked to put on twenty-eight piece

12 This is another lie. Obviously. Of course I've heard of Kasabian.

local support acts or incompatible heavy metal bands playing stripped-down acoustic sets. Apart from it being inconvenient and everything else, it's especially embarrassing for some of the bands. They'd spend the whole gig explaining between every song how they were "usually a lot louder than this."

Anyway, the cumbersome disco light boxes, the drum kit in the wrong place that was only played for half a song, the bubbles, the balloons, the whistles and bells, the bicycle horn, the onstage card tricks – I forgot to mention the card tricks – they were all important to the Stereoworld show and I have always wanted to put on a show. I've never been happy to just turn up and play. When JSSW played at Colchester Arts Centre, just before we went on I was horrified to discover that I'd forgotten to bring my suit, my shirt and my tie. The shops were closed because it was a Sunday and I was wearing a T-shirt and jeans. Not acceptable. I seriously considered pulling the gig. It reminds me of a Carter gig in Cleveland on our final American tour. I wrote about it in *Goodnight Jim Bob*. The venue was full of terrifying people all day and there was no dressing room and no doors on the toilets. That was the night we had to wait for the locals to finish playing pool before we soundchecked in case our music angered them and they shot us. It was also the gig where I went onstage in the jeans and T-shirt I was wearing when I'd arrived. It sounds like nothing but I knew then that it was surely all over for the band.

Once the pool-playing daytime crowd had left, there weren't many people in the audience at the Cleveland Carter gig. Even fewer turned up for Jim's Super Stereoworld in Colchester, but I still wasn't prepared to go on in my civvies. I borrowed the shirt that Pete was wearing and I wore his spare tie. I don't know if that detail is true but I like the idea of Pete having a spare tie with him at all times. I did have to wear my jeans though and I felt like I'd betrayed everything the band stood for and had to apologise for wearing denim in between every song, like I was in a heavy metal band performing a reluctant acoustic set. For Jim's Super Stereoworld, every night may have been Mardi Gras but it could never ever be Mufti day.

I didn't forget my suit for the second Stereoworld gig on the Carling Premier stage at Reading Festival. It was the only thing that didn't go wrong. I'd been working my way down the Reading bill ever since Carter's legendary appearance there in 1991. We played on the main stage that year, going on before headliners James, and although we'd go on to have greater success, with hit singles and a number one album, if we'd split up after playing our encore of 'GI Blues' that evening in a park in Reading, as the sun set over the crepe stall like an Edgar Degas painting, the colour of Ziggy Stardust's hair, and if we'd then waited ten years and reformed, we would have been as big as The Beatles. We went and ruined everything with all our fantastic albums and singles, our videos and live shows and going on *Top of the Pops* and headlining Glastonbury and every one of the other 433 gigs that followed that perfect evening under the David Bowie sky in Berkshire. If we'd stopped right then we would have been huge now. Maybe that's the ultimate goal of a band now. To come back bigger than they were when they went away.

There's a great bit in the Stone Roses film *Made of Stone* when the band are on the way to a gig at an Amsterdam enormodome and someone asks if they've played the venue before. Ian Brown smiles and says, "We weren't big enough to play it before."

In 1995 Carter returned to Reading Festival as a three-piece, this time we were headlining the smaller Melody Maker stage. Fruitbat had hurt his back and had to be wheeled onstage and played the whole gig sitting in a chair. Maybe it was actually this second Carter Reading appearance that that bloke was referring to in 2008 in the back room of a London pub, when he'd reminisced about us getting the whole audience to sit down. Perhaps he'd mixed up his years and had mistaken Fruitbat for the audience.

I don't know how I felt about Fruitbat playing in a chair at the time but I've gone on to wish that we'd cancelled. He was in so much pain and sitting in a chair can't have looked good from an audience point of view. I'm just glad that people didn't film everything in 1994. At least Fruitbat was ahead of his time I suppose. Everyone does gigs in chairs these days. Axl Rose from Guns and Roses and Dave Grohl from the Foo Fighters have both bravely soldiered on in a seated position after an injury recently. Axl Rose had a special seat constructed. It was part office chair and part Davros Dalek. It had guitar necks shooting out at angles like the swords on the *Game of Thrones* throne. Dave Grohl from Foo Fighters had a fancy chair too, after he broke his leg. *WTF! Google Images!* OMG. I've just realised they were both sitting in the same chair. It's a custom built fucking injured rock stars[13] chair. It was probably sponsored by DFS or World of Leather. Jesus Christ. At least Fruitbat's Reading festival chair was a normal wooden one. No stupid guitar necks, no swords, no drinks holder or a special place to put his guitar picks. A punk rock chair. Fruitbat's chair wasn't Bluetooth and MP3 ready. I give it another ten years before no one will be both young and popular enough to headline Reading or Glastonbury festivals standing up.

There's often a stool waiting onstage for me when I arrive for a solo gig (disgusting). I don't think it's because sound engineers think I'm frail and past it. Even though I definitely am. I blame *MTV Unplugged*. It should have been called *MTV Unstood*. If you're playing acoustic music

---

13   There's a great Chris T-T song called 'Dreaming of Injured Pop Stars'. Check it out.

you're expected to sit down. If you're an *Unplugged* drummer you don't even get a chair. You have to sit on a wooden box and slap it with your bare hands.[14]

The last time I played a gig sitting down was in 2003 at Lock 17 (formerly Dingwalls and now Dingwalls again). After the gig I met Eddie Argos from Art Brut for the first time. He told me that I shouldn't sit down. Jonathan Richman didn't sit down, he said. Because Eddie was wearing a pale blue suit that I really liked and as he was uncharacteristically young for a member of my audience, I took him seriously and I never played sitting down again.

The Jim Super Stereoworld Reading Festival gig was on the Sunday and after three days, everyone working on the Carling Premier stage was either too exhausted or bored to make anything work. It took forty-five minutes to get any sound out of our keyboards and DAT machines and we almost ran out of time to actually play. Leeds Festival the next day was less fraught with technical difficulties and in spite of these annoying early issues, our first three live shows felt like they'd gone really well. We'd had some nice reviews. I'd recorded and mastered the second Stereoworld single 'Could U B the 1 I Waited 4'. It had a disco beat and a golf sample. I was feeling incredibly positive. I was going to be a pop star again. And this time I was going to be, not just a bigger pop star but a better one. I would enjoy every single moment. I'd learn from my past mistakes. I'd appreciate the opportunities. Relish the good fortune. When I travelled, I'd see more of the sights this time. I'd meet people and try their food. I wouldn't sit in a hotel room or hide in my bunk on a tour bus all day. And this time I wouldn't become a head of a dick. It's so easy to become a head of a dick when you get a bit of success. With our first single already released, the second on the way and half a dozen live shows in the bag (whatever that means), Jim's Super Stereoworld were well on the way to becoming – at the risk of alienating everyone who's never seen Alan Partridge – only the band Carter The Unstoppable Sex Machine could have been. If Carter were ever to reform, the posters would look like this:

---

14 If The Ballpoints had ever been famous enough to play Unplugged we would have called ourselves The Pencils. Our autobiography would have been called 'Autobirography'.

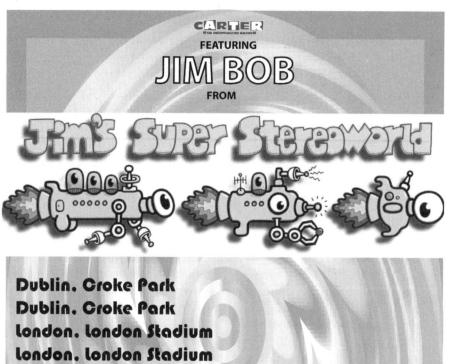

CARTER
THE UNSTOPPABLE SEX MACHINE
FEATURING
JIM BOB
FROM

Jim's Super Stereoworld

Dublin, Croke Park
Dublin, Croke Park
London, London Stadium
London, London Stadium
London, London Stadium
London, London Stadium
Coventry, Ricoh Stadium
Manchester, Old Trafford Football Stadium
Edinburgh, BT Murrayfield Stadium
Cardiff, Principality Stadium
London, Twickenham
Berlin, Olympiastadion
Marseille, Orange Vélodrome
Stuttgart, Mercedes-Benz Arena
Prague, Letnany Airport
Warsaw, PGE Narodowy Stadium

And then we went to Tunbridge Wells.

TUNBRIDGE WELLS

The Tunbridge Wells Forum used to be a public toilet. With the exceptions of Reading and Leeds festivals, it was the public toilet where Jim's Super Stereoworld played their first gig outside London. It was our first gig outside Camden to be more precise. Apart from the two festivals, we hadn't ventured very far from Camden Town yet. After the Bull and Gate and Reading and Leeds, we played two gigs in Camden: one at the Falcon (now a house) and the other at the Barfly (now the Camden Assembly) as part of Camdemonium. Camdemonium used to be called the Camden Crawl and featured '15 bands. 5 venues. 1 ticket.' After our Camdemonium gig at The Barfly we sprinted down the Chalk Farm Road to Dingwalls to catch The Clint Boon Experience! And then we returned to the Barfly to towel off for the Camdemonium aftershow party. I loved The Clint Boon Experience! I felt like we had something in common. I thought we might even be part of a scene. The *NME* agreed: '*as with The Clint Boon Experience, it's embarrassing to watch a man in his 30s still clinging to an adolescent pop dream*'

The opera singer Alfie Boe was at the aftershow that night. He used to sing with The Clint Boon Experience! I got on quite well with him the couple of times we met. If I'd known he was going to one day become so famous I would have made more effort to make something happen that was a better anecdote than this.

Hey, I found an advert for Camdemonium in an old copy of the *NME*:

The Coldplay were supposed to play at the Barfly the same night as JSSW but pulled out at the last minute. Never heard of them since.

The following day the Stereoworld went to Tunbridge Wells. I don't know why I was so surprised there were so few people there. I think I presumed I could simply carry on where I'd left off fame-wise. I figured we'd have a head start and start out at least as popular as Carter were at the end. We arrived in Tunbridge Wells in a fancy tour bus with an unnecessarily large crew for a relatively small gig. We had a tour manager, a sound engineer and a T-shirt seller. When your entourage outnumber your audience, it's hard to not look like your own vanity project.

Realising I wasn't quite the Barry Big Bananas I presumed I was, caught me completely unawares and I was quite down before the gig. I felt sick. With nerves as ever, but made worse by the lack of audience. I felt sick with embarrassment. I didn't even want my band mates and our unnecessarily large road crew to know how unpopular I was. I sat in the dressing room in silence. Admittedly, it was difficult to do anything else as the support band's drummer had a China cymbal that was the loudest thing on earth. Conversation was out of the question. You were probably sitting at home watching TV, wondering what that God-awful racket was. You certainly weren't at the Tunbridge Wells Forum that's for sure. Hardly anyone was. There were bigger crowds when it was a public toilet.

I sat in the dressing room, hoping for a fire or for the Wells of Tunbridge to overflow and wash the venue, the support band's drummer and all evidence of my failure away. After the gig, which I have no memory of, I sulked. The support band's drummer came into the dressing room and turned out to be as loud and annoying as his cymbal. I remember he looked like Rolf Harris, so we called him Rolf. It was less of an insult than it is now to be fair. Then, to worsen my bad mood, the one and only drugs anecdote in this book turned up in the dressing room.

I suppose I should have laid down some rules beforehand. No jeans. No jamming. Don't take drugs in front of Jim. But I hadn't said anything and one of my new crew members had brought out the cocaine. And why not? It was the music business wasn't it? Come on Jim. If you don't like it, join a church granddad. I ended up losing my temper and shouting at everyone.

I don't know what it is about cocaine that bothers me. I've never tried it. Perhaps it's great. But everything about it depresses me. The toilet cisterns, the credit card, the rolled-up banknote, the mysteriously popular strangers in the dressing room, the mirror, the razor blade, the CD case. The thought of anyone racking up a line (street slang) on the cover of one of my albums pisses me right off. That's maybe the one positive thing about downloads and streaming. They've almost totally eradicated the cocaine industry overnight. Multi-bladed safety razors have played their part too of course. Nowadays, hardly anyone does cocaine. If they do, they need to take a good hard look at themselves in the mirror.

We drove home from Tunbridge Wells in awkward silence. I kept insisting that I honestly didn't care. We were all adults. But I think everyone knew I was disappointed. Maybe they thought they'd lost their jobs on the first day. They didn't know I would never have the guts to Alan Sugar anyone.

Okay, so there might be two drugs anecdotes in this book. In 2011 Carter played Beautiful Days festival and someone we didn't know came backstage after the show. He went into our dressing room, moved my crisps to one side and started preparing his cocaine on the table. My daughter was furious. She shouted at him in a way that I've never heard her shout at anyone until the bloke literally ran away. I've been a proud father many times but that day was one of my proudest.

Throughout this section I haven't mentioned the person with the Tunbridge Wells dressing room drugs by name. I decided it was fairest not to incriminate anyone personally. I understand that by not mentioning anyone specifically I've effectively incriminated everyone except myself. Also, if I've made myself sound too much like a vicar, I should point out that I do love a bit of heroin.

The day after Tunbridge Wells I met the rest of the band and crew for the drive to the next gig in Bedford. There was still a bit of a sheepish atmosphere in the van. No one wanted to risk upsetting me again. While we were setting up for the soundcheck I smeared some sherbet from a Sherbet Fountain underneath my nose and waited for someone to notice. And then we all laughed and it was water under the bridge and we never spoke of it again. There was no audience at the Bedford gig either by the way. And no one came to Colchester Arts Centre the day after – where I had to play in jeans. I don't think Jim's Super Stereoworld pulled a decent sized crowd outside London at any time in our short career. I guess we were just too Londony.

That first tour wasn't all doom and gloom and anti-drug lectures though. At York Fibbers, where the audience size hadn't even been increased by the blackboard outside declaring 'Tonight: Carter The Unstoppable Sex Machine', we spent the whole day, both onstage and off, speaking entirely and inexplicably only in Australian accents. Once we'd started it was incredibly difficult to stop. It lasted for most of the tour. I met somebody later who used to work at York Fibbers and they were surprised that I wasn't Australian.

At the Derby Victoria Inn we hid in a cupboard. It was a big cupboard. I didn't measure it. A largish store cupboard I suppose. But with a four-piece band and crew and our tour support Astronaut all in there, it was pretty crowded. We had to sit on vacuum cleaners and boxes of bleach. Derby County were playing Man United that day and the bar of the gig was packed. We were advised by the venue manager to stay inside until everyone left. I think we took it too literally and I suppose it might have been a joke and the venue manager probably didn't expect a group of grown men would be cowardly enough to heed his advice. But once you've locked yourselves in a cupboard, after your initial shame, it becomes quite funny and you don't want to leave. It turns into an endurance challenge. You're competing for crystals in the *Crystal Maze*. If we hadn't had to come out for the gig we'd probably still be there now.

We played in Norwich on my birthday. I've done a lot of gigs on my birthday, including two of the Carter reunion Brixton Academy shows. It was never deliberate. I wasn't after five thousand presents. To be honest, I always felt like a kid whose birthday was on December 25th. There were considerably fewer than five thousand people at my birthday party in Norwich in 1999. The promoter, who didn't know it was my birthday, became increasing irritated by our disproportionate demands at such a poorly attended gig. First we asked for an ashtray for our cigars, then ice and a bucket for the champagne. The spoon and sugar for our Absinthe really cheesed him off. Oh yes, the knife and the plates for our cheeseboard.

We may have appeared to be living beyond our means with our fine wines and cheeses and our crew of sound engineers, tour managers and merch sellers but we, or rather, I, was losing money like nobody's business. And there's nobody's business like show business. We tried to make small savings by only booking two Travelodge rooms every night. Seven or eight of us would arrive at the hotel after the gig to check in and we'd have to keep moving around so the person behind the reception desk couldn't count us. I think we took turns for who got the big bed and who slept on the pullout child's bed or on the floor under the TV. I've stayed in a hell of a lot of Travelodges in my life but in all the years of doing so it wasn't until 2016 that I learned that the pullout kid's bed is called a truckle. It comes from the Latin trochlea meaning 'sheaf of a pulley'. A truckle can also be a small barrel-shaped cheese. And I've eaten a few of those.

I think the first Stereoworld tour was the one when Black Sabbath was playing in the back of the van and Pete Allinson was reading out loud from *The Devil's Dictionary* while everyone else was discussing *The Blair Witch Project*. And then the entire side window of the van suddenly fell out, almost taking Pete with it out onto the M6. Ben held onto Pete's legs but Pete couldn't seem to stop laughing. He was eventually pulled back into the safety of the van, cigarette still in his mouth, still holding his beer can and with *The Devils' Dictionary* in one hand and a tumbler of gin safely in the other. Yes, Pete had three hands. Perhaps I should have opened with that.

I'd remembered that Pete had almost fallen out of the van window when Black Sabbath was playing but Ben had filled me in on the other satanic detail when I bumped into him at a gig recently. I asked Ben what else he could remember from touring with Jim's Super Stereoworld. He reminded me of the kitsch mirrored curtains that Salv had brought along to add to the live show and to annoy sound engineers and support bands even more. We apparently ran a 'Steps versus S Club 7' poll on the T-shirt stall once and there was something about an angry naked businessman complaining about the noise we were making in a Travelodge. But my favourite Stereoworld thing Ben reminded me of, was how, in 2000 we had to get rid of our crew to save money and drive and unload our own van. To maintain the show business mystique that I keep banging on about and to avoid being seen by the audience until we walked onstage to the *J**'ll Fix It* theme, we wore disguises during the changeover. Between bands, me, Ben, Salv and Pete would move the amps, keyboards and drums, wearing glasses and hats and anoraks and dust coats. I wore a hard hat. We gave ourselves names. I was called Ron.

I'M IN THE KAISER CHIEFS AS WELL

Slava and one of the other clowns, I think it was Angela De Castro, signed my programme for me when they came out for their post show beer. When I say they signed it for me what I mean is my daughter went and got the autographs for me because of my overactive orbitofrontal cortex. If we're at a family wedding my daughter always gets two plates of food from the buffet table because she knows that her dad won't go and get one for himself. She knows I'd be too worried I was going to accidentally pull the tablecloth off or wouldn't know which food was vegetarian and end up eating meat for the first time since 1981 rather than embarrass myself.

When I was about twelve years old I used to go to Selhurst Park to collect the autographs of training Crystal Palace footballers, and in 1977, The Boomtown Rats signed my copy of 'Mary of the 4th Form' in the Marble Arch branch of Virgin Records. If you'd told me then, that one day I would be judging a battle of the bands competition with Bob Geldof, I would have asked you what had gone wrong with both of our careers.

Since then I've asked very few people for their autographs. I've asked a few authors to sign their books for me but it's always been at official book signing events, when they're less likely to be put out by the intrusion. When I asked Chuck Palahniuk to write 'To Jim Bob from Chuck Palahniuk' in my copy of his book *Haunted*, he looked at me, raised an eyebrow and said, "Jim Bob eh", as though I was mocking him with my obviously ironic British take on the name. He signed it 'To Jim Bob – no pearl diving! – Chuck Palahniuk.' As I walked away he said, "See you later, Jim *Boawwwb*".

In 2015 I was so nervous when I asked Elvis Costello to sign his autobiography after an event on the Southbank that I mumbled my name. It seemed to really irritate him. He'd been signing books for almost an hour and the last thing he needed was a mumbler. He looked at me like he was my teacher. Which in a way he was. I've got twenty-seven of his albums[15]. I'd met him many years before but I probably mumbled then too. I'm surprised he didn't remember that.

Both Elvis and Chuck were sitting behind tables with Sharpies in their hands and a pile of books next to them, presumably expecting to have to sign them. I would never have approached either of them when they were buying plums in Lidl or watching their washing turn in the launderette.

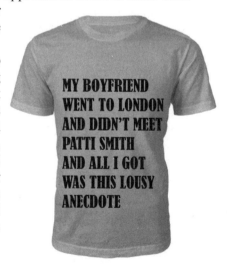

Last year I was in Foyle's bookshop in Charing Cross Road. I was paying for a signed copy of Patti Smith's book *Just Kids* that I was buying for Mrs Jim Bob's birthday. The cashier leaned across the counter to whisper to me, "She's in the store." The fact that I didn't go back into the shop to look for Patti Smith, to ask her to add 'To Mrs Jim Bob, Happy birthday from Patti xx' to the book I'd just bought, is one of my recent life's greatest regrets.

MY BOYFRIEND WENT TO LONDON AND DIDN'T MEET PATTI SMITH AND ALL I GOT WAS THIS LOUSY ANECDOTE

---

15   Twenty-seven *different* albums.

I've asked Mrs Jim Bob if she can think of anyone else whose autograph I've asked for in person. Apparently I got Brett Anderson from Suede to sign something for my sister at Reading Festival in the early 1990s. The last time I saw Brett was in 2009. We were both guests on BBC 6 Music, reviewing new records on Steve Lamacq's *Roundtable* show. Afterwards, me and Brett walked out of the building together. When we were outside I had to wait while he signed autographs for a small group of people. I've never known if the people who wait outside the BBC with autograph books, photographs and copies of *The Guinness Book of British Hit Singles* all open and ready at the relevant pages, are fans, amateur collectors, or whether they get you to sign stuff and then wait until you die so that they can sell it on eBay. Anyway, I waited patiently while Brett signed everything for them. I played with my hair, sculpting my fringe so that it would hang down in front of my face. I whistled 'Sheriff Fatman'. If Phillip Schofield had come out of the building I would have rugby tackled him to the pavement, even though it was never me who did that. Brett finished signing everything and we both walked away, Brett to his waiting taxi and me under the nearest bus, feeling like yesterday's jam.

In my first novel *Storage Stories*, the protagonist, a former rock singer – not me – has run out of money and has to get a regular job. I wouldn't know where to start looking for a proper job myself. I've got no skills outside music and unless an English C grade CSE from 1977 counts, I have no formal qualifications either. When you think about how many former pop stars there are, it's surprising you never see any of them in real life. They're a bit like baby pigeons. I touched on this in *Goodnight Jim Bob - On the Road With Carter The Unstoppable Sex Machine*. I wrote that the only pop stars I'd seen in regular life were Mick Lynch from Stump and Nick Cash from 999. Mick Lynch operated the harness that Phillip Schofield was attached to when he flew onto the stage at the *Smash Hits Awards* and Nick Cash was the attendant at West Norwood Cemetery, where he was a pallbearer at my dad's funeral. I can't think of any other pop stars I've seen in the fourteen years since writing *Goodnight Jim Bob*. Maybe away from their natural habitat, the famous are hard to spot. Maybe there are pop stars working *in* Habitat. Perhaps they're all hiding in plain sight and we see them every day but just don't make the connection. The character in *Storage Stories* gets a job in a self-storage warehouse and at various points in the story he is recognised as 👉 famous 👈

He refers to the indignity of 'when you're still well-known but no longer actually famous.' The book begins with this phone call:

> I was being interviewed for a music magazine. And like the old joke about lawyers, I could tell the journalist was lying, because his lips were moving.
>
> "It's not where are they now?" he said. "It's more where they are now. It's rhetorical, there's no question mark. It isn't one of those has-been round-ups like in other magazines. This won't be a bitchy article about how you're not so famous any more. What we really like to do is let our readers know where you're at, what you've been up to, if you've got anything new you want to promote."
>
> The background noise at his end of the phone line changed. And I knew he was cupping his hand over the receiver. I knew his shoulders were shaking with suppressed laughter, like Edward Heath's used to do. A small damp patch would be darkening the front of his trousers as the music journalist actually started to piss himself.
>
> I knew he was desperate for the interview to end so he could hang up the phone and snort and guffaw and laugh his head off. He wanted to join in with all the other music journalists gathered around his desk in their chant of Haasbeeen haasbeeen before throwing another dart into a picture of me that was pinned to the office dartboard.
>
> "Think of the piece as a map on a bus shelter. One of those maps with a big arrow that says you are here." He said.
>
> What a fucking liar.
>
> Three months later there I was on page five of the magazine, under the heading Where Are They Now? There was a big question mark at the centre of my forehead, in the most acne-splattered and pasty picture of me that was ever taken. The same picture they'd been chucking darts at twelve weeks earlier.

Apart from the dartboard it is a fairly accurate portrayal of a conversation I had with a journalist a few years after Carter had split up and a decent representation of the magazine article that followed. I think that, unless they've received a bang to the head and you're checking if they have concussion, asking a formerly famous person where they are now with any degree of sincerity is impossible. Lauren Laverne from Kenickie used to have a 'Where are they Now?' item on her XFM radio show. She would ring somebody famous up to find out what they'd been doing lately. You can probably see where this is going. I'm not blaming Lauren Laverne. I'm sure she was told that it was as lovely an idea as I'd been told it was when I was asked to take part. I seem to remember a piece of intro music and comic references to various pop stars now being dustmen and working at Tesco's and so on and then a slightly awkward and mercifully short interview for all concerned began. Afterwards, she said goodbye and played 'The Only Living Boy in New Cross'. Or at least up until I put the phone down, when the song was faded and replaced with Feeder or the Stereophonics or someone who didn't require air quotes around the status of their celebrity at the time.

And then on a day off in Norwich during a 2006 solo tour, Team Jim Bob went to watch Norwich play Crystal Palace. After the game we stayed at a guesthouse. We had a drink in the bar and played the trivia machine. The machine had a variety of game choices, one was *Q – The Ultimate Rock 'n' Roll Quiz*. One of the categories within the game was entitled 'Where are They Now?' It was illustrated at the top of the screen with a picture of me and Les.

Do you know what? I think the magazine that was the inspiration for the opening chapter of *Storage Stories* was *Q Magazine*. Perhaps when they interviewed me they were simply compiling future questions for their quiz machine. I can only assume that the magazine's low opinion of me is the reason for my relentless snubbing year after year for a Lifetime Achievement gong at their awards show. I wouldn't mind so much if the Q wasn't the only letter missing from the ornamental alphabet collection on my mantelpiece.

It's possible of course that the autograph hunters outside the BBC recognised Brett Anderson but didn't recognise me. Carter may have reformed the year before and played two sold out shows but there was little publicity around it. And I've always been difficult to recognise. Especially once I'd lost the fringe. If you're going to have a distinctive hairstyle in pop and want to continue to be recognised, it's maybe best to hang on to it. My haircut is more famous than me. It still features in regular 'Worst Haircuts in Rock and Pop' lists. Here's one from the *NME* in 2010:

> Who could forget Carter USM's Jim Bob, whose straggly fringe came to symbolise all that was wrong with guitar music in the unglamorous, pre-Britpop age. He's a writer these days, having just published his debut novel, 'Storage Stories'. You can even follow him on Twitter, if you like.

Oh well, I suppose they do their very best to be nice in the second sentence by mentioning my novel and my Twitter page. But it's such a struggle for the *NME* to not be cynical that they have to add the aside, 'if you like'. Those bloody guys. Still, unless you picked this book up for free from a basket at the front of Sainsbury's, needless to say, I've had the last laugh[16].

When my debut novel *Storage Stories* was published I took part in the *Literary Death Match*, a live club night where authors read a short piece from their work and then have it amusingly judged by a panel of comedians, musicians and other writers. It's good fun. I've taken part both as a competitor and as a judge. The first time I was a competitor and the judges were comedian Terry Saunders, journalist and filmmaker Tessa Mayes and Nick Hodgson from the Kaiser Chiefs.

After the competition (I didn't win) I was having a drink in the bar and chatting to Nick Hodgson and his friend about various things. I talked about my book and about Carter. I was mainly talking to Nick Hodgson, probably because we'd both just taken part in the same *Literary Death Match*. I think I'd be correct in saying that back then, in 2010, Nick Hodgson was one of the more recognisable Kaiser Chiefs. He sang on all the hits and seemed to do all the TV. I'd say at the time he was as famous a Kaiser Chief as Ricky Wilson from *The Voice*.

We chatted for a while and then Nick Hodgson went to the toilet or the bar and I was left on my own with his friend. There was a moment of awkward silence between us. I asked him,

"And what do you do?"

"I'm in the Kaiser Chiefs as well."

The ground could have swallowed me up. I pretended that of course I knew he was from the Kaiser Chiefs and what I'd meant was, what were the Kaiser Chiefs up to at the moment? My God. I actually attempted to hide my embarrassment at not recognising him by asking him where he was now.

In my defence, if you look Simon Rix from the Kaiser Chiefs up on Google, in at least half of the images he has long curly hair and on that particular night he didn't. Perhaps like with the autograph hunters and me outside the BBC, I didn't recognise Simon because he'd changed his hairstyle. Since cutting off my familiar spaghetti bangs I've stood next to friends on a number of occasions while they have conversations about me with somebody else. This has happened most often in venues where I'm either about to perform or have just finished performing. There's probably a joke to be made about how not being easily recognisable is a blessing in a disguise, but there's no time. Here's another bit from *Storage Stories*. 'The Tony Hadley' is the name of an eighties theme pub

---

16 I wrote this sentence before the NME chose to 'expand its digital platforms' (stop printing physical copies to give away in Sainsbury's) and ruin my gag. It seems it was them who would actually have the last laugh.

by the way.

> At The Tony Hadley, Daniel sat in the corner reading a book and drinking a Coke, while I tried to chat the barmaid up by hinting that I might be famous. She politely wondered whether if I had to explain that I was famous, that maybe I wasn't really technically famous.

I often find myself explaining my fame. Not to chat up barmaids of course but sometimes I'll be asked about my job. It might be small talk, like if a taxi driver asks me what I was doing at the radio station he's just picked me up from or sometimes people need to know my occupation to go on a form they're filling in. The enquiry might come from an optician, deciding on the type of glasses best for me, or not long ago, the optometrist who was treating my anterior uveitis, asked me about my job before dilating my pupils. An osteopath might need to know what I do so they can diagnose my back pain and when the dental hygienist always asks me if I've been anywhere nice I usually make the mistake of saying yes, but it was more for work than a holiday. "Oh really, what sort of work is that?"

For years I've had problems with the hearing in my left ear. Blocked Eustachian tubes I believe. The symptoms vary but it's mostly a sort of a muffled sensation, like I'm underwater. Annoyingly it's at its worst when I'm singing with headphones on. Every time I make a record I remember that and wonder if it will be my last record because it's so unpleasant. I think it might be another reason I talk so quietly. Because I can hear my voice inside my head and it doesn't sound like the type of voice I want to share. I realise I'm not alone in that wish.

In 2005 I went to see a specialist about my ear. He did a few tests and asked me if I shot. I thought I must have misheard him. Perhaps that was part of the test. I said pardon, which he must have been used to. He asked me again if I shot. He mimed a shotgun. I said no I hadn't shot. He asked me if I'd been doing any loud DIY and then he asked me about my job. He sat back in his chair. "Musician eh?" he said. He looked over the top of his glasses and down his nose at me. He wrote something down. I knew what he was thinking. "It's more of an acoustic thing these days." I told him. He said something about self-inflicted and how there wasn't a lot he could do. What I remember most was that he really stank of cigarettes and I wanted to tell him about lung cancer and how that could also be self-inflicted. If only I'd waited a few more years, I could have told him I was a writer and he would have thought, hmmm, writing eh? Silence. Thoughts. Long walks in the countryside. Contemplation. Peace and quiet. "Have you shot?"

The most recent stranger to ask me about my job was a physiotherapist who was treating my frozen shoulder (it's a thing). I was telling him how the pain had worsened since coming back from Australia. He asked me if I was on holiday. I said I was working. He asked me what my job was. I said musician. He asked what instrument. I told him guitar. He asked if I was in a band. I said I used to be. He asked me the name of the band. I told him Carter. He said it was probably before his time as he was more into stuff like Blur.

The further away I get from pop stardom the more reluctant I am to boast about it. It feels more and more like a humble brag. Or a lie. I don't want to sound like Billy Liar. Barry Bullshit. It would save time I suppose if I was to introduce myself and declare my genius at the same time, like Oscar Wilde. But I remember the hot flush whenever my mum declared, "My son! He's a famous singer!" to bewildered West Sussex villagers.

Just like the main character in *Storage Stories* – that definitely is not me – once I had to start explaining how famous I was, I probably wasn't famous anymore.

> Knock knock
> Who's there?
> Jim Bob
> Jim Bob who?
> That's show business

In 2016, just two days after my mum's funeral in Devon, I had to come back to London to do jury service. I ended up on a case that lasted for nine weeks, and this will make me sound like the most deluded egotist in the world but every day in court I wondered if someone was going to recognise me, either one of the jury or someone in the public gallery. What if it was one of the accused who was the big Carter fan? Or maybe a barrister would realise who I was, the judge even. Twenty years earlier, Carter had played a gig at the Inns of Court in London for an audience of pissed up trainee barristers and judges. It was one of the worst gigs of my life. Maybe someone from the audience of that Godawful gig was on the case.

Over the course of more than two months together on the same jury, at some point, everyone would ask each other what they were missing to be in court. Did they have to take time off work or were they self-employed? Were they getting reimbursed for their time off or was jury duty going to bankrupt them? Whenever I was asked about my job, I said I was a writer. I thought it would make for a less awkward nine weeks. And after all, I had just spent the last two years writing a novel. So it wasn't like I'd said I was a portrait painter or a gymnast. I was supposed to be finishing the novel instead of sitting on a jury but unfortunately book deadlines, like recent family bereavements, weren't considered reason enough to be excused from court.

The thing is though, you can't just say you're a writer and leave it at that. People are probably going to want details. If I'd said I was a road sweeper or a plumber, it's fairly self-explanatory. You're unlikely to be quizzed on the type of broom you use or whether you mostly plumb toilets or kitchens. I know if somebody told me they were a writer, I'd definitely want to know what it was they wrote – books or plays, films scripts? A journalist?

"Fiction or non-fiction?" Juror number eight asked me.

"Fiction."

"Adult fiction? Or children's books?"

"Adult."

"Have you had anything published?"

At this point in the conversation I can already feel pride is going to come into play.

"I've had a couple published."

See.

"Anything I would have heard of?"

"Maybe," Boasting a bit now. "The last couple did quite well," better dial the boasting back down a little. "Well, on Kindle at least."

"I'll have to look them up."

I can't resist a potential sale.

"The last one is on offer at the moment," there's no stopping me now. "It actually won an award."

"Really? What award did you win?"

"It was for the book's main character," a touch of humility. "The book's main character Frank Derrick, won *Best older person's character in a book, film, TV or radio drama.*"

At this point, taking the award out of my bag to show juror number eight would probably be a little over the top.

"It's very heavy," he says, hefting the weight of the award as though he's about to offer me money for it.

"I beat some pretty impressive people," I've dropped any pretence that it was the character of the book who won the award now. "Sir Ian McKellen, Sir Derek Jacobi, Frances de la Tour and Gemma Jones. Ian McKellen was nominated for two different roles and yet I still beat him."

For a moment there I thought the judge was going to have to adjourn until Monday until I stopped boasting. The next person who asks what I do, I'll say I'm a plumber. Although knowing my luck, they would have needed a bit of work doing in their bathroom and I'd end up having to look at YouTube videos so that I can learn how to fix their shower.

"How did you get into writing?" Juror number eight isn't finished yet. "Did you study it at uni?"
"No. I wrote a non-fiction book and sort of carried on after that."
"What was the non-fiction book about?"
"Stuff I used to do."
"What sort of stuff?"
Here we go.
"I was a musician."
"Oh really. What sort of music?"
"It's difficult to describe," depending who I'm talking to I might say rock or punk or even punk rock. I usually mention drum machines or synthesisers. "It was sort of pop rock. With a drum machine."
"What instrument did you play?"
"Guitar. But I used to sing mostly."
"Were you in a band or was it just you?
"Most of it was with a band. That's what I was most well known for"
Not *that* well known, that's pretty clear, he's thinking.
"Did you make any records?"
"A few."
"With the band?"
"Yes."
"Anyone I would have heard of?"
"Probably not. It was quite a long time ago."
"What was the band called?"
"I doubt you would have heard of them," I won't give the full name.
"Carter."

Juror eight sits forward on seat, studies my hair, checks the length of my trousers. "Not Carter The Unstoppable Sex Machine? Are you Jim Bob or Fruitbat?"
I managed to make it through nine weeks of jury service with only three of my fellow jurors finding out my secret. Or so I thought.

When the case was over most of us went to the pub, which was when I found out it was more like six members of the jury who knew who I was. And then because I was drinking, it suddenly became important to me that everyone knew. I was soon looking up album chart websites on my phone, typing 'Glastonbury headline acts' into Google and showing everyone *that* Smash Hits video.

Luckily, most people aren't too disappointed when they find out who I am. Sometimes they're actually delighted. Sometimes that makes me delighted. Like when Mrs Jim Bob asked Jon Ronson to sign a copy of his *So You've Been Publically Shamed* book 'to Jim Bob', he looked at her and said, "Not *the* Jim Bob."

There are obviously times when I'll go through the whole game of Jim Bob charades and when I finally reveal who I am or was, they'll shrug and say they've never heard of Carter The Unstoppable Sex Machine. I tell those people to fuck off. That's why I was held in contempt of court.

■■■

In the middle of writing that last chapter I received an email from a radio producer. They wanted to know if I would record an interview for a section of a show called 'Still Got it'. The email promised to inform listeners about what I'd been up to since Carter. I've said yes. To be asked to take part in a *where are they now?* interview right now feels too much like fate to turn down. It will be interesting to see if anything has changed since I was last asked the question.

It's a week later. The radio station phoned me and recorded a short interview. It wasn't too painful and the presenter was nice but he didn't seem to be too interested in where I was now. *The Smash Hits Awards* were mentioned quite early on and I was asked about the upcoming Carter gigs even though we'd split up (twice). At the end of the interview the presenter played 'After the Watershed' and dedicated it to 'all the silly cows'.

It's now a few more days after that and the interview has aired on the radio. I was out at the time so I didn't actually hear it but when it was broadcast I did see the radio station had tweeted about it. They called me Jim Bob from 'Carter & The USM.'

PROFESSOR BRIAN COX FROM D:REAM

Towards the end of my jury service, Richard Strange from Doctors of Madness was sitting in the jury assembly area reading a newspaper. I used to know Richard Strange years ago when we both lived in Streatham but there was no way I was going to approach him and say hello. It's one of the reasons I don't have many showbiz friends even though I've met quite a lot of them. If I ever see someone famous who I've met before, unless they say hello first (which they never do) I'll stand there thinking about approaching them, until they inevitably leave. I can't bear the thought of them not recognising me (which they never do) and me having to embarrass us both by telling them.

Wreckless Eric wrote on his blog about the time he played an afternoon show and was eager to leave before Woody Woodmansey from the Spiders from Mars arrived for a later gig at the same venue. Wreckless Eric didn't like meeting his musical heroes unless they knew who he was or at least that he did the same thing as them.

It's hard for me to say that I feel the same, without sounding like Kanye West but I do know I almost didn't join the queue to get Elvis Costello to sign his book because I wanted him to know that I was a singer too. I could have told Elvis that I was in a band called Carter and we once did a cover of his song 'Peace in Our Time' for an album to promote peace in Northern Ireland. But instead, I just quietly mumbled my name, annoyed him, repeated my name, got the book signed and skulked away. All of this isn't new. Here's a paragraph from *Goodnight Jim Bob*:

> Faith No More's bass player Billy Gould came to watch us later on. I got on really well with him. He's one of my celebrity American mates that I never really saw again and he probably wouldn't know me if I said hello to him in the street today. Billy Corgan from The Smashing Pumpkins was another. I'd sat next to him on a panel at the New York New Music Seminar and we got on like a house on fire. We were both too shy for speech making and were completely upstaged by famous transvestite Ru Paul and Shitman, a man in a shit suit (no seriously). I met Nirvana once.

Shitman is round my house all the time by the way. So it's not all bad. We went to Center Parcs together last year. Shared a lodge. Me, Mrs Jim Bob and our daughter Jim Bob Junior and Shitman, Shitwoman and their

Shittwins.

I'm very easily star-struck. If I ever go to the theatre I always look the cast up on IMDb first, to see if they've been in *The Bill*, *Holby City* or *Midsomer Murders*. Basically, if you've been on the telly I'll think more of you for it. If you've written something that's been on the telly or at the cinema, I'll be equally impressed. Years ago I was in a pub in Brixton waiting for Fruitbat to arrive. He was late and I was stuck talking to his friend Tim Connery. Just as I was thinking, I wish Les would hurry up so I don't get lumbered with this boring bloke all night, Tim Connery told me he'd just been working on the script for the film *Plunkett & Macleane*. Suddenly he was the most interesting person I'd ever met. We talked for hours and Tim is now one of my closest friends. In 2018 I executively produced his play about Bill Grundy and in a few chapters time, me and Tim are going to be mugged together and I'm going to blame it on Fruitbat.

I love meeting famous people, and if it turns out they know who I am, although I'm not arrogant enough to not be surprised and flattered, I'm not quite humble enough to boast about my lack of arrogance in a book all about myself.

Andrew Collins has always been a supporter of my work. From when he was the only staff member at the 1989 *NME* staff party dancing to Carter and then later when he was writing for *Word* magazine or when he was presenting radio shows on BBC 6 Music. I recorded a version of ELO's 'Mr. Blue Sky' for Andrew's BBC Radio 4 sitcom of the same name in 2010. And in 2009, when Robin Ince was looking for musical performers for his Christmas show, Andrew suggested asking me.

Every December, from 2009 to 2012, for two or three nights, I'd sing a song at the Bloomsbury Theatre as part of *Nine Lessons and Carols for Godless People*: 'a festive celebration of the Big Bang, evolutionary theory and of music and comedy'. There were some great people on the bill, mostly comedians but also a lot of very brainy people from the worlds of science and maths. Here's a list of those I can remember. I think some of them were actually from another Robin Ince night at the Bloomsbury Theatre called *Robin Ince's School for Gifted Children*. I've arranged everyone alphabetically. Like a scientist or a mathematician would. By the way, if you've ever wanted to feel a bit thick, spend some time in a theatre green room with Professor Brian Cox and Richard Dawkins.

Chris Addison, Helen Arney, Mitch Benn, Ed Byrne, Bridget Christie, Professor Brian Cox, Barry Cryer, Richard Dawkins, Kevin Eldon, Ben Goldacre, Ronnie Golden, Darren Hayman, Richard Herring, Robyn Hitchcock, Phil Jeays, Shappi Khorsandi, Tony Law,

Stewart Lee, Josie Long, Mark Miodownik, Ben Moor, Alan Moore, Al Murray, Joanna Neary, Dara O'Briain, Gavin Osborn, Adam Rutherford, Simon Singh, Mark Steel and Isy Suttie.

Every year at *Godless* I sang one song. I tried to choose something with a bit of a Christmas theme. In 2009 it was 'Angelstrike!' I wore a white suit and had a pair of angel wings in my bag, but the wings never came out. I also had copies of *Storage Stories* in my bag. I'd decided to publish it myself and had three thousand copies delivered to my house, not realising quite how much space they'd take up. We had books in wardrobes and cupboards, under beds and on the stairs. They were piled in every available space in every room of the house. We made furniture out of books and hid them under large pieces of material along the bedroom wall, like a million dollars of Mob money we'd found in a crashed airplane.

In 2009 I put as many copies of the book as I could fit into a bag with my angel wings and I set off for the Bloomsbury Theatre. My plan was to give a copy to everyone else on the *Godless* bill, like a literary Father Christmas. Plucking up the courage to do so made me feel so tense, that on the second night I left the books at home. I did manage to give a book to Chris Addison and one to Isy Suttie. They both sent me great quotes:

"I am totally loving (irritating modern adverbial/ grammatical construction) the book. Really, really

enjoying it." – Chris Addison
"It's fucking brilliant." – Isy Suttie

I didn't know until she told me in the green room of the Bloomsbury Theatre but I'd met Isy Suttie seventeen years earlier. It was backstage after a Carter gig in Derby and she'd given me a cassette tape of some of her songs. There's a more detailed account of that meeting in a chapter of Isy's book T*he Actual One* and how she was so nervous meeting me. The fact that I was as star-struck about meeting Dobby from *Peep Show* in 2009 as Isy was about meeting Jim Bob from Carter in 1994 illustrates how daft this old fame thing is.

Me and Isy Suttie have performed together on a number of occasions now. She's been the special guest at a few of my solo shows and I played the ghost of her dead father in a special orchestral performance of the *Gutted* musical at the Leicester Square Theatre. Isy lives just up the road from me and we bump into each other all the time. She recognises me and everything.

I don't want to spend the rest of the book outing celebrity Carter fans but comic writer, novelist and magician Alan Moore used to live in a flat in New Cross and he and his friends used to sing 'The Only Living Boy in New Cross' all the time. Alan Moore operated a toy bubble machine while I sang 'Touchy Feely' at the Bloomsbury Theatre one time. He's one of the nicest people I've ever met. He gave me a Christmas card two years in a row.

I sang 'Anytime Anyplace Anywhere' and 'The Only Living Boy in New Cross' at Mark Steel's fumftieth birthday party and for my own fumftieth, Chris T-T compiled a collection of Jim Bob cover versions, performed by different people, as a surprise gift. On one of the tracks Richard Herring and Andrew Collins dissected the lyrics to 'Sheriff Fatman'. A little bit like that man in the Irish Bar in Berlin did with 'The Only Living Boy in New Cross'. Richard's comments are in italics.

Sheriff Fatman started out in business as a granny farmer
He was infamous for fifteen minutes
That's a mistake. It should be 'famous'
And he appeared on Panorama
Then he somehow got on board the Starship Enterprise Allowance
Scheme
Loads of mistakes in this.
With a Prince of Wales Award
For pushing valium and amphetamines
I find that highly unlikely the Prince of Wales would not award anything
for that

Moving Up onto second base behind Nicholas Van what's His Face
You can't just change people's names to make them rhyme
At six foot six and a hundred tons the undisputed King of the Slums
Tons and slums doesn't rhyme
With more aliases than Klaus Barbie
He didn't have that many aliases
The Master Butcher of Leigh on Sea
Just about to take the stage
The one and only hold the front page
Fatman's got something to sell
To the Capital's homeless
They haven't got any money, so it's a stupid market. If I was on Dragon's Den I'd be going, well I'm out
At the Crossroad's Motel for the no fixed abodeless
Where you can live life in style you sleep in a closet
And if you flash him a smile he'll take your teeth as deposit
He's written too many words in this. No wonder it wasn't successful

The final night of *Nine Lessons and Carols for Godless People* in 2009 was at the larger Hammersmith Apollo. It was one of the few London venues I hadn't played at. I'd be making my debut there backed by The Mystery Fax Machine Orchestra. It was very much a Jim Bob dream come true. And it was being filmed for television! If the thought of a million television viewers watching didn't make me nervous enough, there were five thousand atheists in the audience and I had to go on after Professor Richard Dawkins.

Performing the song with the heft of a full orchestra behind me was seriously thrilling. I was lucky to sing with The Mystery Fax Machine Orchestra on a few more occasions: in pubs, clubs and in a packed tent at the Latitude Festival. They played on my 2013 album *What I Think About When I Think About You*. Apart from *Jim Bob Sings Again*, which is a collection of old solo and Carter songs recorded with just Chris T-T's piano accompaniment, I haven't made an album since. Once you've recorded with an orchestra, it's difficult to go back to boring old guitars.

The Hammersmith night of *Nine Lessons and Carols for Godless People* was broadcast on BBC4. They'd renamed it *Nerdstock* in case they offended any vicars, while at the same time offending the very people who would be watching the programme. It was good to be on television again though, even if my song had been crudely edited, removing a few verses and chopping out the middle instrumental break that I'd spent rocking the fuck out so that one second I looked all calm and collected and the next I was sweaty and out of breath with my hair all over the flipping shop. Continuity contishmuity. Hey. I wonder if the mystery was that the fax machine used thermal paper and all the pages are now blank.

There are two times in recent years when I've been seriously star-struck. Once at the Barbican theatre and the other time at the penultimate Carter show in 2014 at the Shepherd's Bush Empire. Word had got out that Cillian Murphy was on the guest list. There was a piece of A4 paper with his name on, on a seat in the balcony, and for some reason, the names of Mrs Jim Bob, my daughter, Mrs Ollington and Mrs Spoons on the seats surrounding him. When Cillian Murphy came into our dressing room, he looked a little terrified. I don't think it had anything to do with meeting me. We all fell in love with Cillian Murphy that night.

But the most star-struck I've ever been was in 2012. My friend Herve was doing the sound for a production of *Madamoiselle Julie* at the Barbican. Herve had organised complimentary tickets for me and Mrs Jim Bob. After the play was finished I sent Herve a text to arrange to meet him, so we could thank him for the tickets. When he eventually came out to the Barbican foyer I asked Herve if he had time to go for a drink, maybe to a nearby pub. He shrugged (Herve is French) and said:

"Don't you want to meet Juliette?"

Herve knew I was a fan of Juliette Binoche. In my novel *Storage Stories*, the main character – not me – is infatuated with the woman he works with. He believes she looks exactly like Juliette Binoche. There are drawings in the novel. Here's a particularly bad one of Juliette Binoche:

I did my best to remain calm as Herve led us through a hundred different doors and along countless corridors until we were finally backstage.

"I'll just check Juliette is okay to visit." Herve said.

He went into a room and we waited. I presumed we were about to be led into some sort of meet and greet situation. We'd be in a large green room in a crowd of twenty or thirty other people. We'd stand in a line and Herve would briefly introduce us to Juliette Binoche and we'd leave. Instead Herve took us into Juliette Binoche's dressing room. There was no one else there.

Herve introduced us. He told Juliette Binoche that I used to be in a band he was a fan of. Thankfully she didn't ask for too many details. The thought of Juliette Binoche either hating Carter, or worse still, never having heard of us, would have been unbearable. Herve said Carter had stopped doing gigs and she asked me why and I can't remember what I said but I definitely mumbled it. I was thinking about the copy of my book I had in my hand. I'd brought it to give to Herve. What if he suggested I show the novel to Juliette Binoche and she saw my awful drawings and started beating me about the head with the book until I looked like her in this other equally bad drawing?

Meantime, Mrs Jim Bob chatted with Juliette Binoche about the gold dress she wore in the play. Juliette Binoche said she'd grown to hate the dress and said she would gladly have given it to Mrs Jim Bob if she didn't needed it for the rest of the play's run. Juliette Binoche said she had a bit of a cold and Mrs Jim Bob probably suggested Lemsip or something. How could she be so relaxed and nonchalant and seemingly oblivious to the fact we were in the private dressing room of an Oscar winning actress? I can only presume it was the result of living for almost forty years with such a massive superstar as me.

2 0 0 0

In 1999 everyone was talking about the Millennium Bug. At midnight on the final day of the final year of the twentieth century, planes were going to fall from the sky, the oceans would rise up and the earth would drown. Banks would collapse and the stock market would crash. Basically all the stuff that's happened in the years since then, without any help from a computer software glitch.

At the stroke of midnight on December 31st, Jools Holland from Squeeze would be exposed as a fraud as he boogie-woogied obliviously on into the new millennium, completely unaffected by the lack of electricity.[17] Everyone would have to play unplugged from now on. All the world's musicians would be sitting on chairs or slapping tea chests in the dark. Seasick Steve would be emperor. Anyone meeting up for Pulp's prearranged year two thousand wouldn't be able to find the fountain down the road because the traffic lights wouldn't be working and the road would be gridlocked with broken down cars in need of petrol. The water in the fountain would have been drunk dry by thirsty looters. All over the world there would be blackouts and riots, murders and mayhem, mob rule and anarchy. Inevitably, there would be some people who would find a way to try and cash in on it.

I was approached to write a song for an animated 'Millennium Bug' character. When the world collapsed, it would quickly become the most successful cartoon character since Mickey Mouse. I would write the song and record it with Fuzz Townshend from Pop Will Eat Itself and then Ian Dury would sing the verses.

When I'd written the song ('Y2K. The Bug is Coming') I went up to Birmingham to record it with Fuzz. Fuzz is lovely. I stayed at his house for a couple of days. He had a bar in his back garden. Ranking Roger from The Beat's son popped round for a cup of tea. Carter had always said it was when Fuzz joined Pop Will Eat Itself on drums that it meant it was okay for us to get a human drummer as well. It reminds me how whenever we were unsure about whether to support a particular political cause or charity, we would ask Billy Bragg how he felt about it. Billy was our PC barometer.

Not long after recording with Fuzz, I went to the Underworld in Camden to watch him take on Clint Boon in the 'Featherweight DJ Championship Of The World'. Clint introduced me to Kevin Rowland

---

17 This gag doesn't work because if there was no electricity, how would we be able to watch Jools Holland being exposed as a fraud on television?

from Dexys Midnight Runners that night. I know you're not supposed to meet your heroes but I seem to have met a lot of mine: Ian Dury, Elvis Costello (briefly), Paul Weller (brieflyier), David Bowie (blink and you would have missed it), Nick Cave (he wanted to know the name of our enormous bucket-sized cocktail with the sparklers in so that he could get one too), Joe Strummer (he liked Carter), John Cooper Clarke (liked Carter), Chuck Palahniuk ('Jim *Bob* eh'), Fruitbat obviously, and now Kevin Rowland.

I can remember exactly where I was when I first heard 'Come on Eileen' on the radio. I was working in a silk warehouse in a basement behind Oxford Street. I can even tell you I was wearing a brown dustcoat and my hairstyle was somewhere between Ian McCulloch's from Echo and The Bunnymen and Edwyn Collins's from Orange Juice. I already had the first Dexys album and all the singles but 'Come on Eileen' blew my flipping mind when I first heard it. It still does. If anyone ever refers to it as their guilty pleasure I will fight them.

When I was working in the silk warehouse I went out to get some lunch and I saw Kevin Rowland on Oxford Street. It was around the time that 'Come on Eileen' was released. He was standing just down the road a bit from Marks and Spencer, dressed in dungarees, neckerchief and beret. Just hanging around, all casual like. Not apparently being filmed or photographed. Just being Kevin Rowland. He was like a method pop singer. It was so impressive. When I met him years later in Camden Underworld I wanted to tell Kevin all of that. And when Clint Boon left me alone with him I had the chance. But of course I didn't say anything. I was literally struck dumb until Kevin Rowland found an excuse to walk away.

A lot of my pre-pop star jobs were in basements or windowless rooms just off Oxford Street. I worked in a basement on Soho Square for two years, filing newspapers and magazines onto shelves for an advertising firm. Before that I had a job in the windowless room of a film company on Wardour Steet. I worked with a Russian called Igor and a skinhead who bullied us both. I met the skinhead years later. He'd grown his hair and I couldn't understand why I'd ever been intimidated by him. Hairstyles eh?

The great thing about working in basements and windowless rooms is you can spend a lot of time not working in basements and windowless rooms. I used to sit around, reading the *NME* and daydreaming about my pop stardom until I heard someone from the office walking down or up the stairs and then I'd immediately make myself look busy. When I was 'working' in the silk warehouse[18] there was a goods lift that went

---

18 I've mentioned it quite a few times now without feeling the need to explain, it was a warehouse that housed silk. Not a warehouse a made out of silk. You can relax. This isn't an overly long set up for an alternative version of that joke about the paper shop that blew away.

from the basement up to the street. One day I was standing in the street outside the lift with the warehouse manager, waiting for a delivery of silk – taffetas, georgettes and organzas, I remember all the words – when a car pulled up and parked opposite. A man and woman got out and started walking towards Oxford Street. They called across to us to ask if they were all right to park there for a bit. The warehouse manager, who was a twat, told the man to fuck off and that no, he definitely could not park there. So Paul and Linda McCartney from Wings had to get back in their car and move it. The warehouse manager really was horrible. If someone left the book they were reading lying around, he would tear out the last page. I was very thin at the time and his nickname for me was Belsen. Nice eh. That's my Paul and Linda McCartney anecdote. Next.

The recording, mixing and remixing of 'Y2K The Bug is Coming' probably took longer than it needed to. I think that was because there were too many people involved. Everyone had a different opinion on what the song should sound like. I sort of lost interest a bit and let Fuzz do all the hard work. I didn't go to Ian Dury's house with Fuzz to record the vocals. I think I was scared of what might happen. Ian was quite ill at the time and I felt a bit guilty for making him have to sing my stupid song.

I recently asked Fuzz Townshend what it was like when he went to Ian's to record his vocals. He surprised me by explaining that it was fun and really quick. It was the exact opposite of how I'd imagined it. Fuzz also started telling me a story about what happened after recording Ian's vocals. It involved going to a nightclub with a politician. I said to Fuzz that his anecdote was so much better than my one. All I could say is that I regretted not being there.

Fuzz suggested I should just say I was there. I did think about this for a bit. Nobody would know or dispute it if I claimed Fuzz's anecdote as my own. A lot of musician autobiographies must be at least partially made up or imaginary. I read Keith Richards's autobiography for example. It's a big fat doorstop of a book, packed with details of events and quoted conversations. Considering some of the stuff Keith is describing in the book, I find it hard to believe he can genuinely remember any of it, let alone in such minute detail. I've chosen not to lie though. I won't pretend I was there when I wasn't. If you aren't happy with that, sue me.[19]

I do wish I'd gone to Ian Dury's house with Fuzz though. I hadn't seen him for a very long time. We'd first met in 1992, when Ian came to Brixton, to interview Carter at Fruitbat's house for a BBC television arts show. Not long after that we couldn't get permission to use a sample

---

19 Just to be clear, I'm not talking to Keith Richards there. I don't want to poke that legal hornet's nest again.

from the film *Man of La Mancha* on our song 'Skywest and Crooked', so we made a shortlist of who could possibly replace the irreplaceable Peter O'Toole. Ian Dury was at the top of the list and we were surprised and delighted when he said yes. He came down to Simon Painter's Important Notice Studios in Mitcham. It was where we recorded the first four Carter albums. Notice Studios was a tiny space, basically a concrete shed in the back garden of an otherwise ordinary family house that as far as I know, still has no blue plaque on the wall with our name on. Simon shared the house with three of his old school friends[20]. At Simon's wedding one of his three friends[21] told me about the day he'd come home from work. He came in the back door and walked through the kitchen and into the front room, where he thought to himself: "I'm sure I just saw Ian Dury in our kitchen making a cup of tea."

Ian Dury read from *Don Quixote* for us for almost an hour that day. I've still got over twenty minutes of unheard outtakes from the recording. His voice is incredible. Ian would later feature in the video for 'The Impossible Dream'. We spent two days filming in Madridejos in Spain, where I had without doubt the worst two hangovers of my life. I had to sit on a horse that hated me, at six in the morning in the hot Spanish sun, after staying up all night drinking with Ian Dury in the hotel restaurant. It was in the restaurant that Ian told me about the time he'd almost finished writing a song called 'Do Re Me, So Far So Good'. When he'd heard that Carter were releasing a single with the same name he said he'd considered getting somebody to break our legs. There's a bit in the film *Sex & Drugs & Rock & Roll* where Andy Serkis as Ian Dury has just wrecked a recording studio and is being arrested. As the police drag him away he shouts *Do re me, so far so good!*

Ian Dury was the first person I'd ever heard use the word 'camber'. It's a slightly convex or arched shape of a road or other horizontal surface, as used in this example: "Watch out. There's a fucking camber you fucking skinny streak of piss!" Those two nights of escorting Ian Dury down the camber to his Spanish hotel room while he swore at me is a memory that this fucking skinny streak of piss will cherish forever.

Ian Dury didn't spend his entire time in Spain threatening me and calling me names. We also made plans to work together. Ian wanted us to write a radio play for the BBC. I think my social inhibition must have put paid to that ever happening. I have too many of these artistic near misses in my life for it to be coincidence. Like when I *nearly* went to a recording studio in Tokyo to meet Gilbert O'Sullivan and the time there

---

20 Old school as in, he used to go to school with them. Not retro or vintage friends.
21 I'm not suggesting Simon only has three friends. He is a very popular and loveable guy. There were loads at his wedding.

were plans for me to write songs with Debbie Harry in New York but it didn't happen for some reason. My nonecdotes may be shit but at least they're well travelled.

When Ian Dury came to Fruitbat's house to interview us for the BBC, I remember I made a snide comment during the interview about Charlie Watts from The Rolling Stones and Ian told me off. I can't recall what I'd said but I didn't know Charlie Watts and Ian did. I've always remembered that moment and have tried my best to not be rude about other musicians who I've never met. I mean, obviously, I've largely failed in my efforts to do that, but I have at least tried.

One place I find it most difficult to be nice about my peers is when I'm asked to appear on *Roundtable* on 6 Music. I've been a guest so many times, in many different buildings and with different hosts but mostly with Steve Lamacq. We usually go to the pub afterwards. We complain about the state of the music industry in ways that could never be broadcast.

I've met a lot of great people on *Roundtable* and I'm now going to attempt to list some of them. In no particular order: James Murphy from LCD Soundsystem, Liam Fray from Courteeners, Shappi Khorsandi, Rob Deering, Tim Vine, Steve Levine, Holly Walsh, Toyah Wilcox, Nadia Shireen, Paul Kaye. Paul Kaye is the dead spit of Marc Ollington, who came to the BBC with me that day. I mentioned their uncanny likeness to Paul Kaye but he thought it was nonsense. I don't think he liked me and chose to ignore me and speak to Marc instead, mostly about their mutual love of Arsenal football club. They had a lot in common. Not just their really quite obvious appearance. It must have been like talking to a mirror for Marc, which is incidentally something he does all the time.

Someone else I met on *Roundtable* was Scroobius Pip. It was not long before I went to Edinburgh to appear in a musical at the Fringe festival (don't worry, musical theatre fans. I'll get to that eventually). On one of the musical's nights off I went with my new best friend and fellow musical theatre performer Michael Legge to see Dan le Sac Vs Scroobius Pip at The Liquid Rooms. It was a huge thrill when Pip added "Carter USM – Just a band." to the list of bands in their hit song 'Thou Shalt Always Kill'.

I've been reunited with a few people I hadn't seen for years on *Roundtable*, including Brett Anderson, Clint Boon, Annie Nightingale, Gaz Coombes from Supergrass, Fred from the Family Cat, Carl from Cud and various writers who used to work at the *NME* and the *Melody Maker*.

With Ian Dury's admonishment about Charlie Watts at the back of my mind, I always enter the *Roundtable* room with good intentions and I try my best to not be too negative about the records I'm reviewing.

But I inevitably get bored with the sound of my own noncommittal views, and I hadn't been invited onto the show to tell the nation what wasn't my cup of tea. I'd search for something positive to say about records I didn't like. I'd comment on the drum sound or the chord sequence of the chorus. But soon I'd resort to taking the piss.

I've tried to develop a system. When I get the list of records up for review I'll work out who can most stand a Jim Bob roast. Which acts are too famous or too far away to be listening to BBC radio? I then decide which bands I'm least likely to bump into. I'll Google them to see how many band members there are and whether they look like the kind of people who enjoy fighting. If they've had a recent hit, live more than a thousand miles away and look a bit soft, I'm afraid it's open season for a *Roundtable* dissing from Jim Bob.

This system backfired when I went to derision town on a Bryan Ferry from Roxy Music record. I figured, I was never going to meet him. I couldn't imagine Bryan Ferry would be listening to the radio. And I did genuinely think his new record was rubbish, so I said so. What I hadn't taken into account was Bryan's fan-base, who *were* listening to the radio. For two days I received tweets and messages from irate Bryan Ferry fans, demanding that I apologise immediately.

On one episode of *Roundtable* I had to review a Frank Turner record. I didn't say anything particularly nasty but I definitely didn't give it a favourable review. Four or five out of ten, tops. A week or two later I played at the Midwinter Picnic in Brighton. It was an all day gig organised by Chris T-T and Mrs Chris T-T, Rifa. It was a BYOB and BYOF event and everyone had brought their own couscous and salads, risottos and pasta dishes. Me and Mrs Jim Bob brought a family pack of Walkers crisps, six Mars bars and some £3.99 wine.

Frank Turner was also on the bill. I don't know what food or drink he brought. All day I was thinking, should I go up to him and apologise for slagging him off on the radio or should I take a chance on him not having heard it? It was a right old quandary. In the end, I decided to wait until I was drunk and tell the audience instead. I turned it into a funny story while Frank watched me from the back of the stage. Like I said before, I can't help myself when I'm under the spotlight.

Despite my best intentions I've never left Steve Lamacq's *Roundtable* table without feeling remorse for something I've just said on air and with the sense that I've let Ian Dury down again. It's no wonder nobody wants my autograph afterwards. The *Roundtable* table isn't round by the way and they always put me in the same chair. I think it's the yesterday's jam chair.

The 'Y2K The Bug is Coming' single eventually trickled out without accompanying animation or global catastrophe in January 2000. Clearly the bug wasn't coming. Planes hadn't fallen from the sky, the oceans had stayed where they were and Jools Holland had got away with it for another year. Somebody told me it was the last record Ian Dury sang on. I don't know if that's true. A few months later he passed away. I'm such an idiot for not writing a play with him when I had the chance and for not going to his house. Damn my overactive orbitofrontal cortex.

I think one of the reasons the 'Y2K' single was released so late was because there was a lot of input from all the other people involved in the project and it slowed the writing and recording process down. I had to keep going back to the drawing board. Which is the worst place to record a song, now that I think of it. I should have gone back to the recording studio.

All songs are written by committee now of course. Most often, a songwriting team will be assembled around a massive table with some Danish pastries and water at the centre. Each member of the team will be assigned a particular role: verse, chorus, beat, hook, vibe etc. The performer, if they're lucky, can choose the title and take all the credit – but none of the money – when they explain to a presenter on *BBC Breakfast* how they wrote the song after a difficult break up with an ex.

I PLAYED SIX LIVE SHOWS IN 2000 FOUR OF THOSE WERE IN LONDON AND THE OTHER TWO WERE EMPTY

Carter played the same number of gigs in 1987. It was our very first year as a band and it didn't even start until August. Jim's Super Stereoworld's provincial unpopularity had bruised my ego enough to make me lazy. I preferred staying at home where I was still relatively famous, even if Mrs Jim Bob would sometimes forget to applaud me when I entered the room.

I'd been spoiled by my previous success. Spoiled in the bratty sense of the word. Without sounding bigheaded – okay, *with* sounding bigheaded – once you've headlined Glastonbury[22], sitting on the wheel arch in the back of a van and sleeping on a Travelodge floor after an empty gig in a former public toilet is bound to feel like a step backwards.

It's greedy isn't it? I'd already had my turn at the top. Chris T-T once pointed this out to me when I was moaning about how unsuccessful my latest solo record was. He told me that at least I'd been successful once. Maybe that should be the rule. Once you've had your success, you don't get a second go at it. No reformed bands, no heritage acts, no anniversary rereleases.

I've often wished I could be content just playing music purely for the love of it. Instead of always looking for validation or approval or chasing some dream or other. I hope Les doesn't mind me saying this, but his band Abdoujaparov have been going for longer than Carter, with many different lineups, including one with me on guitar[23]. But I don't think Les has ever had any real driving need for the band to be successful. He just loves being on stage playing guitar. The size of the crowd watching him is almost irrelevant. In fact I know he's enjoyed a lot of the emptier Abdoujaparov gigs more than the sold out ones. As I write this he's the guitarist with Ferocious Dog. He stands back and simply plays his guitar and I've never seen him happier. I'm clearly way more needy than Les.

---

22 Every year when Glastonbury is on television people go on Twitter to make snide comments about the days the festival was so shit that Carter The Unstoppable Sex Machine actually headlined! I've always resisted naming and shaming Colin Paterson for saying the same thing (twice) on BBC television. I think it would be unfair to do so now.

23 To date there have been sixty-eight different line-ups of Abdoujaparov. As Andy Warhol once said: 'In the future, everyone will be a member of Abdoujaparov.'

If I ever tell you that I'd be happy if just one person liked my music, I'm definitely lying. I want lots of people to like it. I wouldn't have been satisfied for Jim's Super Stereoworld to change just one life. I wanted us to change lots of lives. My own included of course. My own in particular really. Me, me, bloody me.

Anyway. It's the year 2000, we're all still alive and I've got another album to finish. Jim's Super Stereoworld have just signed to Musicblitz. com, who are a digital record label based in Los Angeles. They've already released 'Pear Shaped World' as an exclusive online only single on something called an MP3, which you couldn't physically touch or make an ashtray out of. It was an exclusivity that sounded a bit more futuristic to me at the start of the millennium than it does now. Nowadays saying something is exclusive is less a boast and more of a pre-planned worse case scenario. I think it took me until the end of the 1990s before I realised that 'limited edition' meant as many copies as you could sell.

Musicblitz.com were going to build up a large roster of acts and then float the company on the stock market for a bazillion dollars. They were going to be the next Google and I was going to get in on the ground floor. The floor where the fusball table, basketball hoop and ball pit were. The trouble with the dot-com bubble was that it was inevitably going to burst. They should never have called it a bubble.

For a while though, it was exciting to think of all these unseen things that were apparently happening to me on the other side of the Atlantic. I decided not to question too rigorously whether it was true that my music was going to be used to soundtrack major coverage of US television sports or soundtrack popular primetime TV shows and adverts. Home runs would be hit to the sound of my voice I was told. All those muppets who blamed Carter's lack of American success on my accent and the songs being too English were about to eat humble (apple) pie when they heard Jim's Super Stereoworld on *Dawson's Creek* and *Buffy the Vampire Slayer*. When the MP3 of 'Pear Shaped World' was downloaded by billions of people all over the world-wide-web.

As it turned out, a lot of what I was told must have been nonsense. Flannel FM as Carter's old tour manager Nimar used to say. Jim's Super Stereoworld's American success certainly didn't materialise in any tangible bank-accountable-buy-an-island way. But I was happy to believe it at the time. All egomaniacs really require is to *believe* that they're popular. I'm reminded of the time when I learned that Chrysalis Records always made sure that the posters for Carter records went up on walls close to where we lived, to guarantee that we saw them. The posters themselves apparently didn't make a great difference to record sales and were mainly there to keep the bands happy.

At the end of 2000 I saw the American band At the Drive-In perform on *Later…With Jools Holland*. They started their first song '*One Armed Scissor*' like most bands end their last. It was amazing. I didn't know the song and I wasn't entirely sure At the Drive-In did either. The guitarist wasn't so much playing his guitar as having an argument with it. The singer was standing on the drum kit, jumping off the drum kit, standing on an amp, jumping off the amp. He was up and over the monitors and going into the audience, returning with a chair he'd found somewhere, which he then gets his feet caught up in. And that seems to anger him and so he throws the chair across the stage, almost tripping the guitarist up. The guitarist is now even more possessed than he already was. He's kicked the chair and he's thrown his guitar towards the audience, almost decapitating Robbie Williams from Take That on the adjacent stage.

At the Drive-In finish their song, probably, I don't know, who could possibly know? The cameras focus on Robbie Williams, who looks like a deer caught in the headlights of the car crash he's just witnessed. A car crash that he now has to try and follow with his new, let's face it, dull by comparison single. Poor old Robbie Williams knows that no amount of gurning, antibacterial gel and pointing the microphone at the audience to let them do all the hard work, is going to stop his song from sounding lame compared to what's just happened. I knew how he felt. And I'd only watched it on telly.

At the next Jim's Super Stereoworld gig I turned the volume and the distortion on my guitar up full and I threw it around like it was on fire. I didn't bother to play the right chords. It probably sounded terrible. I hope it did. It was outside London so there was nobody there anyway.

Just before the willful self-destruction of my disco pop band we played a gig at the Barfly in – where else? – yep, Camden. It was the gig where the support band upset Salv. After they'd finished their set and packed up and left without watching the main band like all local support bands do, I played a short acoustic set. It was the first time I'd played completely solo since about 1982. I remember the 1982 gig more vividly. It was at the Thomas A Becket pub on the Old Kent Road and I was so nervous before the gig that I couldn't stop throwing up. I'd never been onstage on my own and I was absolutely terrified. I performed under the name Jamie Wednesday and two of the songs I played would later be rewritten as 'Sheriff Fatman' and 'After the Watershed'. Nothing is wasted. That's what authors are always advising each other. It all gets used eventually.

If I was especially nervous for my next solo performance eighteen years after the Thomas A Becket, it might have had something to do with Fruitbat being in the audience. I was going to end my set of solo acoustic songs with 'A Prince in a Pauper's Grave'.' It would be the first time I'd sung a Carter song since we'd split up. I don't know how Fruitbat felt about it at the time but after that day, when I started performing on my own more regularly and including more Carter songs in my set, he didn't like it.

When I knew Fruitbat was going to be in the audience at my gigs, I dreaded it. I used to tell him in advance that I was going to play Carter songs, like I was warning him strobe lighting would be used in the performance, or the time when Carter played at York Barbican and the venue insisted on putting up a sign that said: 'PARTS OF TONIGHT'S CARTER USM PERFORMANCE WILL BE ON PRE-RECORDED TAPES'.

I might have told myself there was no difference between playing a Carter song or one of my solo ones because I'd at least partly written them both. But when Les was watching, I felt like I was doing something dirty or wrong. Like I was cheating on him in public. I'd make self-deprecating onstage jokes about my guitar playing before a Carter song, proving my point by getting the opening riffs to 'Everytime a Churchbell Rings' or 'Good Grief Charlie Brown' wrong. And even more wrong than usual, because I was so anxious that Les was watching me.

I'm sure it must have been particularly annoying for Les because it was easier for me to play Carter songs. I certainly don't mean because I'm a better musician. I mean because it's my voice on the records. Les told me recently the reason he still didn't perform many Carter songs at his own gigs is because they sounded like cover versions with him singing them.

When I played 'A Prince in a Pauper's Grave' for the first time, it was three and a half years since Carter had broken up. Maybe it was too soon. I don't know when it's acceptable to start playing your old songs. Because everyone who was once in a successful band will end up playing their old material at some point, especially the singers. Morrissey from The Smiths has done it, Liam Gallagher from Oasis, both Roger Waters and Dave Gilmour from Pink Floyd, and Paul Weller from The Jam.[24]

I'd recommend easing yourself into the old material gradually, hoping no one will notice. Maybe begin by playing one of the more obscure

---

24 Not to be confused with 'From the Jam', a group comprising of Bruce Foxton and Rick Buckler from The Jam, playing Jam songs but with a different singer. Rick Buckler has now left From The Jam. If Bruce Foxton goes too, From The Jam could easily end up in a Sugababes situation of being a band with none of its original members. Like the anti-Who's the Daddy Now? who you can read about in a couple of chapters time. Or if Bruce Foxton leaves but a new band emerges, they'll be called From From The Jam and made up from discarded members of one of the two Bucks Fizzes and either of the UB40s. From From The Jam will perform The Jam songs with a reggae twist and pull each others' skirts off during 'Down in the Tube Station at Midnight'.

songs from your back catalogue, working your way up to playing the hits but still only playing them in the encore. Before long though, you'll be performing nothing but your old back catalogue. In 2018 someone will go on Facebook and accuse you of being 'Shit acoustic Carter karaoke'.

I just watched an interview with Paul McCartney from The Beatles, where he was explaining why he'd started performing Beatles songs for the first time since the band broke up twenty years earlier. Paul said for a long time it would have been like singing his ex-wife's songs after their divorce. I hadn't even realised The Beatles were married.

Jim's Super Stereoworld went on at the Barfly after I'd played a Carter song for the first time in three and a half years. It was a struggle to win the crowd over as I'd just blown myself offstage. The whole gig was filmed and streamed live on the Internet by Channel Fly. We called it 'World Tour in a Day'. The idea being that I was playing to a potential audience of everyone on the planet all in one go and without needing to leave the comfort of my own Camden. I have no idea how many people actually watched it or how jittery the pictures were. I imagine there was so much buffering in 2001 that the live stream of the gig hasn't quite finished yet.

DAMON ALBARN FROM BLUR

In 2001 I was changing lanes again. I'd just finished making a disco-pop-punk record and before it was even released I was moving on to the next thing. An album of mostly slow acoustic songs called *J.R.* I'd changed my name again. Not quite ready to return to the full Jim Bob yet but I was now James Robert Morrison. By the time *J.R.* was out, I was back in Stereoworld, working on a collection of bubblegum punk rock songs about fast cars and girls. My manager Adrian told me how difficult it was to promote me if I kept changing my mind about what I wanted to do every five seconds.

Dennis @Snafflebold_Den69 . 6m Just fucken reform Carter.
#youfatbastard!

I was as impatient as Dennis. Not for a Carter reformation, but my return to the top. It was taking too long. Things had happened so quickly when we started Carter. We'd formed the band while our last one was still going. We had our first gig at a big London venue booked before we'd written a single song or chosen a band name. We wrote seven songs in a couple of days and made our live debut a few days after that. We recorded a demo tape and the very first label we gave the tape to released our debut single. If it had all taken a bit longer I wonder if I would have got bored and tried something else.

With things now moving at a slower pace for me I had too much time to think and too much time for doubt. Maybe if Jim's Super Stereoworld's second single 'Could U B the 1 I Waited 4' had spent a second week at number ninety-nine instead of just one in the UK singles chart, or if it had moved up the chart instead of down, I wouldn't have panic-recorded an acoustic album.

I was also involved in a second animated project. After the Y2K nonstarter I was working with Dave Reading on a 'virtual pop band'. Dave had designed the Jim's Super Stereoworld sleeves, including the first album (which features photos of me taken by Grant Gee who made the Radiohead documentary, *Meeting People is Easy)*. Dave Reading took the photo of my daughter on the cover of the first Carter single 'A Sheltered Life'. He had an idea for a group of cartoon characters called 'Heds'. They would 'perform' the songs I was writing for them. So many inverted commas. It would be my voice actually singing the songs but Heds would be the face of the band. Basically: Gorrilaz.

Professional jealousy isn't very professional, so I'll pretend I don't mind that Damon Albarn from Blur is so much better at getting his ideas funded and off the ground than I am. Years after Heds vs Gorllilaz, I was going to arrive at the launch party for my novel *The Extra Ordinary Life of Frank Derrick* dressed as a milkman and riding on a milk float. I bought a white coat and a milkman's cap on eBay for twenty pounds but then the budget[25] ran out. Without the milk float, my cheap milkman outfit looked ridiculous. I didn't even look particularly like a milkman. I looked more like an ice cream man.

Luckily I kept the white coat and cap, because there was an ice cream van on the cover of my next novel *Frank Derrick's Holiday of a Lifetime* a year later. This time I was going to turn up at the launch party in an ice cream van. But even though I'd saved money by already owning the ice cream man outfit, lack of budget again and the difficulties of parking in Crystal Palace meant that I got a bus to the bookshop instead. As it happened the publication of *Frank Derrick's Holiday of a Lifetime* coincided with the release of Blur's *Magic Whip* album. And of course, for their promotional campaign, Blur not only had an ice cream van, they also had their own special brand of ice cream.

I have to admit there are times when I feel sorry for myself. When I wonder why I'm not appreciated more and why there hasn't been a *Jim Bob Night* on BBC4. But I try my best to keep any feelings of professional envy to myself. And sometimes it's quite hard. Not long ago I'd written a new novel but couldn't find anyone to publish it. I was starting to feel disillusioned with everything and reading on the Internet about all the authors who'd just signed book deals didn't help. When Jarvis Cocker and Brett Anderson both signed huge book deals I wrote this on Twitter:

> *If everyone could shut up about their six-figure book deals until I've got one, that would be much appreciated.*
> *Thank you.*

Why couldn't I just be happy for them both? The Germans have a word for the sick feeling in the stomach when hearing of someone else's success: Gluckschmerz. It's the opposite of schadenfreude. Morrissey wrote a song about it – 'We Hate It When Our Friends Become Successful'. And Brett was a sort of friend. We'd only spoken when we'd bumped into each other in the guest bars of festivals in the 1990s and that one time on *Roundtable*. But still, why couldn't I just be happy for him?

The same applies to any envy I have of Damon's success. We always used to get on. There's even a piece of Googleable photographic evidence of our friendship. The picture was taken at the launch party for Blur's

---

25 Twenty pounds.

Parklife album at Walthamstow dog track. We both look quite drunk and I appear to be ever so slightly smaller in scale than Damon. It looks like I've photoshopped the picture and put it on the Internet to make it look like we're mates. Ironically, most of my work that is similar to Damon's – animated virtual rock band, musical – have also been on a much smaller scale.

I was such a Blur fan, especially around the time of *Modern Life is Rubbish*. Justine Frischmann from Elastica once physically attacked me in a bar because she thought I'd stolen the Carter song 'Lean on me, I Won't Fall Over' – musically and lyrically – from Blur's 'Advert'. I've just listened to them both and maybe she had a point.

As for my relationship with the other members of Blur: I did get very drunk with Dave Rowntree from Blur at the NME Awards once. I have a story about that but I'm saving it for if he ever becomes leader of the Labour Party. Graham Coxon from Blur was the first person outside of a Hollywood movie I heard use the word 'dweeb' – as in "Why are you speaking to these two dweebs?" – a question he put to Damon when he discovered him in conversation with me and Fruitbat at a festival in Germany[26]. I don't remember ever meeting Alex James from Blur but I have eaten some of his cheese. It came in a box as part of a selection that someone bought me for my birthday. And I'm genuinely not saying this for effect or as a pithy metaphor for how I feel about the members of Blur, but the Alex James cheese was my least favourite out of the selection.

---

26 This was the festival Carter played the day after headlining (yes, headlining) Glastonbury. We were ejected by security from both. Yes, both.

RAY WINSTONE

WHO'S THE DADDY NOW?

www.~~v~~
Phone: ~~~~
email: ~~~~

J.R. was the first record released on my own Ten Forty Sound label[27]. In conjunction with Who's The Daddy Now?, a label consisting of Ten Forty Sound, Fruitbat's Spinach Records and our Australian friend Jason Bootle from the Invisibles's Pop Gun Records. I found a short WTDN 'mission statement'.

> *To pool the resources of three likeminded labels.*
> *To obtain good distribution.*
> *Strengthen OZ/UK ties with reciprocal tours/releases.*
> *To make serious casheroonie.*

We achieved at least two, maybe three of those aims. By combining our three small labels to make one slightly bigger label we were able to get a better distribution deal and get our music into more shops, and Fruitbat did play an annual tour of Australia with Abdoujaparov. The serious

---

27   The origin of the label's name is like a cryptic crossword clue or one of those 'my first is in Jim but not in Bob' type riddles. My birthday is the 22 November, that's 22.11. Which is twenty-two eleven, or twenty to eleven, which is ten forty.

casheroonie I don't recall. Unless Les and Jason trousered it all. I'd ask them about it but they're both on holiday at the moment in their adjacent luxury condominiums in the Seychelles.

On a Monday in February 2001 we had our inaugural Who's the Daddy Now? business meeting in the Wetherspoons in Crystal Palace. There was a sign on the bar celebrating the pub's regular 'Monday Club' and from then on, as our record company meetings were regular Monday events too, we called them our 'Monday Club'. After WTDN were no more we still went to the 'spoons on Mondays. We still do, although less frequently and not always on a Monday. And we've moved pub because we're a bunch of snobs now and the 'spoons just isn't good enough for us anymore. Our club membership has changed a bit as well. The current regular Monday Club membership consists of three musicians, an author, a scriptwriter, a television marketing executive and a bubble machine operator. Imagine a South London Bilderberg Group. An elite art new world order that meets every first Monday of the month to dress in robes and set fire to a 30-foot high owl statue. That's why we have to keep changing pubs.

When we aren't shouting at each other at Monday Club, about television and films and the brilliance of the 1970s, we still discuss a bit of business. All the Carter reunion shows for example, along with their accompanying themes and T-shirt designs have originated there.

We had such big plans for Who's The Daddy Now? In August of 2001 we put on the first of many (one) Who's the Daddy club nights at the Windmill in Brixton. Spinach Records band Malowski and Jason's own Pop Gun band Invisibles played. Me, Fruitbat and Jamie Suburban played records. I was MC. It was £3 to get in. Doors were 7.30pm until late. The Windmill is left out of Brixton tube, just off Brixton Hill. Can you tell I've just found the flyer?

Mrs Jim Bob painted a life-size boxer onto a wallpaper-pasting table and cut a hole into the table where the boxer's face would have been. The audience at The Windmill could stick their head through the hole and have their photo taken. Damon Albarn would have had a real boxer at the club. The audience would have been able to have their faces projected onto a hologram of Sylvester Stallone. Sylvester Stallone would have been DJ'ing. Damon would have got Arts Council funding and a *South Bank Show* out of his club night. We just did the one night in a Brixton pub, three quid to get in. Left out of the Tube.

Who's The Daddy Now? had an obsession with boxing. All the gigs were billed as heavyweight title events and the bands were usually advertised as 'versus' one another. We called our press department 'Aggressive Marketing' and the WTDN logo was a big fist. In our publicity picture, Les, Jason and me are all duffed-up like extras from

Fight Club. Maybe it shouldn't be so surprising that the whole thing would come close to fisticuffs when we took it on tour.

The WTDN tour was inspired by the Stiff Records package tours in 1977, 78 and 1980. The acts on the first Stiff tour were Elvis Costello, Ian Dury, Nick Lowe, Wreckless Eric and Larry Wallis. The idea was that everyone would muck in, with musicians being shared – Ian Dury played drums for Wreckless Eric for example. The running order would rotate each night and everyone would come back onstage at the end and play 'Sex & Drugs & Rock & Roll'. I've got the superb live album they recorded on the tour. I quoted from it in the prologue of this book.

On the Who's the Daddy Now? tour, the Invisibles, Abdoujaparov and Jim's Super Stereoworld would play our own sets and then we'd all join together at the end of the night to play a few Carter songs. And just like my solo acoustic shows, the more dates Who's the Daddy Now? played, the more Carter songs crept into the set, eventually almost annexing the rest of the show. With me and Fruitbat in Who's The Daddy Now? (and also Salv and Ben) we jokingly billed ourselves as the only tribute act containing all the original members of the band that we were paying tribute to.

In his book *Unfaithful Music & Disappearing Ink*, Elvis Costello talks about how competitive the Stiff Records tour was, particularly between him and Ian Dury. There was definitely an element of competition on the WTDN tours. I know Jim's Super Stereoworld went onstage every night with the intention of being the best act on the bill. And as we went on before the Who's the Daddy Now? free-for-all at the end, technically I wanted to blow myself off stage again. I know the Invisibles felt the same as us. They definitely wanted to be the best band every night. I'd say it was only easy-going Fruitbat who wasn't too fussed about competing. As usual he was happy to be doing what he loved, playing guitar, being on stage, on tour, on a tour bus.

Tour buses are expensive. Especially when you consider they don't even have the facilities for going for a poo. The advantages are obvious though. They're still cheaper than booking hotels and hiring transport and drivers for twenty people and you can get halfway to the next date on your badly routed tour while everyone's still in bed. You can stay up late and get drunk, knowing that your bed is within staggering distance. But they really are very expensive, especially if you're the one who's paying. I paid for the bus on Carter's last American tour, and Les and Jason might dispute this if I bothered to check it with them, but I think I also paid for the tour bus on the first Who's the Daddy tour.

In *Goodnight Jim Bob* I wrote about the bus games we played on tour with Carter. Like when we stuck cigarette papers to each other's heads and guessed the names of the popular celebrities and world dictators written on them. We had 'Freddie Mercury nights', when everyone wore black gaffer tape moustaches and sung along to *Queen's Greatest Hits*. One particularly memorable tour bus driver called Eric took us all to Blackpool Pleasure Beach for the day before a gig in Manchester once. The same bus driver stood with me one night as we watched Fruitbat – who'd just played a gig sitting in a chair because of his sciatica – kicking Carter drummer Wez who was lying on the floor in the aisle of the bus, literally asking for it. "Kick me then, kick me," Wez said. There was that time on the same tour, during the general election, when Wez's brother and Carter guitarist Steve climbed on top of the bus in Farnham and dropped his trousers to moon local tory MP Virginia Bottomley.

I'd lost any enthusiasm I once had for sleeper buses by the time of the first Who's the Daddy Now? tour. I didn't want to play video games or watch *The Blues Brothers*. I didn't want to stay up all night drinking and I associated the bunks with loneliness and melancholy. Also, I think we took some of the onstage inter-band rivalry onto the bus with us after the gigs. I don't know if any of Abdoujaparov or the Invisibles talked about Jim's Super Stereoworld behind our backs but we definitely did behind theirs.

I recall a lot of serious crisis meetings in the upstairs lounge of the bus on the Daddy tours, usually to do with people not pulling their weight at load-ins or load-outs. There seemed to be a meeting every night about whether the bus should drive to the next town after the gig or park up outside a nightclub so that half the passengers could go inside while the rest of us sat on the bus and sulked. We could never agree what music should be playing on the bus.

I'd like to say the mood on the tour bus started out well and then deteriorated, but it was doomed from the first night of the first tour. We were parked up outside Harlow Square (offices and apartments now) and at some point the table in the downstairs lounge got broken and peanut butter sandwiches were thrown at the wall. I overreacted. I shouted at people and then I sulked. That's why I'm so sure it was me who must have paid for the bus. I wanted to go home immediately. I seriously considered walking to the train station and cancelling the tour. As with the Tunbridge Wells drugs story I've chosen to not name and shame anyone for breaking the table and throwing the sandwiches and once again that makes everyone look guilty except for me. Hooray!

Musicians are expected to trash at least one tour bus or hotel in their careers I suppose but I've never been one of those people[28]. And I don't like watching others doing it either. The worst case of rock 'n' roll destruction I've witnessed was when Carter were part of the Big Day Out tour of Australia in 1993. Using my 6 Music Roundtable theory that I can

---

28   Musicians.

get away with slagging bands off if they live a long way away from me and therefore I'm unlikely to bump into them, I'm going to name them. It was Mudhoney. Every night they'd smash things up and it started to really bother me. Not enough to say anything. I'm British. I remember them running along the corridor of a hotel smashing every single light bulb one night. I think it was in Fremantle, where they later threw the hotel manager in the swimming pool.

The Fremantle hotel where Mudhoney threw the hotel manager into the pool was the same hotel I'm pictured perched on the balcony of, on the front cover of *Goodnight Jim Bob*. At the end of my 2018 solo tour with Pop Will Eat Itself, me and my roadie/friend/tour manager/ swimming coach Mister Spoons stayed on in Fremantle for a few days to eat ice creams. Totally by coincidence we booked into the same hotel I'd stayed at on the Big Day Out tour. We worked out which room the book cover photo had been taken from and the staff let us in to recreate it. Sadly, because of age, my fear of heights and my frozen shoulder (*it's a thing*) I couldn't make it up onto the balcony and Mister Spoons had to do it for me, just like he has to do everything else for me.[29]

---

29   Mister Spoons = Spoons = Wetherspoon's = Witherow = Neil Witherow. Neil has been my 'butler, babysitter, hand-holder and designated driver' since the third Who's the Daddy Now? tour. Apart from tuning my guitars and operating the bubble machine at gigs, Neil also designs and hosts my websites. He typeset my first novel and sometimes goes swimming with me. We've been to football, Australia and Center Parcs together. He cooked meals for everyone during the recording of at least two of my solo albums and starred in the video for my single 'Battling the Bottle'. Neil is a sometime wedding DJ and used to be the eagle mascot at Crystal Palace football club. He is a keen ukulele player. But nobody's perfect.

It's not only musicians who can be badly behaved on holiday. In 2017 I played a solo acoustic set of Carter songs on a cruise ship from Hull to Rotterdam, along with Dodgy, James from EMF, Clint Boon from the Inspiral Carpets and Peter Hook from New Order. I'd last seen Peter Hook in 2014. He'd played on the same day as Carter at Bearded Theory festival. Shortly before it was time to go on, Peter Hook arrived in his sports car. He pulled up behind the stage but didn't get out of the car until it was time to go on. After the gig he got straight into his car and drove away. I was disappointed he didn't pull up beside the cruise ship halfway across the North Sea in a speed boat, climb up a rope ladder, play the gig and then walk straight off the stage into his waiting speed boat. Actually, I didn't see him arrive or leave, so perhaps he did exactly that.

Everyone onboard that big boat, with the exception of me and the captain (I like to think) were off their faces. I was too scared to drink because I was so paranoid about getting seasick and not being able to perform. I had managed to play a gig on a boat once before without getting seasick, but it was only a barge, and it was moored to the shore in Battersea. Before boarding the ship to Holland I double-dosed on Kwells and avoided the all-you-can-eat buffet. I felt fine.

Before it had left the port the ship took on the appearance of that mad bar in *Star Wars* or all of *Blade Runner*. Everywhere I went there was yet another room full of insanely drunk people. The only real escape was to jump overboard. The audience was pretty rambunctious during my set and the ship's crew tried to contain the rambunctiousness. The sight of them all in their crisp white epauletted shirts, looking like a cross between airline pilots and shopping centre security guards, attempting to stop the audience from dancing, was bizarre. Eventually they put one of those red VIP ropes across the front of the stage, which everyone kept falling over because they were so drunk. In the morning I was talking to the purser (the dude who looks after everyone's purses during a voyage, the captain takes care of the caps and the first mate is everyone's best friend) and I asked him about the badly behaved audience the night before.

I said I bet he wasn't used to such a mental crowd. On the contrary, the purser told me, the regular weekend crossings were a hundred times worse. The passengers on the regular trips from Hull to Rotterdam were worse than Mudhoney.

Everyone should perform a gig on a ship at least once in their lives. It was certainly an experience and my old next-door neighbour would have been pleased that I'd finally taken his advice. He was a chauffeur and used to drive real proper showbiz stars like Shirley Bassey around. Every time I saw him he always used to tell me how I should play hotels and cruise ships. "And the holiday camps Jimbo," he'd say. He always called me Jimbo. I was too polite to ever tell him my name wasn't Jimbo but I did tell him I wasn't the type of artist who would be seen dead performing at holiday camps or on cruise ships. Seven months after the gig on the cruise ship I played a gig at Butlin's. I'll tell you someone who'll never perform on a cruise ship. Seasick Steve.

The first Daddy tour ended in London at the Mean Fiddler (formerly the LA2, the Astoria 2 and the Buzz Club) on Charing Cross Road (now part of the same big hole in the ground as the Astoria)[30]. For the second leg of the same tour we moved upstairs to the larger Astoria venue and by the end of the third Daddy tour a year later, we were back downstairs. I do like my rags to riches and back again stories to be concise.

I've played at least two of London's legendary Marquee Clubs and neither of them was the original one. Carter played at the Marquee on Charing Cross Road (now a Wetherspoon's). The picture of Carter on the back of the 'Sheriff Fatman' sleeve was taken at the Marquee on Charing Cross Road. I also played a short solo set at a different Marquee in 2004, this time in Leicester Square. It was a benefit gig to encourage Americans in the UK to vote in the US election. George W Bush was re-elected that year. I suppose I'm at least partially responsible for that.

One of the gigs on the last Daddy tour was at the Cavern in Liverpool. I remember being quite depressed about everything that day. It wasn't just that the venue wasn't full or that it wasn't even the original Cavern in Liverpool. It was both of those things. I'm not even sure it was the Cavern in Liverpool that replaced the original Cavern in Liverpool. You know, the one where The Beatles used to play. I'm surprised the venue doesn't mention that more.

My memories of the third Who's The Daddy tour are of emptier rooms in general, and judging by the posters on the walls, we were very much on the tribute act circuit. At least we had a witty name for our tribute act. Surely one of the main reasons for forming a tribute band is so you can come up with a funny name. Maybe it's the only reason. Names like By Jovi and Leonard Skinhead. Nowadays tribute bands are all called 'The Rolling Stones (tribute)' and '(Tribute to) Queen.'

When we (spoiler alert) reformed Carter, the promoter of one of the London aftershows paid for a Carter tribute band to fly over from Tokyo and play. Clinton USM are fantastic and a far better Carter tribute act than the one with all the original members of the band in.

---

30 During the excavation for the new Tottenham Court Road Underground station Crossrail builders discovered a vault beneath the Astoria. Archaeologists unearthed hundreds of 19th and 20th century earthenware jam jars – quite literally yesterday's jam. The vault had been part of the former Crosse & Blackwell bottling plant and also contained pickle pots, glass catsup bottles and mustard bung jars, which explains at last why people were always shouting you fat mustard at us.

I can remember so little about the final Who's the Daddy tour. Which could mean I was having too much of a good time I suppose. The things I do recall don't really qualify as anecdotes. They aren't going to get me a spot on *The Graham Norton Show* any time soon. I'm not sure they'd even get me a spot in that red chair at the end of the show.

For the second Stiff Records tour they hired a train. I remember discussing doing the same for a third Who's the Daddy tour. It's probably just as well it didn't happen, what with the state of today's railways.

TEAM BUILDING

I've always surrounded myself with enablers. Normal people might call them friends. Without Adrian Boss managing us, Carter would never have got anywhere. Literally, because neither me or Fruitbat could drive at the time (I still can't). For the first Carter gigs, Adrian would hire a car and drive us there and back. He did so much more than that of course. Adrian was metaphorically driving us as well. Giving our demo tape to the right people, getting us gigs that weren't at the Cricketers in Kennington, arranging people to interview us, making phone calls (Les was about as good as me at using the telephone). Adrian featured a lot in *Goodnight Jim Bob*. I told the story of his 'Magic pants', how he hallucinated a white horse on the M3 and fell asleep in a bonfire and that time he threw beer in an American security guard's face.

Adrian carried on as my manager after Carter broke up in 1997, right up until sometime at the start of the two thousands. There was no great falling-out or disagreement between us. It was just time for a change. I was already doing a lot more of my own admin by that point anyway. The anonymity of email helped me. And I still had one of my Stereoworld sock puppets working with me. Good old Kenny continued replying to emails on my behalf until Marc Ollington took over.

Marc had already been helping out with my PR, which he did under the name Marcus Tandy, a character from the short-lived BBC soap opera *Eldorado*. I've known Marc for close to two decades and I'm not sure I've ever asked him why he called himself Marcus Tandy. On the first Carter album *101 Damnations*, Adrian Boss is credited as the third Beatle. If Adrian was Brian Epstein, Marc Ollington is Murray Hewitt.

Murray managed the band Flight of the Conchords in the hit TV show of the same name. Like Marc, Murray also had a day job. He worked as Deputy Cultural Attaché at the New Zealand consulate in New York City. Marc was International Marketing Executive for the National Geographic Channel. Luckily they never found out he'd been using their A3 photocopier to print hundreds of my tour posters or giving away all the company's promotional merchandise as Jim Bob competition prizes. When I played Glastonbury, Team Jim Bob slept in National Geographic tents and carried our belongings in National Geographic bags. It was a fine line between theft and corporate sponsorship.

According to Wikipedia, Murray Hewitt is 'passionate about Flight of the Conchords and aspires to be a successful manager. He lacks basic competence in the field' and is 'unaware of the proper name of the bass guitar (he calls it the "dad guitar")'.

Marc used to write letters to me when I was in Carter. Sadly, I haven't kept any of them but Marc has kept my replies (I believe that tells you something about our individual characters). Marc has kept six of my replies. Here's one of them. Morty is Morty from Sultans of Ping:

> Dear Marc,
>
> Thanks for writing and for sending the lovely photos. Straight in with the bad news I'm afraid though as Morty was unfortunately mucho mistaken and we aren't actually looking for a bass player at all. Very sorry about this. I hope it's not too much of a disappointment. Anyway, I hope you are well, we're involved in intense exercise – 15 mile runs every morning, 200 press ups, strict diet etc, in preparation for the upcoming touring which kicks off in a couple of weeks. Also it's interview schminterviews and round the block bullshitting and having our ugly mugs photographed for crap magazines to accompany the misunderstandings and slaggings of our new and brilliant record. So you are better off out of it really, it's overrated. Enough of my gibberish, we're actually glad to be doing something as we've been incredibly idle lately and bored shitless. Looking forward to the touring part and playing the new songs to see if anyone likes them or not.
>
> Anyway, more news soon.
> Yours truly,
> Jim Bob

Marc couldn't play bass. To be honest, knowing him as well as I do now, I wouldn't be surprised if, like Murray Hewitt, he didn't really know what a bass guitar was. I presume he'd looked at a picture of me and Fruitbat and compared us to another band, say, The Beatles or The Rolling Stones, he'd ascertained what was missing from the picture and decided playing the drums looked a bit too strenuous.[31]

Marc used to write regularly to three other people apart from me. He wrote to Arsenal manager George Graham, sending him his tactical observations. George always replied and Marc still has twenty letters from him. Marc sent ten letters to David Bowie but Bowie never replied. And Marc wrote to Uncle Pigg, the editor of the comic *Oink!* Uncle Pigg replied every time and Marc's jokes made it into the comic twice. In 2013 one of Marc's letters went viral. Yes Dennis, I know, technically an email isn't a letter.

---

31 Andy Burrows from Razorlight once offered to be Jim's Super Stereoworld's
   drummer. I can picture the conversation vividly. It was in the back room
   of a pub in Winchester. He was wearing a blue parka and had long hair. He
   was young and looked cool. It almost didn't matter if he could play the
   drums, which it turned out he could of course. He must have joined
   Razorlight not long after and he's played with other bands since, including
   We Are Scientists and Foregone Conclusion – David Brent from The Office's
   band. Doc Brown was also in Foregone Conclusion. Me and Doc will be in a
   musical later in this story. When I Wikipedia'd Foregone Conclusion, I
   discovered that two members of The Dum Dums were also in the band. Jim's
   Super Stereoworld played at the LA2 with The Dum Dums. It's a small world
   isn't it.

THE BUZZCOCKS LETTERS

I was one of the guests on the un-broadcast pilot episode of *Never Mind the Buzzcocks*. It had a different title at the time: *Give 'Em Enough Ramones* or something. I was on a team with Sean Hughes and Keith Allen. I think Nick Heyward from Haircut 100 and Ashley Slater from Freak Power were on the other team. I don't know who else was on their team. Let's pretend it was Ozzy Ozbourne. He'd never know any different. I think Mark Lamarr was hosting.

The Buzzcocks pilot was recorded downstairs in a West End building where I'd coincidentally had my first ever full time job at an advertising agency. I started there as a foot messenger and eventually became the dispatch manager. I was also in charge of ordering stationery and I used to order myself a lot of Letraset for making badges, imaginary posters and record sleeves for my band Jeepster. I worked there in 1977, the year that *Never Mind the Bollocks, Here's the Sex Pistols* was released. I returned twenty years later to record a pilot for a show called *Never Mind the Buzzcocks*. It's all so neat isn't it?

I was told the wrong time to arrive for the Buzzcocks pilot and got there after everyone else had watched all the clips and written their adlibs. During the show I barely said a word. Sean and Keith cracked zinger after woofer and I just sat there in silence. Afterwards, as we were leaving, this little skinhead kid who was there with Keith Allen told his dad off for being mean and not letting me get a word in. Alfie Allen from *Game of Thrones* ladies and gentlemen.

Some years later – and before Carter had even split up for Christ's sake – we started to receive requests to appear in the 'Identity Parade' section of *Never Mind the Buzzcocks*. Every year they would ask and every year we'd feel a little more insulted but still, politely decline. The offers to appear on the Buzzcocks ID Parade shared a lot in common with the Where Are They Now? interview requests. Particularly this bit from 2011:

> In the ID Parade part of the show, we play out some footage
> of a particular musician/artist, normally from Top of The Pops
> or a music video and our celebrity panel teams will be asked
> to correctly identify the musician/artist hidden in a line-up of
> extras in our studio. Not only is this hugely popular and a good
> opportunity to reminisce about great music, it has also become an
> opportunity for artists/musicians to promote any current projects
> that they are working on.

This was Marc's 2011 reply:

> Hi ******
> I hope you are well this afternoon, and many thanks for your email.
>
> I'm a huge fan of Buzzcocks (I ruddy love it!) but I would never let Carter go on the ID parade – nor would they want to. They would poke horrible spiky sticks in my eyeballs if I signed them up for this. As you may know Carter recently headlined the Beautiful Days festival to 15,000 people and they are about to play sold-out shows at venues like Brixton Academy. And Jim Bob is now a published author with his second novel on the way. He has also hosted shows on 6music, appeared in musicals etc.
>
> What I'm basically saying is that they are too famous to be lumped in with the normal has-beens & freaks that appear on that section of the show. And if I'm honest Jim Bob is now more famous than 50% of actual show guests!
>
> Many thanks for asking. This is actually the fifth time (ha ha). Please do ask again next year though because even though I will say no again Buzzcocks is genuinely my favourite TV show and it's a thrill getting emails from you.
> All the best,
> Marc

In 2012 they asked again. Marc replied:

> Hello ***,
> I hope you are well this sunny Friday.
> Thank you for your email but I will cut to the chase like a man with a crazy axe. The answer is very much a 'no'. And not any old 'no'. A 'no' that is a little weary and sad. Perhaps this 'no' is even a tad disappointed.
>
> You are probably wondering why Mr No isn't full of the joys of this late Summers day? It may be to do with the fact that this is the seventh (I am guessing this number, but it seems as good as any and I like the number seven) time Jim has been asked. That may explain the lethargy of his refusal? Who can tell? Numbers aren't the easiest people to work out at times.
>
> Anyway, I have always enjoyed 'Never Mind The Buzzcocks' (especially the Simon Amstell period – did you see his sitcom 'Grandma's House'? An underrated gem!). As a viewer though, and you as an exec producer I think we can both agree that the section of the show isn't always that kind to the person on parade. At times it's almost like laughing at a disabled person who has fallen out of a wheelchair. But don't feel bad – it isn't as bad or exploitative as The X Factor as you do things like pay expenses.

Money can often change everything! You have to pay your own expenses to look like a banana on Simon Cowell's cavalcade of cruelness.

In my humble opinion I think Jim is too good for this part of your show. That sounds arrogant but I don't think that's a bad thing. At times I don't think the British are arrogant enough. We should say what we mean more perhaps? It hasn't done the Americans any harm, but I digress. You may not know this (why would you? You aren't God. You can't know everything!) but Carter still play sell out gigs at venues like the Brixton Academy. 5,000 people pay £25 British pounds to see them, at just that one show. In Scotland we only charge £20 as they aren't so flash with the cash up there. An amazing fact – they even headlined the Beautiful Days festival recently to 20,000 odd people. Don't get me wrong it was full of old crusty dudes but they paid over a hundred quid to get in. So not to be sniffed at eh?

Jim also has a successful solo career and is about to release his eighth album (I probably have that figure wrong too and Jim will sack me. Numbers schmumbers). He may not sell as many compact discs as U2 but he does what I would class as 'ok'. And unlike Bono he isn't going bald. Nor does he always wear sunglasses. If he goes on the identity parade he may as well say on the show "This is the only bit of publicity I can get to push my new album that nobody cares about. Please mention my new album, it will make the hilarious jokes about my old haircut all be worthwhile." But of course he couldn't say that because I don't think you allow the Identity Paraders to speak. Good job too ***. Most pop stars just talk rubbish! As it is though Jim already has a fair bit of publicity planned so I don't think we need to do this. I won't lie, it could be better. The One Show won't book him and that gets six million viewers. They are fuckers quite frankly. Six Music are a lot more amenable you'll be pleased to know.

The last thing to mention that Jim also is now an author and is onto his third novel, and his latest with a major publisher. This isn't 'Barry's Books' giving Jim 20p to write some load of old tosh. This is one of the big publishing guns giving him shit loads of money (he won't tell me how much exactly to avoid paying me properly) to write his new tome. You wouldn't find J K Rowling up on Parade. And now Jim is a published author I have a motto "Only do what the Harry Potter lady would do". I think this will hold him in good stead.

That is it from me you'll be pleased to know. Sorry for such a long response but before you emailed I was having to do something with numbers and budgets and it was hurting my noggin. I think I am doing that deflection thing my psychiatrist often talks about.

Anyway, have a great weekend ***. I hope it brings you happiness and general warm vibes.

Marc x Jim's Manager.

Marc's Buzzcocks email was shared a lot on social media and ended up on the front of the Huffington Post. Other musicians commented on how they they'd been fielding the same annual requests. Because of his Buzzcocks letter, for a while Marc was more famous than me. I was a guest on a political talk show on LBC radio and – as usual – I was trying to explain who I was to a friend of one of the other guests. I went through the whole aforementioned, "I'm a writer, I used to be a musician, I was in a band, we headlined Glastonbury, here's a video of the *Smash Hits Awards*," but was met by the same blank look. And then suddenly, their eyes lit up. "OMG," they said. "You're managed by that Marc Ollington guy. His Buzzcocks letter was *hilarious*." Marc's stupid fucking email gained so much publicity that the producers of *Never Mind the Buzzcocks* accused us of using a private correspondence for cheap publicity and of getting a cheap joke at their expense. If you've ever heard a better example of a pot calling a kettle black, I'd like to hear it.

LAUGHING AT FUNERALS

In the summer of 2002 we put on three 'Goodnight Jim Bob' club nights at the Hope & Anchor in Islington. Jim's Super Stereoworld fan, the fire-eater and children's entertainer, Tony De La Fou suggested the club idea to us and also put us in touch with a promoter. Funnily enough, Tony De La Fou *was* part of an identity parade on *Never Mind the Buzzcocks*. He's the one on the unicycle. To be honest, if I'd known we were allowed to unicycle I would have definitely said yes.

There were three Goodnight Jim Bob club nights. In June, July and August. Every night I'd compère and play an acoustic set, sometimes accompanied by a few friends. Apart from my own songs, I also attempted various ill-advised cover versions, including Busted's 'What I Go to School For', Blink 182's 'All the Small Things', Status Quo's 'Caroline' and David Bowie's 'Sorrow'.

Fruitbat played one night as Uncle Fruity, a sort of acoustic version of his band Abdoujaparov. They dressed up as sailors for some reason. Ben from Carter and Jim's Super Stereoworld did a set as 'Leads and Wires' and our friend Bransby read his blog about his holiday in Ibiza. Rob Newman and Martin Millar also read from their novels. It was quite the variety show. All three nights were rammed but we'd agreed to such a tiny fee – I don't think anyone appearing was getting paid – and Marc ended up in a huge row with the promoter because he asked for more money for the third night.

Without getting into the ins and outs of how performers are paid – mainly because it's something I know very little about – I remember playing two identically sold out shows within a few months of each other at a venue in the Midlands. After the first gig, it was suggested we should do the second one for a share of the door money rather than a flat guarantee fee. I'm boring myself here. Obviously, my share of the door money would be after costs, which seemed to include everything from the door staff to the promoter's mortgage payments.

When Marc went to collect the money after the gig, he questioned why the amount was so small. The promoter must have pressed a secret button under his desk, because a burly security guard (why are they always burly? You never hear of anyone apart from security guards being described as burly) appeared like a *Mr. Benn* shopkeeper. He didn't need to do anything. He just stood there looking burly until Marc had no option but to take the paltry sum and leave.

Sometimes I feel like the least rewarded person in the room I'm responsible for filling with paying customers. I remember I was standing at the aftershow bar at one of the Carter Brixton Academy reunion gigs. The aftershows were always sold out in advance and packed until four in the morning. I was having trouble getting served at one of the club's bars, I stood there for ages waving my twenty pound note and then I thought to myself, what the hell am I doing? I must have moaned about this to somebody because the following year there was a roped-off area for me and Les and a case of lager. They don't call me the Indie Mariah Carey for nothing. Did I ever tell you Mariah Carey used to be able to open an electric garage door with the pitch of her voice?

In August 2002, Islington was hit by a biblical rainstorm and the cellar of the Hope and Anchor flooded. Maybe that was why Les was dressed as a sailor. It was touch and go whether the night would go ahead and for the sake of this anecdote I kind of wish it hadn't.

I must have enjoyed the freedom of playing solo those nights at the Hope & Anchor. I didn't need to book rehearsal studios or hire vans. There were no heavy amps or drum kits to carry. Soundchecks lasted five minutes and I could play whatever songs I wanted, from Busted to Bowie, often dropping or adding songs in the middle of the set. After the final Who's the Daddy Now? tour and after Salv threw his bass in the air in a cinema in Welwyn Garden City (still not come back down), a couple of months later, four years of Jim Bob solo acoustic shows began in earnest.

If you think I'm going to make a lame joke about a place called Earnest you're half right. My four years of acoustic touring actually began in Rotterdam though. Mister Spoons, who'd been driving the Jim's Super Stereoworld van in the UK, was unavailable for the Dutch trip (a Crystal Palace under elevens reserves B team friendly, according to Marc) and so me, Marc, Louis Eliot from Rialto and our two guitars all squeezed into Richy Crockford from Abdoujaparov's hatchback and we drove to Holland.

I'd met Louis Eliot at a benefit gig we were both doing at the Betsy Trotwood in Clerkenwell a few months earlier and we got on like a flipping house on fire. Going to Holland together seemed to be the next logical step in our friendship. It's been said that Louis and I look alike. Louis also went on before me in London at Lock 17 (formerly, and now once again, Dingwalls). When he came onstage, my daughter thought Louis Eliot was me. He played nine songs before she realised he wasn't. And that was only because I was sitting next to her by then.

I don't know if Mister Spoons had paid Richy Crockford to get deliberately lost so that he would seem indispensable as a driver, but that's what Richy did. First he got lost on the way from London to the Eurotunnel terminal in Kent and then again – because none of us had thought about bringing a map – he got lost in Holland too. After circling Rotterdam for almost two hours without finding a route in, Richy took a photo of a map on a bus stop and we managed to navigate our way to the first gig. Louis Eliot must have wondered what he'd agreed to, going on the road with such a bunch of amateurs. He got his revenge by refusing to get up in the mornings.

I didn't know what to expect from a solo acoustic gig in Rotterdam. I wasn't playing Carter songs. If an audience turned up, they might hate me. I was too nervous to eat before the first night. We sat in the venue's café and were served some vegetarian concoction. I tried eating some of it, moving the food around my plate, trying to push it over to one side or hide it under the lettuce to make it look like I'd eaten at least some of it. Eventually the waitress cleared our plates and I breathed a sigh of relief, only for her to return with another plateful and a message from the chef, saying that as I'd obviously enjoyed his cooking so much I could have another helping.

The next day, during Louis's set in Den Bosch, me and Marc were overcome with – and I realise how un-punk-rock this sounds – a fit of the giggles. It had nothing to do with Louis's performance. He was brilliant. It was the silence in the room during the quieter songs. The audience was being respectfully quiet. The bar staff weren't even filling the ice machine or making cappuccinos. It was during those quieter moments that me and Marc started laughing. Once we'd started, we couldn't seem to stop. I can only describe it as being like when the teacher tells you off at school and warns you against laughing and then not laughing becomes the hardest thing in the world. Or at a funeral. Who hasn't almost burst out laughing at a funeral?

This childish Pavlovian response to acoustic music would be triggered time and again at my gigs, especially if the local support act was one of those John Lewis Christmas advert style singers. If they sang their plaintive and poignant songs quietly enough, with their eyes closed, being wistful and sensitive, when it was quiet enough to hear a pin drop, me and Marc would be in absolute stitches.

I remember an acoustic night upstairs at the Bedford pub in Balham. We were there to see Bransby. I was going to join him for 'The Only Living Boy in New Cross' and the Captain Kirk from *Star trek* version of 'Common People'. The singer on before Bransby had an unbelievably fragile voice. He softly stroked his guitar strings, never breaking into a proper strum, as he whisper-mumbled his words in that way I've always thought singers do to hide how awful they know their lyrics are. And I could see Marc's shoulders were already starting to shake. I knew we were in trouble. I was soon shaking too. There was no way out of the room without walking past the front of the stage. I know people can die from laughing but I thought I was going to die if I didn't. In the end we both simply had to leave the room. We went to the gents and let it all out. Sweet blessed relief. Good Lord almighty Jesus. The poor fella onstage must have heard us roaring and guffawing as he felt his way through another whispered song.

DAVID GILMOUR FROM PINK FLOYD

We were halfway through the first UK solo Jim Bob tour, eating breakfast in the Wigan Wetherspoons and reading the *NME*. Now I'm not naïve enough to be surprised that everything I do will be reviewed to a certain extent as something by 'Jim Bob from Carter'. Whether it's a song or a book or the cure for cancer, I expect the connection and the reference to be made. Once an elephant gets in the room, it's notoriously difficult to get them out again. But the *NME* journalist who used his review of my new solo album *Goodnight Jim Bob* (at this point you've probably realised that a lot of my stuff has the same title) to tell the world how much he'd always hated Carter, was a bit much. He gave the album three out of ten.

Three out of ten seemed a little harsh to us that morning in the Wigan Wetherspoons. If he'd given it six out of ten, even a five, Marc probably wouldn't have phoned the *NME* and asked to speak to the reviewer. And when the journalist wasn't in the office, Marc wouldn't have said, in his best American accent (which is roughly the same as everyone else's worst American accent) that he was the reviewer's friend Barry and could he have his mobile number. If the review had been a five out of ten, Marc wouldn't have rung the *NME* and been so surprised they gave him the reviewer's phone number that he felt compelled to have it printed on three hundred strips of paper and distribute them among the audience at my London Borderline gig at the end of the tour.

> *** ********** **gave Jim's new album 3/10 this week. Here is his mobile number...**

Apparently three weeks of phone calls from people ordering pizzas and asking if a Mister P Ness Head lived there followed. I feel quite bad about it now. It's not something I'd countenance these days. Especially since social media has turned us all into pitchfork wielding revenge merchants.

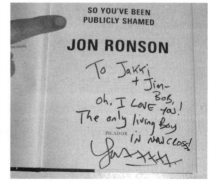

These days the only reviews I get – good or bad – are from Amazon customers who've read my novels. Authors aren't supposed to read their Amazon reviews but I've read all of mine. Here are the latest stats I've prepared:

There are currently 544 Amazon UK reviews for *The Extra Ordinary Life of Frank Derrick*. 296 reviewers gave the book 5 stars, 137 gave it 4 stars, 63 people gave 3 stars, 28 people gave the book 2 stars and 20 people on Amazon thought *The Extra Ordinary Life of Frank Derrick* was only worth 1 star. The average review is 4.2 stars out of 5.

That's not such a bad average. And 544 is a lot of Amazon reviews. I should be happy. And yet I can't help focusing on those two and one stars. In the summer of 2014 I went to Latitude to read from *The Extra Ordinary Life of Frank Derrick*. My publishers Pan Macmillan had their own area at the festival. They had a pop-up bookshop, deck chairs and a small tent with beanbags and scatter cushions inside. That was where I would do my reading. I was on after Jon Ronson. I wanted to say hello and tell him how much I liked his work but my overactive orbitofrontal cortex made that impossible. It was before I knew he'd been a fan of Carter and because I was billed as J.B. Morrison, he had no reason to know who I was.

People not knowing that J.B. Morrison and Jim Bob are the same person makes it difficult for festival organisers to know how to bill me. If I'm billed as the author J.B. Morrison, there's a strong chance nobody will turn up but if I'm billed as Jim Bob, people might expect songs. I could play songs as well of course, but then shouldn't I be getting paid more?

My dream is for the author J.B. Morrison to become so successful that he attracts an audience as large as Jim Bob the singer. I'd like to appear at a literary festival in a packed tent that's split equally down the middle between the two audiences and watch the faces of the J.B. Morrison fans when I walk on and half the audience start calling their favourite author a fat bastard.

When Jon Ronson finished I took my place in the Pan Macmillan tent. I sat on one of the beanbags. It may have been a scatter cushion. It was very nice the Pan Macmillan area at Latitude. If I was in charge I probably would have booked a small PA system and a microphone but that's just me.

Billy Bragg was on the main stage when I started reading. Dutch techno was thumping away in the nearby dance tent, and right next to where I was reading from my book without amplification, something called 'Noisy Toys' was in full flow. On the Noisy Toys website they describe themselves thus: 'Music Scientists and Noise Technicians will show you what to do while Booming, Bleeping, Zapping, Squeaking, Farting, Screeching fills the air!'

There were only a handful of people there for my reading and at least half of those only came because the beanbags were so comfortable and they couldn't be bothered to get up. If anything, me reading from my novel was spoiling their pleasant afternoon in the sun. The Pan Mac tent was in such a convenient spot for listening to all the stages that surrounded it. The relentless thud of Dutch techno, Billy Bragg's 'Sexuality' and the booms, bleeps, zaps, squeaks and farts coming from the Noisy Toys tent. It was hard to hear myself read. I was practically shouting the book at people. It was embarrassing and I speed-read to make it end sooner. When it did I asked if anyone had any questions. The first one was can you speak any louder? The second question was about the forthcoming Carter reunion shows. Me and Mrs Jim Bob went and bought a horrible lager, drunk half of it and drove home.

I was annoyed with myself for how I let everything get on top of me so easily at Latitude. I should have shouted louder, I wished I'd thrown cushions around. Scattered those scatter cushions. I should have told a joke. Abandoned reading from my book and sung 'Sheriff Fatman'. But instead, I just gave in. It bothered me for days afterwards. A bad gig always does. The only way I can get it out of my mind is to redeem myself with a good gig, preferably two.

My next book reading was at Wilderness festival. I'd treat it like I was headlining Glastonbury. I wore my loudest shirt and bounded up to the microphone like the Beastie Boys, shadowboxing and air Kung fu-ing. I had a little plastic box with sound effects in it so I could start my reading of the moment when Frank Derrick is run over by a milk float with the sound of breaking glass. I'd tell loads of jokes. My book reading would be like The Who *Live at Leeds*. When it was over, if there was a microphone, I'd drop it. If there wasn't a microphone, I'd kick the lectern over. No lectern and I'd punch one of the other authors.

I was chatting with the other authors at Wilderness before I went on. They all said they were hoping that just a few people, or ideally nobody, turned up for their talks. I on the other hand wanted the tent to be packed. Further evidence that I was still very much Jim Bob from Carter I suppose.

I started my Wilderness 'set' by reading some of my bad Amazon reviews to the audience. And then read the reviews for the things the same people had given five stars to. The reviewer who said of my novel: 'I'm going to try and delete it from my Library' gave five stars to *This is Your Land* by David Fitzgerald. They said: 'David Fitzgerald playing the saxophone is like liquid drops from heaven – a molten stairway that takes you there. Has Heaven realised one of its musicians is missing?'

The reviewer who simply said my novel was: 'Rubbish' gave four stars to a litre of DOFF Ivy and Brushwood Weed killer. Although to be honest, they weren't entirely happy with that either: 'When I received it, it had been sealed in a plastic bag at the sorting office as it was leaking due to the top not being screwed on securely.'

I felt a little sorry for this next person because page thirteen is where my novel really takes off: 'Didn't do it for me, I put it down after about a dozen pages.'

This idiot found *The Extra Ordinary Life of Frank Derrick*: 'Dreary, boring, not very funny. No recommend from me.' But they did give five stars to: Two hundred Blue Disposable High Density Aprons on a roll. 'I bought these mainly to protect clothes whilst grooming our cats. But have found them useful in other ways e.g. when cooking or baking.'

Here's a good one. First my book: 'The most depressing book I have read in a long time and only made me laugh at the end when I had finished.' They did love their 235 millilitres of Astonish Pro Granite Shine and Sparkle Cleaner though and gave it five stars, describing it as: 'Brilliant on my granite work tops and leaves a great protective coat and more importantly a fabulous shine!' And finally, the reviewer who gave my novel one star because it was: 'A bit of a disappointment', gave five stars to a Jake Bugg album.

My experience of literary festivals and in particular, my appearances on literary stages at bigger music festivals, is mixed. One I did really enjoy was Curious Arts in 2015. I was interviewed on stage by comedian Simon Evans. Simon's live intro music used to be 'Do Re Me, So Far So Good' but I hadn't met him until just before the festival.

Curious Arts is the poshest festival I've ever been to. On the night after my interview with Simon, me and Mrs Jim Bob went to help ourselves to cheese and wine from the 17th century manor house, whose grounds the festival was held on. I walked into a large sitting room. At first I thought there was no one else there but I could hear the sound of gently played piano music. I nodded hello to the man playing it and I left. I imagine there are people who would kill to be alone in a room for what was effectively, if only briefly, their own private piano performance by David Gilmour from Pink Floyd. I wondered if he'd ever heard what Carter had done to his song 'Another Brick in the Wall'. I was tempted to hang around and wait for a pause in his piano recital and shout 'mutha *fucka*!'

A little later that evening, I was sitting at a long table outside the 17th century manor house, eating cheese and biscuits with David Gilmour and the actor who played Peter File in the 'Dinner Party' episode of *The IT*

Crowd. John Illsley from Dire Straits was playing 'Money for Nothing' on the nearby main stage. It was what people in the *X Factor* would probably have called surreal. My favourite moment of the evening was when a musician from one of the bands playing at the festival went into the house to look for more wine. After he'd been gone for a while David Gilmour tipped his head back and announced, in a lovely posh way, "Where's that boy with my wine?"

Me and Mrs Jim Bob glamped in a huge white tent with a double bed and a fridge that night. David Morrissey was in the tent next to us. But you know, it really doesn't matter how luxurious the accommodation is or who your neighbours are. Estate agents are right. It's all about location, location, location. If it's a festival, you will still be surrounded by inconsiderate, drunk arseholes and you won't get a wink of sleep.[32]

I know the *Goodnight Jim Bob* album is not perfect by the way. Maybe not as bad as a three out of ten. I'd give it six. The lyrics are a bit vague. That's what I don't like about it. It has a lot in common with Carter's *I Blame the Government* in that respect. I think I only wrote and recorded it because it was *time* to make a new album. It was what I did once a year or so. Like putting out the bins. I should have waited until I really *needed* to make another record. I'd like to write songs that can be pulled apart by German etymologists or English stand up comedians. Carter songs like 'Midnight on the Murder Mile' and 'Twenty Four Minutes from Tulse Hill', that both describe journeys between two specific points with such accuracy, you could almost use them as satellite navigation.

I don't want to be one of those songwriters who when asked about their lyrics has to lie. Claiming they didn't know what their songs were about until ten years after they'd written them. Or the lyrics can mean what anyone wants them to mean. I don't want to be that songwriter. Not long after the *Goodnight Jim Bob* album was released I made a promise to myself that I wouldn't write songs or release another record until I had something worth writing about. I'd wait for my muse. Something was bound to come along eventually.

---

32 I should clarify that David Morrissey wasn't one of the inconsiderate, drunken arseholes. I did find my ego wondering, as it does with all famous people of a certain age, if he was ever a Carter fan.

MY NAME IS MICHAEL CAINE

Michael Caine said something once that I've been misquoting ever since. I don't mean: "You're only supposed to blow the bloody doors up", or "My name is Michael Caine and not everybody knows about it." I'm talking about something Michael Caine said in a movie acting masterclass I saw on television years ago. The gist of the anecdote (maybe that's what I should have called this book) was that as Michael Caine was waiting to make his stage entrance during rehearsals for a play, an actor in the preceding scene threw a chair that blocked the door that Michael Caine had to walk through. The play's director instructed Caine to "use the difficulty". If it was a comedy, the director said, he should fall over it, if it was a drama, he should pick the chair up and smash it. It apparently became Michael Caine's philosophy for life. Whenever there was a problem, he would 'use the difficulty'. I misremembered it as 'using the obstacle' but the results are the same. In the summer of 2003 I found my difficulty.

I was walking home from the pub with Fruitbat and our friend and movie scriptwriter Tim Connery. We were laughing loudly and hysterically about something when we were stopped by a large group of…now this is where I struggle to find a less humiliating way to describe what it feels like to be beaten up by children.

My intended way of dealing with muggers would be to give them what they want and send them on their way. They're just doing their job after all. And it's better to get kicked in the self-esteem than in the balls. That's always been my motto. Les had a different system however and he told them to fuck off, which was when the biggest child punched us both really hard in the face. And I do mean really hard. Not a child's punch at all. The kid had what Henry Cooper might have called, "a good right hand".

When I was the same age as those kids I was making badges and fake record sleeves for my latest imaginary band. I would have left school with no qualifications, taken a week off (what I like to refer to as my 'gap week') and then looked for a job. I went to two interviews and got both. It was probably easier to be a teenager then. Like a reverse of that Monty Python 'Four Yorkshiremen' sketch. I'm really trying hard to empathise with my assailants here.

After having my rapidly-expanding face X-rayed and after being told I had a couple of broken cheekbones, I was sent to the maxillofacial department of St George's Hospital. I seemed to be able to lift one side of my skull up and down with my hand. It felt detached. The maxillofacial department couldn't really help me. So I wrote this song:

VICTIM

It's said that men look cool and hard
When their faces are all bruised and scarred
Not like some badly drawn cartoon
Of a kid that's swallowed a balloon
Or looked into a telescope
The victim of a schoolboy joke
I don't care what people say
That's how I looked that day
Now everywhere I go it's changed
Places that I know seem strange
Every patch of park or green
Looks like a future Crimewatch scene
Down every alleyway and path
An ugly crime scene photograph
Something deep inside me changed
On the day that I became a victim

A victim of a so-so crime
Not worthy of a yellow sign

To match the bruise around my neck
Changing colour as I slept
Now there's a part of me that shakes
With every car that overtakes
The Jeremiah in my head
Says everybody wants me dead
Like the audience at a pantomime
He tells me I should look behind me
Tells me I should run and hide
Move out to the countryside
"Just get yourself away from harm
Sell the farm and buy a farm"
Things would never be the same
From the day that I became a victim

Everyone I knew was sure
I should report it to the law
I'd get financial compensation
If I went to my local station
But because of cutbacks staff were short
And since what happened in New York
The police station I told my friends
Only opens at weekends
So in the year Charles Bronson died
I got my bad self organised
I bought a book on martial arts
Enrolled in a karate class
And I wish some day a rain would come
And wash the streets of the all the scum
Everybody says I changed
On the day that I became
A victim in his early forties
Unprovoked and unreported
Looking for someone to blame
On the day that I became a victim
Everybody says I changed
On the day that I became a victim

Apart from the verse about learning karate, the lyrics are pretty factual.
Charles Bronson did die that year and I definitely had a face like a
kid who'd swallowed a balloon. And yes, it changed colour as I slept.
I couldn't eat anything except grated cheese for a while and I was afraid
of my own shadow. I suddenly didn't want to live in London anymore

and I spent a lot of time browsing estate agent websites. It seemed worse that I'd been mugged so close to my home – and even closer to a police station (see final verse).

After I was mugged I'd remembered what Michael Caine had said in that acting masterclass. I decided that if I had to be a victim I could at least get something productive out of it. The mugging would be the catalyst for my longest solo album *Angelstrike!* The mugging would also be a pivotal moment in the life of the protagonist (not me) of my first novel.

Apart from 'Victim', there were songs on *Angelstrike!* about how the street where I lived had turned into a hangout for teenagers with nothing to do but do nothing ('Feral Kids' and 'The Children's Terrorism Workshop'). One night, the house a few doors along was attacked by kids with machetes and baseball bats. They threw paint over the front door. That led to the song 'Come on Smart Bomb!'

Our orange VW Beetle – the car that featured on the front cover of the Carter B-sides collection *Starry Eyed and Bollock Naked* – was vandalised outside our house so it wouldn't drive anymore, and then the car's windows were smashed and we had to get it scrapped. We forgot about it until we saw the beautiful orange car rising up in the air on the other side of our hedge, in the claws of a scrapyard tow truck. It was like a metaphor for how I was feeling at the time. If we'd hung onto the car for another few years, Carter would have been popular again, and like the M1 keyboard that the 'Sheriff Fatman' bass-line was played on, the Beetle would be priceless.

The album's title track is exactly what you might think it's about. A song about the time the angels went on strike and the resulting chaos and dystopia. 'Closure' is a song about a missing girl being found murdered. '55 Cards' was inspired by the pack of playing cards given to US troops with pictures of the most wanted members of Saddam Hussein's government and army on. 'Tongue Tied' is based on the story of Tony Martin, the farmer who shot and killed a burglar. 'Georgie's Marvellous Medicine' is about how drugs destroy friendships. 'The Hippies Were Right' and 'We have the Technology' feature a theme I'd return to a lot in my lyrics – *why can't we all just get along?* 'Soulmates' was a short piece of optimism about the importance of friends and family. I wrote about my mild obsessive compulsions (more on that later) on the song 'Obsessive Compulsive'. And I wrote about how basically fed up with everything I was on 'Ray of Light', a reworked Jim's Super Stereoworld song.

Unlike *Goodnight Jim Bob* with its directionless and vague songs, every song on *Angelstrike!* was about something and with the exception of 'The Revenge of the School Bullied', they were all brand new songs and traceable back to that walk home from the pub when Fruitbat told a child to fuck off. I'm not saying I'm glad that I was mugged that night but it did lead to one of my most popular albums. And I had to do something with all those lemons?[33]

There was a bit of light relief on the *Angelstrike!* album. I wrote the song 'My Face Your Arse' as a fictional account of me and Les falling out, leading to the break-up of Carter. We recorded it as a back-and-forth conversation duet, in the style of The Pogues' 'Fairytale of New York' or 'A Little Time' by The Beautiful South. Or more obviously 'Can't Stand me Now' by The Libertines, which I can't deny it does sound quite a lot like.

I lost my 2003 pocket diary in that night of inner city violence. But as is probably apparent to you if you've made it this far, that was no great loss. It wasn't as though Samuel Pepys or Alan Bennett had been mugged. Also – swings and roundabouts – I used my difficulty. I might have been punched in the face and lost a diary but not only did I have an album's worth of material and a scene in my first novel, I still had the thirty quid I'd hidden in the Johnny pocket of my 501s.

One other thing I remember Michael Caine saying in his acting masterclass, was how on cinema screens, the close-ups of your face are absolutely massive.

---

33 I've just realised that Michael Caine's director could have said, 'When life gives you lemons make lemonade' and it would have meant exactly the same thing.

MAX MAYHEM

I said earlier, there was a reason why there isn't a prime time Saturday night TV show called *Britain's Got Authors*, but I did once see a BBC documentary called *Scribbling*. It followed Robert Newman over the course of the three years it took him to write his new novel, from research to final draft. There was a memorable bit in the programme when Rob talked about sitting at his desk in front of the window working on his new novel when two people walked past his house. He heard one of them say something like, "Rob Newman lives there. He used to be famous."

Like Rob Newman in the TV documentary, I spend a lot of my time preparing to write. I'll buy notebooks and pens, pads of Post-it notes and more recently, note-taking apps. I've written on a desktop computer and on laptops. I've used an iPad and an iPad mini. I send myself emails written on my phone. I used to use a dictaphone[34]. But the real gold dust is the stuff I write on the back of my hand.

When you become a published author you'll eventually be asked to write a short piece for the *Guardian* website about how you write. Sometimes it will take the form of a list of tips or advice. Like my *Desert Island Discs* choices and my Nobel Prize for Literature acceptance speech, I thought it would be prudent to have my *Guardian* piece prepared in advance. I still haven't been asked for it. I better hang on to it just in case. Here's a similar 'how I write' piece I prepared for *Time Out* magazine instead. I say at the end that my daughter is twenty-four so I must have written it sometime around 2011. I don't know if it was ever published but let's face it, even if it was carved into an eight-foot high stone tablet like that one with Ed Miliband's election pledges on, no one would have read it. Except maybe a few other authors and then only so they could tut and scoff at how wrong I'd got it all and how pointless these things are.

---

34   See first book for dick-to-phone joke.

HOW I'LL WRITE HOW I WRITE
FOR HOW I WRITE

There's a regular feature in the books section of Time Out magazine called *How I Write*, where authors explain their working routines. For quite some time now I've been thinking about what I'd write for the magazine when they surely and inevitably asked me to let them in on what my secret was. Ever since the publication of *Goodnight Jim Bob*, my first book – I've been planning what I'd say.

A lot of the *How I Write* pieces tend to be fairly similar – get up at five, walk the dog, put pot of monkey digested coffee on, go into office overlooking the sea and write (insert amount) thousand words before the kids come home from school.

I either read somewhere or heard it said or more likely I just imagined it or made it up but apparently there's a male and female way of writing. The male way is to plough through from start to finish without reading what you've written and then do the editing afterwards. The female way involves editing as you go along. Or maybe it was the other way round. It's not important and is no doubt bollocks anyway. But since you asked, I write the lady's way.

Words read differently on paper than on the computer screen, it's also easier to miss errors on the computer. So I write and rewrite and then print and read and then edit and print again. I waste a lot of paper. I was thinking recently about whether we'd need home printers if nothing we read is actually printed anymore. Very quickly I decided that soon the only people using printers will be writers, and if the Mars/Venus theory has any truth to it, the writers will mostly be women. I'm going to print this now, read it and come back to it in a minute.

I'm back. It's not brilliant but I'll carry on. I'm currently writing a second novel and it's taking a long time. I'm doing it the lady way again: editing as I go, printing and throwing away a lot of A4 paper, I have been selecting the 2 pages per sheet option in the print layout menu though, so I'm not quite B.P.

I write with music on (usually The Jam or Elvis Costello) or I write without music on or while someone's talking on the radio. A lot of the time I'm writing when I'm away from my desk. I write a lot on trains – not *on* trains, I'm not Banksy[35] – and I've also been writing a fair amount in my head when I'm swimming. As a by-product, parts of the book will be set in a swimming pool and there's also a bit on a train. Anyway, got to stop now. The tide's out and I have to get the kids from school*

  * Jim Bob lives in South East London nowhere near the sea. His daughter is 24.

---

35   Or am I?

There's never really been any method or order to the way I write, and certainly no fixed hours to my working day. While I was writing *Goodnight Jim Bob* two tax inspectors came to my house. I was claiming Working Tax Credit at the time and the Inland Revenue wanted to know how I managed to live on such a small amount of money. I secretly recorded the conversation.

> Tax inspector 1 – "How much do you spend on clothes on average per week?"
> Me – "I don't really buy a lot of clothes."
> Tax inspector 2 – "Just an average amount will do."
> Me – "I really haven't bought any clothes for a long time."
> Tax inspector 1 – 'I'll put ten pounds a week. Okay?'
> Tax inspector 1 – "What would you spend on entertainment in a week? How many times do you go to the cinema?"
> Me – "I haven't been out a lot lately."
> Tax inspector 1 – "Let's put fifteen pounds a week. How often do you eat out at restaurants? On average?"
> Me – "I really haven't been out a lot."
> Tax inspector 2 – 'Takeaways then?

They asked me how many hours a day I worked and I told them it varied. I was working on a book and I usually started writing first thing in the morning and last thing at night. But I wouldn't be working for the whole day. I was waking up at three am a lot and looking for a pen in the dark.

> Tax inspector 1 – "What would you say your average weekly earnings are?"
> Me – "It's difficult to say."
> Tax inspector 2 – "What is your annual income?"
> Me – "Hmm. I'm not actually earning anything at the moment. Hopefully when the book is published I'll get some royalties from that. My earnings vary throughout the year. It also depends on whether or not I'm doing any gigs."
> Tax inspector 1 – "Gigs?"
> Me – "Concerts. Playing music."
> Tax inspector 2 – "What sort of music?"
> Me – "It's difficult to describe. Sort of punky pop rock."
> Tax inspector 1 – "What instrument do you play?"
> Me – "Guitar mostly. And I sing."
> Tax inspector 2 – "On your own?"
> Me – "Yes. I was in a band before."

Tax inspector 1 – "Anyone we might have heard of?"
Me – "I doubt it."
Both tax inspectors look at me, waiting.
Me – "Carter."
Tax inspector 1 – "Not the Unstoppable Sex Machine?
Are you Fruitbat or Jim Bob?"

When people used to tell me I should write a book, I never thought they were saying my words were so fantastic I should write more of them. I thought they meant that I should stop writing songs.

After the break-up of Carter, when there was enough distance between me and the past to be subjective about it all and I tried to write a book about my time in the band, I soon realised how dull another book about a bloke in a band would be. I didn't want to write about sex and drugs or stab all my friends in the back and I also didn't want to write a boring diary, cataloguing every venue and town I'd been to and the songs I'd played and the make and the model of the guitars I'd played them on.

It was after I read *A Heartbreaking Work of Staggering Genius* by Dave Eggers that I realised there was another way. The Dave Eggers memoir was self-deprecating and funny and irreverent. There were drawings and graphs in it and the back of the book is upside down. Dave Eggers says a particularly brilliant thing in the book's introduction. He advises a friend who doesn't want to read about real people, to 'Pretend it's fiction'.

Even though *Goodnight Jim Bob* is nothing like *A Heartbreaking Work of Staggering Genius*, Dave Eggers showed me that I didn't need to follow any rules. I could include drawings and recipes, ignore the timeline and go off at tangents, like this one about the time in 2018 when Marc Ollington rang the Shepherd's Bush Empire and introduced himself as Max Mayhem, PA to the actor Tom Hardy. Marc said that Tom was a big Jim Bob fan and wanted to go to my gig there. He also wanted to know if it was possible for the venue to arrange a meet and greet between Tom and me. The woman on the phone at the Shepherd's Bush Empire was incredibly excited. She told Max Mayhem that he should speak with my manager. She gave Marc his own phone number and said that if Jim Bob's manager couldn't sort it out then Max Mayhem should ring her back and they would get Tom Hardy into the show. I should stress, that there was no audience for this prank phone call. It was just Marc sitting on his own amusing himself. He told me afterwards that even though he knew Tom Hardy wasn't coming to the gig, he was excited because it really felt like he was.

Before I read the Dave Eggers book, tangents like that would have been impossible. I have to admit to another twinge of Gluckschmerz when Brett Anderson's recent memoir was described by one of my other literary heroes Douglas Coupland as 'This decade's *Heartbreaking Work of Staggering Genius*'.

And talking of Suede books, or books about Suede: Just after *Goodnight Jim Bob* was published, I was in a pub in Brixton where I was introduced to a friend of Fruitbat's (not a euphemism) called David Barnett.[36] He wrote the official Suede biography *Love and Poison* and Fruitbat introduced us because we'd both written music books. Me and David were both quite drunk and after chatting for a while we swapped books. I've often wondered if there was a moment later on, when David sobered up and remembered the bit in his book about the alternative scene being dominated by under-achievers like Carter and other bands whose names said it all.

When *Goodnight Jim Bob* was finished, I sent it to a few publishers but none of them were interested. One publisher suggested I turn the book into a novel. I told them to take Dave Eggers's advice and just pretend that it is. They didn't reply. After you've spent God knows how many hours (I haven't kept time sheets) working on something, suggestions like that are kind of annoying. I was reminded of when Carter were looking for a new record deal and a major label A&R man told us how much he loved us and everything we did and how unique it all was but wondered if we'd considered getting a drummer.

Marc Ollington was a season ticket holder at Arsenal and had a seat next to Adam Velasco, who happened to be the managing director of Cherry Red Records. Marc told him about *Goodnight Jim Bob*. I don't exactly know what he said but I imagine Marc would have exaggerated the sales potential of the book. During quieter moments at Highbury[37], Marc would have told Adam Velasco that I had a mailing list of fifty thousand fans and Tom Cruise was keen to play me in the film adaptation of the book and so on. Whatever it was, Cherry Red wanted to publish it.

---

36   David and Fruitbat would both later be regular members of Keith Top Of The Pops & His Minor UK Indie Celebrity All-Star Backing Band. I sung a bit on Keith TOTP's album *Fuck You! I'm Keith Top of the Pops*. Other members of Keith's Minor UK Indie Celebrity All-Star Backing Band include Eddie Argos, David Barnett, Jo Bevan, Rob Britton, Chris Cain, Ian Catskilkin, Micky Ciccone, Emma Cooper, Sue Denim, Mikey Drums, David Fade, Johnny Fade, Jasper Future, Luke Haines, Charlotte Hatherley, Julia Indelicate, Simon Indelicate, Arec G Litter, Jackie McKeown, John Moore, Keith Murray, Sarah Nixey, Adie Nunn, Dee Plume, Melissa Reardon, James Rocks, Sara, Charley Stone, Nathan Thomas, Tim Ten Yen, Phil Whaite, Dyan Valdes, Johnny Yeah, Zachary Amos, Jennifer Denitto and Mikey Georgeson.

37   This is a football joke. Arsenal's ground used to have the nickname 'the Highbury Library', because it was so quiet.

My first live reading from *Goodnight Jim Bob* was in Berlin. I'm not sure why I chose Berlin. I was probably hoping for another etymological essayist to be in the audience. On stage, I would read a bit from the book, play some songs, read another bit, play lots more songs. It became the pattern of my live show for a few years. Some people liked the songs more than the readings, others preferred the reading while most didn't stress a preference. I don't have the exact figures.

A particularly difficult gig in Bristol springs to mind of how off-putting a handful of drunk men shouting 'Sheriff Fatman!' and 'you fat bastard' every time you open a book and attempt to read from it can be. My favourite heckle came at a gig in Newcastle. Technically it wasn't a heckle, as I wasn't supposed to hear it. It was more of a thought that an audience member had accidentally said out loud. I was on tour with my *Driving Jarvis Ham* novel. I'd do my usual, come on stage, read a bit, play some songs, read a bit more, play loads more songs. In Newcastle I walked on and picked up the book. The audience were library quiet and the very first thing I heard was – it works much better in a strong Geordie accent – 'Oh no. He's going to read from his fucking book.'

Three published novels later and I still feel like a musician who's written some books. When *Storage Stories* was published, I wrote this for Crystal Palace's *Transmitter* magazine.

A MUSICIAN WHO'S WRITTEN A BOOK

To be recognised as a serial killer you have to murder three or more people. I think it's the same for authors and books. You need to write at least three before you can start calling yourself an author. It's more for musicians who write books, four books or five, and even then you're going to have to win the Booker Prize or something before people stop referring to you as Paul McCartney from The Beatles and you can stop taking your guitar along to book readings. My second novel is out in May and I'm currently writing a third. I've published a twelve thousand-word short story and an autobiography – but that was about my band so it doesn't count, and the short story came as part of an album of music, so that's cheating. I'm still a musician who's written a book.

I'm going on tour soon. I'll be playing songs and reading from my new book. I have no real idea what people are buying tickets to hear: Whether they've paid to see an author or a singer. I overcompensate for this by giving them neither and veering towards stand up comedy.

Sometimes during the reading bits I think I can see people checking the time on their phones. I read way too quickly, rushing to the end so I can pick up my safety blanket and play 'Sheriff Fatman'. One day somebody will shout, "Stop playing all the old songs! Read some more!" I'll have to come back on for an encore and read something from my first book.

There were no figures on Wikipedia for how many murders a musician who writes a book and then decides to embark on a further change of career as a serial killer needs to commit. I guess I'm going to have to keep killing until somebody tells me to stop.

WOTCHA-WA-WA-WA

In 2004 I started writing an occasional blog. I'm gong to include selected snippets here and there from now on, but only if I feel they add some insight into how I was feeling at the time. I'll use a different font so you'll know that's what's going on. I'd hate for you to think I still hold the same abhorrent views now or that I thought I could get away with simply cutting and pasting my way to a Costa Book prize[38]. My first blog entry was written in November of 2004. I'd been asked to take part in a BBC Radio Two musical comedy show called *Jammin'*. I've just found the show's script and have discovered that Robin Ince was Programme Associate. I hope he doesn't read this.

BLOG – MY NEW BAND 9/11/04
A busy week for Jim Bob as I rehearsed with my new band: Rowland Rivron from French and Saunders on drums, Richard Vranch from Whose Line Is It Anyway on keyboards, Dave Catlin Birch from the Bootleg Beatles on bass and Robert Newman on banjolele. We formed briefly for a BBC Radio 2 programme called Jammin' – a mixture of music and gags. I won't tell you what I did as that would spoil any enjoyment you might get out of it when it's broadcast at the start of next year. Anyway, I had to learn a lot of new guitar stuff and become a musician for a day. Despite ridiculous pre-rehearsal nerves I enjoyed myself and hope this is my big break into the world of BBC light entertainment.

My 'big break into the world of BBC light entertainment' hinged on my performance of George Formby's 'Leaning on a Lamppost' in the style of a thrash metal song, playing the *James Bond Theme* (both wrongly and badly) and the theme music to *Film 2000* equally badly and wrongly. I also sung the first song that I'd ever written 'The Planet of No Return'. The title was genuine but I made the rest up. I can't remember what I did last year, let alone a song I wrote about the end of the world when I was fourteen for Christ's sake. I'm not proud of such deception but this was a few years before Sachsgate and those faked *Blue Peter* competitions. Minor fraud on the BBC was still acceptable.

---

38 I do occasionally have a coffee in a Costa. You have to be so careful though, as their medium sized cup is more like a Nero's large and too big. Also, Costa's gimmick is to have the cup dimple bit off centre on their saucers. It can make carrying your coffee to your seat a bit like returning from the bar on a North Sea ferry.

On *Jammin'*, the band played 'Sheriff Fatman' and Rowland Rivron challenged me to place board games into the lyrics and change the words 'Sheriff Fatman' to 'Simon Cowell'. I played Chas 'n' Dave's 'Rabbit' in the style of Radiohead's 'Creep'. I'm sorry to all concerned: to Chas and to Dave, to Radiohead and to anyone listening to the show. I think it was the kind of thing the audience laughs at because it's a comedy show, rather than because it's funny.

Whenever I'm in a room like the one where *Jammin'* was recorded, where everyone else is a proper musician and they call out chords to me or suggest dropping a tone or adding an augmented sixth or they say things to me in Italian or Latin that mean speed the song up or play it at half the tempo or something – *grazioso Jim, glissando!* – I have absolutely no idea what they're talking about. But I'm so ashamed to admit it and instead I'll try and bluff my way through and hope no one notices.

In case you were wondering by the way, my appearance on *Jammin'* wasn't my big break into the world of BBC light entertainment.

HESTON BLUMENTHAL

I played forty-four solo gigs in 2003 and 2004. I wish something more dramatic had happened. There was that one time when Mister Spoons put petrol in the car instead of diesel by mistake I suppose, but otherwise it was mostly forty-four days of service station cheese ploughman sandwiches and crisps. Meal deals and Grab bags.

Every night the three of us would sleep in a Travelodge. Three to a room, Marc on the pull-out half-bed underneath the tabletop where the TV and the kettle were, me on the sofa bed and Spoons keeping us awake all night with his loud snoring on the double.

In the morning we'd eat another Little Chef breakfast, one time we went to the one that Heston Blumenthal had jazzed up. I'd seen a television documentary about it and I quite liked Heston Blumenthal. The Little Chef he'd transformed looked a lot better than all the other Little Chefs. In the toilets there were pictures of animals on the wall that made baa and moo sounds when you touched them.

Little Chefs were the inspiration for the chain of roadside restaurants in my second novel *Driving Jarvis Ham*. I'd rename them Mister Breakfasts and people would get murdered there. No one was murdered at any of the actual Little Chefs while we were there. Selfish bastards. I could do with the anecdotes. Heston Blumenthal had murdered the Little Chef menu though. Presumably because vegetarian sausages didn't make any sense to him, they were the first thing he got rid of. All the other vegetarian options followed.

"Is there no vegetarian breakfast?" I asked the waitress in her all new Blumenthalled uniform and hat. She looked at the menu.

"Macaroni cheese?"

On stage every night after that I talked about how Heston Blumenthal had ruined Little Chef and how much I hated him. I went as far as saying removing the veggie sausages from the menu was an insult to the memory of Linda McCartney and all cancer sufferers. Jim Bob does say the funniest things.

Occasionally at one of those 2003 or 2004 gigs, the venue's bar would stay open for a while after the show and we'd get drunk. In Aberdeen Mister Spoons got on stage at one in the morning and did his Gary Numan impression and after a gig at the Worcester Marrs Bar Marc left the whole tour's merch and gig money in a taxi. I asked him about it.

"I have never really been someone who can just carry on drinking. A few shandies and I am gone. For some reason though that night in the

Worcester Marrs Bar I got a taste for the sauce like never before. Beer, wine, dodgy whisky and even vodka (that I really can't stand) all tasted so delicious. The after show drinks ended up lasting until the early hours of the morning, and resulted in a jamming session with the staff and support band. I took the guitar and started making a song up about the promoter. I can neither sing nor play the guitar and he was a big bloke who should have punched my lights out. Instead he got us more drinks.

I was carrying the tour takings around in my merch bag. We didn't do sensible things like go to banks. I think it was around ten thousand pounds, though it could have been five hundred. These things do build up in your head. We got a cab from the venue to the hotel, which I seem to remember was madness as it was only a two-minute walk. The hotel was a shithole. As I got to my room I had the sudden realisation that I'd left the money in the taxi. I was so drunk though that I didn't care. My way of dealing with it was to tell Mister Spoons and ask him to go and find the money. I then put my head down and went to sleep and thought very little of it until the next morning. Spoons makes out he was searching for the cash for hours and ended up nearly dying of pneumonia. I think he just does this to make me feel guilty, even all these years later. He did find the money though, so fair play to him. But where was he a couple of years later when I left a load of German tour money in the seat pocket on a flight back from Berlin? He didn't get that money back."

I forgot about the money that Marc – and let's remember here that he's my manager – left on the plane. We'd spoken to the airline afterwards and they said they could probably get the wallet back eventually but the cleaners would have taken the cash by now. It seemed like quite a cavalier attitude to take but what do I know about running an airline? I'm not Richard Branson. Despite the rumours.

The morning after Marc left the money in a taxi in Worcester was horrible. I was so hungover. We had to drive to Devon for a gig at Ivybridge Rugby Club. It was a charity tribute to my big sister Vicky. I spent the whole day trying not to throw up. I'm sure she would have been proud.

Out of the forty-four venues I played in 2003 and 2004, some would have been full and others empty. In the car on the way there we'd play the million pound game and Mister Spoons and Marc Ollington would talk about *Doctor Who* and they'd talk about football. I'd pretend to sleep in the back. I never really slept though. I couldn't risk falling asleep. What if Spoons and Ollington murdered me? They never did. Selfish bastards. I could do with the anecdotes.

We'd make in-car compilations, mine always including something by The Jam and Elvis Costello, Marc with his obligatory Morrissey and David Bowie songs and Spoons with his Mick Thomas and Gary

Numan tracks. We had a great time in the car, the three of us and later, four, when Chris T-T became a permanent part of what became known as Team Jim Bob. Chris did his best to bring politics and culture to the long car journeys but ultimately it was like broadcasting Radio Four into a monkey enclosure. Tim Ten Yen travelled with us on one tour. Tim altered the dynamic for a short while but resistance to our futility was useless.

I hate to break years of rock touring tradition but sometimes the gig was the part of the day I was least looking forward to. I liked being in the car with my friends, chatting shit and eating crisps. One time we bought a lottery ticket and agreed that if we won the jackpot we would spend it all before the end of the tour and we wouldn't tell our wives. We'd stay in the most expensive hotels and arrive at the venues by helicopter. We'd have the most amazing light show the Southampton Joiners had ever seen. I'd change guitars between every song and give them all away at the end of the gig. The audience wouldn't have to pay to get in. We'd pay them. Every night of the tour would be sold out. We were going to spend, spend, spend our way to popularity. We'd bring our own rider. We'd have a chef and a sommelier, serving the finest wines money could buy. The promoters would be happy, if a little confused, by an extravagance not seen on the pub and club circuit since 1999 when Jim's Super Stereoworld played Norwich Arts Centre. At the end of the tour we'd go home just as poor as when we'd left, as though none of it had ever happened.

Eventually on tour, we would try and spend some of the daytime between gigs more productively than just eating sweets and talking nonsense. We'd go to the cinema, usually in Manchester. I think once we'd been to the Trafford Centre Odeon twice, it became a tour tradition. The first film we saw there was *Children of Men*. Our car had broken down. The Fiat Multipla came second in a *Daily Telegraph* list of 'The 100 Ugliest Cars', but what do those pricks know about cars. We loved that car. We called it the Popemobile and the Neilmobile and some other names that I can't include here for reasons. We parked our broken vehicle at the cinema and couldn't believe it when Clive Owen from *Children of Men* was in the exact same car as ours! And Clive's broke down too!

My biggest regret from my time touring the world with Carter is how I saw so little of it. When I think about the architecture I could have seen and the oceans I could have swum in. All the cathedrals and museums and the art galleries and the parks. I just wish I'd been a better tourist. I wish I'd seen the Statue of liberty and the Grand Canyon, the Guggenheim and the Louvre, the Anne Frank Museum and the White House. How could I go to Barcelona three times and not see the Sagrada Familia once? When Fruitbat and the road crew were climbing to the top of a famous tower in Canada, I chose instead to sit in the dressing room looking at the penis drawings on the wall and reading the names of the bands that had drawn them. My reluctance to get out more was partly due to my mind being so fixed on the show ahead that I couldn't relax enough to enjoy much else. But still, I feel shameful for the opportunities I wasted. For all the sights I didn't see on tour when I had the chance. The kind of chance that's unlikely to come again. I didn't even get to see what half of the venues looked like, because I arrived and left through a back door up a pissy alleyway. I might as well have been blindfolded. In a similar way to the Queen thinking everywhere smells of paint because it would have been repainted just before she arrived, I thought the world smelled of urine.

If we'd stayed in one place for a little longer, I expect I would have made more of an effort to sightsee. When Carter were in East Germany the first time, we stayed for a whole week in somebody's Berlin flat and we did a lot more walking around than usual. All in all, I've probably seen more of Berlin than most other cities I've been to. Even when I went back there as a solo performer, we walked to the Brandenburg Gate, through the Tiergarten and climbed to the top of the Peace Tower, where I had to hang on to the walls to stop myself jumping off, because that's what my irrational fear of heights was telling me I really needed to do.

The first time I went to Berlin as a solo artist, Mister Spoons was at a German football match and the gig's promoter asked me and Marc what we wanted to do in the daytime before soundcheck. We told him to surprise us and take us somewhere interesting. He picked us up from the hotel and drove us through Berlin, pointing out monuments and war leftovers. He drove past Checkpoint Charlie and Potsdamer Platz, that was nothing but grass surrounded by flats when Carter were there in 1990 but was now all skyscrapers and office complexes, banks and hotels and Europe's largest casino.

After being driven around town for forty minutes, both me and Marc wondered if we would ever reach whatever the destination of our 'something interesting' was. And was it going to be a museum or an art gallery? A fun fair or the zoo perhaps? And then we turned a corner and we were back at the hotel. If we'd known the journey and not the destination was the something interesting, we would have paid closer attention to it.

The Berlin promoter was Tim Schneck. Tim was a longtime Carter fan. He was probably with us in the Irish Bar on at least one occasion. Tim is one of a handful of people to have stayed at my house. It was when Carter took part in a pop quiz against the Family Cat and the Senseless Things. I think it was at the Mean Fiddler in Harlesden. Tim had brought a large keg of German beer with him. I remember him hammering a screwdriver into the keg with the end of his shoe, sending a fountain of

German everywhere. It's not a great anecdote but at least it happened.

The pop quiz was broadcast on the pirate radio station Q102, the same station that organised the infamous Subbuteo competition Carter were disqualified from. Me and Fruitbat guest DJ'd on Q102 when it was still a pirate station, broadcasting from radio boss Sammy Jacob's flat. It was early on a Saturday morning and Sammy woke up wondering who the hell was playing all the Gilbert O'Sullivan and Frank Sinatra records on his indie radio station. When Q102 was granted a licence it changed its name to XFM and later it became Radio X, 'the first truly male-focused, fully national music and entertainment brand for 25-44 year olds.'

I haven't played many solo shows outside the UK. I've been to Berlin, those two shows in Holland, Athens a few times, a gig in Dublin supporting the Sultans of Ping, an Australia tour in 2018 with Pop Will Eat Itself and two gigs on the Isle of Man. If I went to some of the places I'd been to with Carter now, I'd make sure I was a much better tourist. When Team Jim Bob went to Athens we walked for miles. We went to the old part of town and swam in the Aegean. Mister Spoons climbed up onto a rock and picked up some sort of hideous rash on his buttocks (thankfully no picture available).

On the UK solo tours, whenever Marc had to return to his proper job as Cultural Attaché work at the New Zealand consulate (I think that's right) me, Spoons and Chris T-T took the opportunity to see a few sights. Marc was stubbornly resistant to experiencing any culture on tour. He really enjoyed the time in the car. He preferred motorways to scenic routes and favoured huge homogeneous Motos over nice little greasy spoon cafes in the middle of nowhere. But when Marc wasn't there we seized the day. We carpe-diemed the shit out of it. We went to a model village, to the Angel of the North and the Yorkshire Sculpture Park where years before Chris T-T ate his first curry, took MDMA (whatever that is) and got his nose pierced.

We visited a whisky distillery in Scotland. It was a great little tour, led by an old dude who showed us how the whisky was made. Towards the end of the tour he talked about the distillery's green credentials and how they had to offset the carbon footprint to do their bit for the good of the planet. He clearly resented having to say it and when he'd finished, he added: "For me. It's Clarkson every time. The gift shop is this way ladies and gentlemen."

I've still got the expensive bottle of whisky I bought from the gift shop. Exactly like an exotic green drink you try on holiday, the whisky that tasted amazing in the sampling part of the distillery tour was undrinkable when I got it home.

I went to the *Doctor Who* exhibition in Cardiff with Mister Spoons and we all went to the National Space Centre in Leicester, even Marc, although he did spend a lot of the time there posing with all the phallic rockets and telescopes as though they were his penis.

On the tour to promote my novel *Driving Jarvis Ham*, we did so much sightseeing during the day that I had enough photos for a slideshow at the Borderline in London at the end of the tour. We went to the Blue John Cavern in the Peak District on that tour. It's the underground home to Blue John stone, a 250 million year-old semi-precious mineral. I think the Blue John Cavern is where The Beatles first started out. Me, Neil and Chris (AKA the Pet Shop Boys) went on a guided tour of the mine. The guide was an old miner and he kept dropping these semi-racist innuendos. He also told a story about how he was propositioned by a transvestite on one of his cave tours. We reported him for both of course.

My favourite tourist trip on the *Driving Jarvis Ham* tour was Mother Shipton's Cave, in North Yorkshire. The main attraction there is a petrifying well. The water is so rich in sulfate and carbonate that if you leave a teddy bear or Paul Daniels' glove in the well for long enough, they'll become petrified. There's a collection of objects in the Mother Shipton Museum. They include Queen Mary's shoe, John Wayne's hat, Agatha Christie's handbag, Paul Daniels' sock[39] and Fruitbat's hat (thrown in by Mark Morriss from The Bluetones) [citation needed]. In the museum there was a hangman's gibbet containing a waxwork man. It was hanging right above the ice creams. The gibbet also had a model crow sellotaped onto it and when you walked nearby, the hanging man cried out something like "Help me I'm done for!" and the waxwork crow would say "Caw! caw!" It was funny because it was clearly the same person doing the voice of both the hangman and the crow. It's probably my favourite museum in the whole world. Those pricks on TripAdvisor don't know what the fuck they're talking about.

After a day of sightseeing we'd head to the venue for the soundcheck. We'd play the gig. It would either be full or empty, or half empty or half full, depending on our mood and then we'd go to the Travelodge. We'd get some snacks out of the vending machine. At some point Travelodge would introduce the ice cream hoover to their hotels. For a while a machine that sucked our chosen ice cream out of a fridge before dropping it into a tray for us seemed like magic. We'd take our vending machine snacks up to our room, we'd each drink half a bottle of Becks before going to our beds to sleep, to sleep – perchance to dream – ay, there's the rub, for in this sleep of death what dreams may come when we have shuffled off this mortal coil, must give us pause. There's the respect that makes calamity of so long life. Shakespeare, ladies and gentlemen.

---

39 The late magician once part owned the attraction and presumably kept dropping his clothes in the well when performing tricks.

THOM YORKE FROM RADIOHEAD

The 2004 *Goodnight Jim Bob* tour ended in December at the Bloomsbury Theatre. It was my biggest solo show so far. I think we'd sold about five hundred tickets. It was an all-seated venue and I wanted to do something special. Tony Shea, who I first met when he came backstage at a Carter gig with a message from Phillip Schofield – a nice message, not a bag of burning dog shit or an envelope full of Anthrax – Tony did the lights for the production of *Joseph and the Amazing Technicolor Dreamcoat* that Phillip Schofield was in at the time and he would often pass on messages to us from Phillip to break a leg[40].

We met Tony Shea, who for some reason we'd renamed Tony O'Shea, at subsequent gigs, both Carter and solo Jim Bob. I asked him if he'd like to do some theatrical-style lighting at the Bloomsbury show. It was also time to attempt another balloon drop. The last one hadn't gone so well. About fifty billion *Love Album* balloons had been dropped from the ceiling of Brixton Academy in 1992 and they'd all landed on the stage. We had to perform the remainder of the gig in what was essentially a children's ball pit. If anything, it looked selfish.

At the Bloomsbury Theatre show, I would do what I'd been doing on the rest of the tour. I'd read a bit from my book, play a few songs, read another bit, maybe the *Smash Hits* chapter (very much the 'Sheriff Fatman' of the book) and then finish with a load of hits. I'd end the gig with my song 'Touchy Feely'. That would be when Tony O'Shea would drop the balloons.

There was a puppet show or an NUS meeting or something going on in the theatre during the day and we couldn't get access to the venue until quite late, so we were in a hurry. The soundcheck ran right up until the doors were due to open and then, when the balloons were finally secured in their netting on the ceiling, they immediately fell straight back down again. We had to further delay the doors while we frantically chased balloons around the auditorium and put them back in their net. It sounds like a lot more fun than it was.

Fruitbat had just made a short feature film with Tim *Plunkett & Macleane* Connery and we thought that instead of the usual apologetic acoustic heavy metal support band, it would be nice to premiere the film before me. There was a big screen at the theatre, it would be perfect. Les came onstage to introduce the film. He first apologised that things were running a bit late, blaming it on "Jim's balloon drop", which he

---

40 Insert your own joke

pointed at. The whole audience looked up at the ceiling. It was quite the spoiler alert. The only surprise really with the balloons was mine, when they were released two songs earlier than they were supposed to. The gig hadn't been going well up to that point to be honest. I was having the worst ever onstage sound issues and I don't think the audience liked having to sit down. They all stared up at me, feeling very alone on that big stage, dying on my arse. I totally forgot to use my difficulty that night. It was going to take at least three or four amazing gigs to erase the memory of such a disaster.

I felt a bit sheepish returning to the Bloomsbury Theatre for *Nine Lessons and Carols for Godless People* five years later. I was particularly anxious about meeting the manager of the venue who was still working there. I must have shouted at him for about fifteen solid minutes after my 2004 gig.

I ended the year with another humiliating experience. It was just before Christmas and I went up to the West End to record an interview and a few songs for Virgin radio. I had a stinking cold and had to battle my way through crowds of Christmas shoppers, avoiding tourists and trying not to slip over on the slush. When I got to the radio station the DJ I was there to see wasn't in the building and I sat in reception while they tried unsuccessfully to locate him. I think the receptionist thought I'd just turned up on the off-chance they might let me on the radio. As though it was my lifelong dream. I felt this small. I could have pulled all the stupid Hard Rock Cafe style memorabilia off their wanky reception wall and smashed their idiotic Stratocaster shaped clock. Instead, I said, oh, okay. That's no problem. Thank you. Bye. Merry Christmas. When Marc spoke to the DJ later, he said he was sorry but something else had come up and he'd forgotten I was coming. Seriously. *This* small.

Also:

BLOG – STICKS AND STONES 21/11/04
'The Revenge Of The School Bullied' from Angelstrike! was
reviewed on BBC 6 Music the other day by Mari Wilson (80s
star/big hair), some bloke from Rough Trade and the editor of
Word magazine. The general Roundtable opinion was Carter were
rubbish and therefore so was my new album. Anyway, it's nice
to still be judged on my ridiculous haircut and big shorts, I really
must get some long trousers and a date with my barber.

After some of the bitchy things I'd said on the same show, I suppose I was asking for that. It's a weird feeling though, finding out somebody you like doesn't like you. I owned Mari Wilson records. I still do. I didn't immediately burn them or turn them into ashtrays because she gave me a bad review on the radio. But it was upsetting somehow. I'm reminded of the time years ago when I famously chased James Dean Bradfield from the Manic Street Preachers around the bar at The Astoria because he didn't want to shake my hand. I was a big Manics fan. Or the time in Paris when I attempted a conversation with Thom Yorke from Radiohead. I'd met him years before and we didn't get on then. But I was a massive Radiohead fan. Listening to *The Bends* on my Discman over and over again had helped me through a difficult American tour. I say helped. More like accompanied. But I bloody loved Radiohead. In Paris I had to tell Thom Yorke how much I loved his band. I waited for the right moment. Until he was alone in a corridor. He completely blanked me, ladies and gentlemen. And this was years before Chas & Davegate. Jeez. A fellah could develop a complex if this carries on.

JIM BOB IN THE HOUSE

Nowadays, apart from playing pianos on station concourses, the only way bands can afford to perform live is to arrange private shows in the houses of secret millionaires. There are literally no more venues open to the public anymore. They've all been closed down because of noise complaints. They've been bulldozed and turned in to apartments for Russian oligarchs and people who hate music. The entire live pop music audience now consists of just four hundred well-offs and their closest friends. I might be to blame. I invented playing gigs in secret millionaires' houses in May 2005 when I auctioned a live Jim Bob performance for £1200 on Ebay for charity.

> **BLOG – THE EASYJETSET 15/05/05**
> On Monday I was in a man named Carl's house in Brighouse
> West Yorkshire, performing for 80 minutes (my manager times
> everything) to around thirty people in Carl's front room. Carl
> bought me on ebay, it was a strange experience but enjoyable, the
> house was lovely as were the biscuits and the guests and so on, we
> filmed a bit of it for my future DVD release so you can see some
> of what went on then, including my fantastic goal scored against
> a small boy. The train journey there was slow – British railway
> slow – we missed our connection at Wakefield and had to wait for
> an hour. During that Wakefield hour we noticed a teenager with
> a canvas bag with the words CARTER USM written on in biro.
> I thought he must be too young to be a fan of anything I'd been
> involved in but I think I was wrong, he walked past us a couple of
> times and gave us sideways looks. I wish I'd spoken to him and
> who knows, maybe he feels likewise.

I don't know what twelve hundred pounds is in today's money. By the time you read this it might be worth nothing and we'll be bartering Pokémon cards for food. And I don't know if Carl was a secret millionaire when I played the gig at his house, but he certainly was when he was on telly.

THE FIVE SECOND RULE

I don't know when it's acceptable for a band to get back together after splitting up. I don't think there's the equivalent of the five-second rule for dropped food, where if a band splits up and reforms quick enough for nobody to have noticed, they can just continue as they were. The last thing you want to do though, is mistime your comeback and end up being ridiculed because you've had to cancel two nights at the O2 after only selling a hundred tickets. And you want to be ready. Looking as good as you possibly can, or as close to how you used to look as your body will allow. You don't want it to be like that time Boyzone got back together and couldn't get off their stools in the key change.

I'm sure Carter had been asked to reform before 2005 but the first time I remember it being suggested by a promoter who could actually make it happen was at a friend's party on a boat on the Thames. I think my answer was that I would "rather eat my own legs." I had a few stock answers for when people asked me if Carter would ever get back together: Not for a million pounds. Over my dead body. Over Fruitbat's dead body. That sort of thing.

One time, I was a guest on a BBC 6 Music show to discuss bands reforming. They played an audio clip of people in the street being vox popped on the subject. One bloke they spoke to said "Carter USM should get back together. Although they must be in their late fifties now." Not realising my microphone might still be on in the 6 Music studio, I said "Oh fuck off you cunt." A panic filled the room as everyone ran around, trying to find out if my swearing had been broadcast. Apologies were issued just in case. I was so against the idea of Carter reforming at the time, I was prepared to end my career in a 'Filth and Fury' style stream of rude words.

Although Jim's Super Stereoworld didn't officially split up, we did reform briefly in 2005, to appear at one of the three nights I played at the Water Rats in King's Cross. Every night I performed a different set, both solo and Carter songs. I'm not suggesting I was the first person to ever play albums in their entirety but as you can see from these set lists below, I clearly was:

TUESDAY
101 DAMNATIONS POST HISTORIC MONSTERS ANGELSTRIKE! NIGHT

SOULMATES
SPOILSPORTS PERSONALITY
CHURCHBELL
PECKHAM 123
SMART BOMB!
VICTIM
SCHOOL BULLIED
24 MINUTES FROM TULSE HILL
LENNY & TERENCE
SING FAT LADY
DUMB AND DUMBER
OBSESSIVE COMPULSIVE
TONGUE TIED
CHARLIE BROWN
CHILDREN'S TERRORISM WORKSHOP
GEORGIE'S MARV MED
SUICIDE ISN'T PAINLESS
UNDER THE THUMB
THE HIPPIES WERE RIGHT
THE MUSIC THAT NOBODY LIKES
ANGELSTRIKE!
FATMAN
GI BLUES

WEDNESDAY
30 SOMETHING, WORRY BOMB, GOODNIGHT JIM B & J.R. NIGHT

SURFIN' USM
COOL
SECOND TO LAST WILL
CHEAP 'N' CHEESY
GOOD HAIR DAY
IN THE FUTURE
LET'S GET TATTOOS
YOUNG OFFENDER'S
NEW MAN IN THE MORNING
DEFEATIST ATTITUDE
GLASGOW KISS
CRUEL

A TIME TO KILL
SENILE DELINQUENT
YOU CAN'T TAKE IT WITH YOU
SHOPPERS' PARADISE
THE ONLY LOONEY LEFT
ONE TOO MANY
SAY IT WITH FLOWERS
CEASEFIRE
A PRINCE IN A PAUPER'S
ANYTIME ANYPLACE
SO LONG FAREWELL
EVERYTHING IS GOING TO BE ALRIGHT
BLOODSPORT
FALLING ON A BRUISE
THE FINAL COMEDOWN

THURSDAY
1992 THE LOVE ALBUM, A WORLD WITHOUT DAVE NIGHT

ENGLAND
IS WRESTLING FIXED?
A WORLD WITHOUT DAVE
AND GOD CREATED BRIXTON
SUPPOSE U GAVE A FUNERAL
WHILE YOU WERE OUT
NOWHERE FAST
LOOK MUM, NO HANDS!
SKYWEST AND CROOKED
THE ONLY LIVING BOY IN NC
DO RE ME, SO FAR SO GOOD
IMPOSSIBLE DREAM

(JIM'S SUPER STEREOWORLD)
CANDY FLOSS
HAPPIEST MAN ALIVE
BUBBLEGUM
YOU'RE MY MATE
BONKERS IN THE NUT
HEADS WILL ROCK
YOUNG DUMB AND FULL OF FUN
WHEN YOU'RE GONE PARTS 1 & 2
A BAD DAY

MY NAME IS JOHN
BIG FLASH CAR
JIM'S MOBILE DISCO
COULD U B THE 1
TOUCHY FEELY
PARTYWORLD

Everyone expects a setlist at the end of a gig these days don't they? If you don't come home with a picture of yourself with your back to the band and a signed setlist, it's like you were never there. If you want to pretend you were at one or more of these Water Rats gigs, just print out one of the above lists, scribble out one or two of the songs and then step on the paper with your dirtiest shoes, tear a bit off the corner to make it look aged and genuine and spill some tea on the paper and then sign it Jim Bob. That's what I do when people ask me for a signed setlist.

MUSICAL THEATRE

When we first began Carter, me and Fruitbat would cite a variety of influences: L.L. Cool J, Public Enemy, AC/DC and Tom Waits – but also the musicals *West Side Story* and *Cabaret*. We loved musicals. We recorded 'The Impossible Dream' because it was a song we used to busk in a subway leading to Croydon Whitgift Centre, where we also attempted 'Supercalifragilisticexpialidocious' and 'Chim Chim Cher-ee' from *Mary Poppins*. I wonder if the waltzy Carter songs like 'The Taking of Peckham 123', 'A Prince in a Pauper's Grave' and 'England' would exist if I hadn't heard 'Oom-Pah-Pah' from *Oliver!* so many times when I was growing up. In fact, 'England' might not have started at all, without its opening line stolen from *Paint Your Wagon*. And where would 'The Only Living Boy in New Cross' be without *Evita*?

The film musicals from the sixties that I saw so often when I was a kid are still my favourites. I saw *Mary Poppins* and *The Sound of Music* at the cinema not long after they first came out. At Streatham Odeon. I remember forcing a straw through the lid of an intermission Kia-Ora. Peacocks of Balham. *John Collier John Collier the window to watch.* A dry cleaners just five minutes walk from this cinema.

Years later I'd play the soundtrack albums of *Cabaret* and *West Side Story* as often as my Elvis Costello and Clash records. Carter sampled 'Tomorrow Belongs to Me' from *Cabaret* at the end of 'Is This the Only Way to Get Through To You'. The title and chorus are samples from *West Side Story*. The sleeve for *A World Without Dave* is a straight homage to the *West Side Story* soundtrack LP sleeve. I could go on.

People have frequently suggested there should be a Carter jukebox musical, in the style of *We Will Rock You* or *Mama Mia!* But I'd rather write a musical from scratch. In 2005, the Jim Bob solo album *School* was the closest I'd been to writing a full on musical. After *Angelstrike!* I'd been true to my word about waiting for the songwriting muse to come and get me before I made another record. For some reason when it arrived, the muse wanted me to write an album about a failing school being saved by a new headmaster when he starts up a school orchestra. Once I'd written the first song 'The First Big Concert for the Orchestra', the other songs were easy. It must have only taken me a couple of weeks to write the whole album.

I wanted to stick to a strict concept when it came to the songs and the recording. My dream was that *School* would one day be performed by kids in schools all over the country. The songs needed to be easily replicated by schoolchildren, whatever their musical abilities and available instruments were. This made more sense to me than it does now, as every day I see another video clip of a seven year old playing a guitar blindfolded or a whole band of shredding seven-year old metal-heads playing with a level of skill I could only dream of.

The chord progressions and arrangements of the songs on *School* were kept deliberately simple. I realise when I pictured out of tune recorders, glockenspiels and nylon strung acoustic guitars and a box of percussion instruments, I was probably basing my idea of what a school orchestra consisted of on my experience from a long time ago. I'm guessing today a school orchestra would be twenty-six DJs with laptops and a stylist.

Anyway, it's my concept. So there are recorders and acoustic guitars, drums and piano, glockenspiels and xylophones on the record. There's also a mouth organ, a cello, a trumpet, a saxophone, a trombone and a flute. The only traditionally played rock song on *School* is 'Asbomania!', which I imagined was being played by the school rock band. Every school has one. They still play the same set of songs as when you and I were at school: Amy Winehouse's version of 'Valerie', 'Seven Nation Army' (the Oh Jeremy Corbyn song) and something by Nirvana or the Smashing Pumpkins.

I bought a cheap glockenspiel and a triangle, a couple of tambourines and some castanets. I also bought one of those vibraslaps with the bendy piece of metal that you ping so it goes boi-yoi-oingggg. I bought a Swanee whistle (*The Clangers*) and I found an instrument that sounded like rain and a 'thunder box' to create the sound of thunder. You can hear the thunder and the rain on 'Storm in the Staff Room', a song about the geography teacher Mr. Moon, dreaming of the day when he exacts his revenge on all the other teachers and the pupils who, when given the choice, drop geography in favour of history or the performing arts.

Mr. Moon was inspired by my daughter's geography teacher. Mrs MacMurphy, the food technology teacher who can't stop swearing on 'Mrs Fucking MacMurphy (Teaches Food technology)' was, not so much inspired by, as an autobiographical account of my daughter's incredibly angry food technology teacher. Some of the teachers on *School* are named after characters from my favourite novels, including Mr. Durden from *Fight Club*, Mrs. MacMurphy from *One Flew over the Cuckoo's Nest* and the English teacher Miss Fontaine, from *The Virgin Suicides*.

When it came to recording the album I needed to find musicians and a studio that was better equipped than my spare bedroom. About a year earlier Fruitbat had recorded the soundtrack to his own musical *Tommi and Chris* at Earth Terminal Studios in an old Hop Kiln in Hampshire. I'd sang on one of the songs. I went back to Earth Terminal a year or so later to record *School*. Les played bass on 'Asbomania!', Richy Crockford who'd got us lost in Holland played guitar and the insanely good *School* drummer Damo Waters was also occasionally in Abdoujaparov.

Chris T-T plays piano on the record. Ben from Jim's Super Stereoworld and the six-piece version of Carter had introduced me to Chris's music on the Who's the Daddy Now? tour bus. Chris went on to support Jim's Super Stereoworld a few times and has been a part of every Jim Bob record and tour I've done since. Chris brought his friend Jon Clayton to Earth Terminal to play cello. Jon also played cello on the *A Humpty Dumpty Thing* album and engineered my most recent solo records.

I still needed somebody to play the brass instruments on *School* and most importantly, the recorders. I didn't know anyone. I decided to learn how to play the recorder myself. I'd played one at school. It was probably like riding a bike. Not literally. You know what I mean. To help, for Father's Day my daughter bought me a book called *Play Recorder! (A first book for beginners of all ages)*. I looked at the cover of the book and saw it was written by somebody called Simon Henry. The inside cover informed me the book's Editorial Director was Lindsey Lowe. O to the M to the G# minor. Simon and Lindsey were the saxophone and trumpet players in Jamie Wednesday. I hadn't seen them for years. Serendipity-doo-dah! I got in contact with Lindsey via the book's publisher and the rest is history (Mr. Durden/*Fight Club*). Simon and Lindsey had a friend called Vicky Johnson who played the trombone. It was meant to happen.

We recorded *School* in Autumn of 2005 and performed it live just once at 'Jim Bob's Christmas School Concert' at the Islington Academy.

From back to front (left to right): **Kate Grimaldi (recorder), Holly Morrison (recorder), Lindsey Lowe (trumpet), Simon Henry (sax, flute), Jason Powdrill (glockenspiel, percussion), Vicky Johnson (trombone), Damo Waters (drums), Richard Crockford (guitar), Arran Goodchild (percussion), Mr Spoons (grumpy face trying to look sexy), Chris T-T (piano), Jon Clayton (cello and bass), Tucker Jenkins.**

It was because of *School* that I ended up writing two songs for a pantomime.[41] Uber Jim Bob enabler Andrew Collins had given a copy of the album to the Barbican Theatre producer Andrew Collier (I reckon they met when they sat next to each other at school). The Barbican were putting on a production of the pantomime *Dick Whittington and His Cat*, written by Mark Ravenhill and directed by Edward Hall. Rather than the usual method of shoehorning songs from the current pop charts into the production, they wanted to commission original songs. It was because of *School* and the type of record it was, that I was asked if I'd like to write a couple of songs for *Dick Whittington*.

I can't begin to tell you what a big deal it was for me. I took it very seriously. I read up on the real life Dick Whittington, visiting the Museum of London, buying Dick books and learning all about the Worshipful Livery companies of merchants and makers. Once I'd started writing the songs, like with those for *School*, I couldn't stop. Two of my songs ended up in the finished production, 'The Evil Victory Song', sung by Nickolas Grace and 'The Lord Mayor's Show'. Another would eventually be rewritten as 'Cartoon Dad' on my *A Humpty Dumpty Thing album*, hence the 'I thought the streets were paved with gold' lyrics.

I explained earlier how easily star-struck and shallow I am. And how if I ever went to the theatre I always looked up the cast on IMDb to see if they've been in *The Bill*, *Holby City* or *Midsomer Murders*. Imagine my delight when I saw the cast of *Dick Whittington and His Cat* included actors who'd been in all three. As well as actors from *Only*

---

41   Oh yes I did.

Fools and Horses, *Bergarac* and *Balamory*, *Lovejoy*, *The Professionals* and *Porridge*. And they would be singing my songs!

It's a great thrill to hear something you've written, being sung by somebody else. There've been a few Carter cover versions of course. The Sultans of Ping recorded a couple and the Family Cat did a great version of 'Lean on Me I Won't Fall Over' for example. More recently, Ian Dury sang on 'Y2K The Bug is Coming'. All amazing. But at the opening night of *Dick Whittington,* when I heard the arrangement of my first song in the show 'The Lord Mayor's Show', all properly arranged and professionally performed and sung and even choreographed, I'd never felt so damn proud.

I'd met the Musical Director and arranger Sarah Travis at a press thing at the Barbican a few weeks earlier. She'd just won a Best Orchestrations Tony Award for Stephen Sondheim's Sweeney Todd on Broadway. Having re-orchestrated what the Internet describes as 'one of the most celebrated scores in musical theatre history', Sarah Travis was now going to have to work on my half-arsed nonsense. I was a bit embarrassed meeting her, knowing that she'd heard my home demo recordings. At the press thing though, Tony Award winning genius Sarah Travis confided in me, that she didn't really know what she was doing and had been winging it and making it up as she went along for years. Brilliant.

When I arrived at the theatre for the press thing I shared a lift with Roger Lloyd Pack. He was playing the pantomime dame Sarah the Cook. We posed for press photos together and he took hold of my arm in a supportive actor kind of way. There's a picture of us on the Internet looking like best mates but I can't afford to reproduce it here. Me and ~~Trigger from Only Fools and Horses~~ Roger Lloyd Pack were interviewed together for BBC2's *Culture Show* but as usual the BBC cut me out of the edit.

The whole thing was an amazing experience. My demo recording of 'The Lord Mayor's Show', with my crappy old voice on, was played over and over again on the Barbican's float at the actual Lord Mayor's Show that year. I watched it live on television but the second the Barbican float went past the cameras, the BBC cut to a short film about plumbers (seriously). They really will do anything to keep me off the telly.

There was a party after the opening night. It was the first time I'd been to anything with a free bar for such a long time that it's surprising I didn't make an absolute idiot of myself. At the party I met some of the cast, including Miles Jupp, who told me his first live music experience was when he won tickets for the *Smash Hits Poll Winners Party* in 1991.

Not quite such big fans of my music were the people who reviewed *Dick Whittington and His Cat* on BBC2's *Newsnight Review.* One particular reviewer really hated it. He described the songs as 'awful sub-Disneyesque' or something along those lines. I hated him so much then and he's done nothing in the years since to redeem himself, or to change my opinion of him. Michael Gove, ladies and gentlemen.

Just as my appearance on *Jammin'* wasn't my big break into the world of BBC radio light entertainment, my two songs at the Barbican didn't set me off on the successful career in pantomimes and musical theatre I was hoping for. I would get to act in a musical though. But that's another story.

THE *Musical* THAT NOBODY LIKES

In a distant and yet local future there are no thirty-somethings left alive. At the age of twenty-nine, life abruptly and violently ends. All that is except for the life of the 'evil' Sheriff Fatman, a six-foot six and a hundred ton post historic monster of a dictator. His reign of terror is feared by everyone, even those sycophants who praise his every move, hailing him with their chant of 'you fat bastard!' For to do otherwise, to show any hint of resistance or defiance would result in certain death at the hands of Fatman's heavily armed and brutal 'Glam Rock Cops'.

Fatman's reign continues unchallenged. As he passes yet another draconian law as part of what will be known as his '101 Damnations', there is perhaps only one person who can save us from his tyranny. Believed to be long dead and buried, a true 'prince in a pauper's grave', our hero comes out at night, 'after the watershed', from his hideaway in the 'rubbish' left behind in the abandoned 'Shoppers' Paradise' hypermall. Born thirty years ago on the fifth of November. His name is Johnnie Walker, 'the only living boy in New Cross'.

BLOG – THE MUSICIAN'S FEAR OF THE MUSIC SHOP RETURNS 13/01/06

So, here's what happened. When I was rehearsing for the School Orchestra gig, my guitar started making farting sounds. I swapped guitar leads and the flatulent sounds stayed. I diagnosed a broken pick-up. For the Islington gig I taped an emergency pick-up to my guitar, which I'd take back to the shop after Christmas. It was still under its 12-month guarantee and I was also entitled to a free 'set up', which for the non-musos is like getting your car serviced (of course for the yes-musos, it's nothing like that at all).

I've talked before about my phobia of music shops and the people who work there and how I got over this somewhat when I successfully bought my new guitar last year. Anyway, I went back to the shop yesterday and after being ignored by the six people behind the counter for five minutes I was 'served' by a grumpy bloke who reluctantly took my details and then reluctantly tried to find the phone number of the guitar's manufacturer for the next 30 minutes, until he got bored and handed me over to somebody else. This new assistant took my details again because the grumpy geezer hadn't saved them on the computer.

To cut what's a pretty boring story that I wish I hadn't started short: after one hour in the music shop, with my details taken twice, the guitar maker's phone number finally found and telephoned, all to the accompaniment of some kid playing Coldplay songs on a piano keyboard, we found the battery. There's a fucking battery? I had a flat battery in my guitar. I felt stupid. I felt like someone who'd put petrol in his diesel car, like the man who took his fax machine back to the shop because every time he fed a fax message into the machine it came back out the other end. To add a little insult to my injury it was then pointed out via the shop assistant's guitar twiddling, diddling, harmonics and showing off – playing the guitar so much better than I ever would – it was pointed out to me that it didn't need a free set up either. And so I left the music shop with my guitar between my legs. As I climbed the stairs I swear I could hear all the many, many staff pissing themselves laughing at the nob jockey who'd just been in the shop, they'd dine out on the story for years. I'd never go into a music shop ever again. My only consolation was that I was a sort of pop star and they all worked in a shop.

I did a gig at Wimbledon library. It was in a room upstairs and the audience had to carry their own chairs up from the library. The bar consisted of two boxes of wine and an honesty box. I was supposed to be reading from my as yet unpublished *Storage Stories* novel and playing a few songs, but I chickened out and read from *Goodnight Jim Bob* instead. I'd often do a similar thing when I reached a new solo song on my setlist and feeling I was losing the audience, I'd play 'Sheriff Fatman' instead.

I drank more than my fair share from the library wine boxes and was less than honest with the honesty box and I thought it would be amusing to start by reading from the Elton John biography on the windowsill behind me. I know all of this because I wrote in my blog how, *'I chickened out of reading anything from my new unpublished book but did have a stab at a passage from an Elton John biography. I resisted saying that I had a stab at Elton John's passage there, I hope you're proud of me.'*

When I was reading from *Goodnight Jim Bob* I was aware of a couple of older well-dressed ladies at the back of the room. I became very conscious of all the F words and C bombs I was dropping and hoped they wouldn't be offended. After the gig they approached me. I prepared myself for a telling off. They in fact told me they thought I was very entertaining and one of the ladies said I had a charming manner. She said it was the kind of manner that would allow mc to gct away with saying any old nonsense. They particularly liked my reading of the 'Adrian's Magic Pants story' in the book, which is mostly about poo. While she was talking to me one of the women mentioned her father a few times. She said he would really have liked what I was doing. It was only as they started to leave that her friend whispered to me, "Her father is Dylan Thomas."

Apart from writing two songs for a pantomime, that may have been my highlight from 2006. I played twenty-seven gigs and stayed at an equivalent amount of Travelodges. I stopped at service stations and ate in Little Chefs. We drove on A roads and B roads and motorways. I went on three different boats, one of them moored to the shore by the Thames and another to the Isle of Man on such a rough Irish Sea that virtually every single passenger was sick. Mister Spoons took almost two full days to recover and had to put Chris T-T on his driving insurance to drive the car two hundred yards from the ferry terminal to the gig venue.

While we were in the Isle of Man, we were sitting in a café on the seafront having a baked potato, talking about the island's most famous resident Norman Wisdom. I looked out of the window and there he was. Doing his Mr. Grimsdale walk for the tourists.

Of the twenty-seven gigs I played in 2006, some were empty, others were not so empty and very few were full. Every night at least one person would ask me if Carter would ever reform and I'd say no. It had been nine years now and more people were asking the question and more frequently. Among all my grand declarations and dismissive exclamations about eating my legs and never in a billion years or not for a million pounds, I hadn't considered there might be a bad reason for getting the band back together again.

JIM BOB EATS HIS OWN LEGS

On 6th December 2006, after returning from a US tour and collapsing at a band rehearsal, Wiz from Mega City Four was taken to St George's hospital, where he sadly died from a blood clot on the brain. The following February, Carter's former live booking agent Paul, rang to ask if me and Les would perform some acoustic Carter songs at a tribute show. I said yes. Without needing to think about it for a second. I loved Wiz. I don't know anyone who'd met him who didn't. He was such a sweet and lovely guy. And if it hadn't been for Mega City Four, Carter would never have toured as relentlessly as we did. Apart from anything else, the Megas gave us a copy of their famous list of venues and contacts. It would take us everywhere from Ipswich to Banja Luka. So I told Paul that I'd need to speak to Les but then I'd get right back to him. I didn't tell Paul I hoped Les would say no – and before Dennis takes this out of context on Twitter:

I'd released six solo albums. I was about to record a seventh. I'd written songs for a major theatre production and started work on my first novel. When I went on tour, the Carter logos on the posters were finally getting smaller. Sometimes they weren't there at all. The last thing I wanted to do was remind everyone who I used to be. I didn't want to show them what they could have won. To me, it just seemed so much simpler if I played the four Carter songs for Wiz on my own. I was still eleven years away from being referred to on Facebook as shit acoustic Carter karaoke but I did play a handful of Carter songs in my live solo shows. And Jim Bob playing Carter songs would be just that. Jim Bob playing Carter songs. Jim Bob and Fruitbat playing Carter songs would be Carter The Unstoppable Sex Machine.

I was pretty sure Les wouldn't be keen anyway. We'd played twenty minutes of acoustic Carter songs together at the Mean Fiddler's birthday party in 2002 and it hadn't really worked. The only song I remember us doing was 'My Defeatist Attitude', which I imagine we played because it was already an acoustic song. For Wiz, I would have wanted to do something from the earlier albums. I was always the crowd pleaser in Carter. Les would probably have insisted on playing 'My Defeatist Attitude' four times in a row.

As it turned out, Les did say no. And in the words of Tony Blair – "this is not a day for sound bites" – but it would change the course of history. Because he suggested we use electric guitars instead. And backing tapes.

It would be the first thing we argued about when we got the band back together. What would we play the backing tapes on. The last version of the band hadn't used tapes at all and before that we were using eight-track ADAT machines, which took VHS-sized tapes that rarely worked properly, especially if the room was too hot, too cold, a bit damp or slightly dry. Before ADATs we'd used DAT machines[42] and before that, analogue cassettes.

Ever the pioneer, for our four songs for Wiz, Fruitbat wanted to use an MP3 player. He'd been using one with his Abdoujaparov side project Idou. It seemed like a bad idea to me, because – techno speak alert – the output was a mini earphone socket and the sound wasn't great. I was convinced an MP3 player would fail in the middle of a song or we'd lose it on the way to the gig because it was so small or Fruitbat would break it when he sat on it in the back pocket of his jeans.

The backing tape media would be an issue every time we played another reunion show. By 2014 we had so many different forms of back-up because of my paranoia that one of them would malfunction. We had two laptops, two hard disk players and three DAT machines. I didn't tell anyone but I also had CD copies of all the backing tapes in my bag as well. Whatever we played the music on though, no matter how digital or lossless it was, some of the backing tapes we used in 2007 and for every gig until we stopped in 2014, like 'The Taking of Peckham' or 'G.I. Blues' for example, were the exact same recordings we'd used at our first gig at the Astoria in 1987, tape hiss included.

For the Wiz gig, Les won the argument and we used an MP3 player. We booked a rehearsal session in a studio in Streatham. It was just five hundred feet from where the Orchestra Pit, the rehearsal studio where I first met Les in 1979, used to be. It's a Job Centre Plus now. Which is fitting, as none of the bands that rehearsed there ever had a job. The rehearsal studio we went to in 2007 was just up the hill and round the corner (not a euphemism) from the Orchestra Pit. It was above the Silver Blades ice rink, featured in 'Twenty Four Minutes from Tulse Hill'. Not long ago the ice rink was moved along the road, to where the bus garage used to be and the original Silver Blades is an enormous Tesco Extra. There's a Marks and Spencer Foodhall a few doors along, next to the train station. It used to have a Café Revive at the front of the store but it was recently turned into a self-service restaurant. The Veggie Percy and Colin the Caterpillar sweets seem to be on a permanent two for £3 offer.

When I was a teenager I used to skate at the Silver Blades. I say skate but it was mostly smoking fags and trying to talk to girls. There was a nightclub above the ice rink, called the Bali Hai. I think it's where Mick Jones from The Clash went dancing 'down Streatham on the bus'

42 Digital Audio Tape (DAT or R-DAT) is a signal recording and playback medium developed by Sony in 1987. Using 3.81 mm magnetic tape, DAT is smaller and less hissy than the analogue cassette tapes in a machine on a chair or two beer crates that the band Carter The Unstoppable Sex Machine used previously. Nowadays all pop acts use Spotify or Deezer. Unless they are performing an 'unplugged' set. Or 'offline' or 'Away from Keyboard' as it is now known.

in The Clash song 'Stay Free'. Mick Jones went to the same school as Fruitbat and it was only a few years ago that Les remembered that Tim Roth went to his school too. Les is not as easily star-struck as I am and there may be other famous alumni he's forgotten about. Tom Cruise or all of the Sex Pistols may have been in his class as well. It just hasn't occurred to Les yet.

Like Mick Jones, my mum used to go down Streatham on the bus (a 137 then, either a 159 or a 50) to the Bali Hai. She went there for the reggae. For the Dennis Brown and John Holt records they used to play. My mum liked lover's rock and Bob Marley dub versions. She was quite the enigma, my mum. She grew up in a fairly posh part of Surrey during the Second World War and had to go to a boys' school because that was the only school available. In the nineteen forties she was a speed ice skater and also appeared in a synchronised swimming show with Olympic gold medalist and Tarzan actor, Johnny Weissmuller. My mum lived a life that sounds made up.

In the fifties she sang in a close-harmony act called the Four in a Chord. You may have their recording of 'Rudolph the Red-Nosed Reindeer' on a Christmas compilation LP in your attic. Who's the Daddy Now? sampled a bit of it at the start of our second single 'Daddy Christmas'. As a member of the Four in a Chord my mum appeared on the Morecambe and Wise show, *Running Wild* and she sang with Benny Hill and Stanley Baxter. In spite of such a white show business background, my mum loved black music. When I gave the undertaker the list of songs to play at her funeral, they probably thought it was me who'd chosen Bob Marley, R. Kelly and Ladysmith Black Mambozo. But it was my mum. It could equally have been Gregory Isaacs playing in that Plymouth crematorium. Or Delroy Wilson or Dillinger, Leroy Smart, or anyone else Mick Jones's band-mate Joe Strummer sang about in '(White Man) in Hammersmith Palais'. My mum loved reggae. If Carter wrote a song about her it would probably be called '(White Mum) in Streatham Bali Hai.'

A month before the first Carter rehearsal in ten years, a teenage boy was murdered at the ice rink. I was still jittery going out at night after being mugged and so rehearsing upstairs from a murder scene added to the anxiety. I was also anxious about playing in a band with Les again. It was only four songs but what if they sounded dated or awful? And I used to say that after we stopped being in a band together, me and Les became friends again. What if Jim Bob and Fruitbat didn't get on as well as Jim and Les? The thing I remember most from the rehearsal is how weirdly uncomfortable it felt being alone in a room together with no windows. It was like a blind date. Like we were strangers meeting for the first time. Thankfully we could break the ice (no pun intended©) with very loud music.

It was surprising how well we remembered the songs. I even got the chords wrong at the start and the end of 'Twenty Four Minutes from Tulse Hill' just like I used to. Muscle memory is an amazing thing. We didn't need to rehearse many songs. Everyone at the Four 4 Wiz gig – The Megas, Ned's Atomic Dustbin, Senseless Things, Andy Cairns from Therapy? Reuben and us – played four songs. Ours were 'Tulse Hill', 'The Only Living Boy in New Cross', 'A Prince in a Pauper's Grave' and 'My Second to Last Will and Testament'. There was no 'Sheriff Fatman' because Les had always sort of resented the way we *had* to play it. Even when we reformed properly I'm pretty sure I had to bully him in to including it in the set. We very rarely rehearsed it.

There was more love in the room for us and our four songs at Islington Academy than I ever could have imagined, even after the MP3 didn't work properly at the start – I knew it! Naturally, there was talk backstage about us doing more gigs and playing for longer. Our old booking agent thought we could probably sell out one night at the Shepherd's Bush Empire. That really seemed to annoy Marc Ollington. He thought it was almost defeatist. Marc had other ideas. It was only recently that he told me he'd been planning a Carter reformation ever since seeing Pop Will Eat Itself do theirs so well two years before us in 2005. He knew me and Les still weren't keen to fully reform. He needed to find a way to convince us to change our minds. He waited until after we'd reformed, played nineteen sold out gigs and then split up again, before confessing how he'd tricked us into it.

It was never just about the money but when I'd proclaimed that we wouldn't get back together for a million pounds, I was probably secretly hoping somebody would call my bluff. No one ever did though. It made it easier to come out with grand statements about eating my legs etc. It's easy to refuse things that aren't being offered. As long as there were no gig promoters offering large sums of money for us to reform, we could carry on being proud and stubborn by refusing them.

I've always been a bit uncomfortable talking about money. If Marc or Mister Spoons weren't at my solo gigs, I'd never collect my fee at the end of the night. I'd be too embarrassed to go and ask for it, especially if the gig hadn't been full. I've played quite a few gigs when the promoter has said he hadn't made enough money on the door to pay me. If Mister Spoons wasn't there to accompany the promoter to the cash point, I would have fallen for such an old show business (lack of) confidence trick.

The mere fact that I'm now on the third paragraph about how unimportant a factor money was in Carter getting back together, demonstrates how uncomfortable I feel about the subject. My guilt about money and not wanting to be seen as a bread-head is why, when Dennis has a go at us on social media later in this story, when he accuses us of selling out and cashing in, with yet another reunion gig, so we can add to our sports car collections and re-tarmac our helipad, when I actually needed the money to pay to get my mum out of the flat she was so lonely and unhappy in and moved into sheltered housing, my discomfort with money is the reason I'm not going to tell Dennis to go fuck himself.

Having said all that, obviously we weren't about to reform the band for fuck all. We're not communists.

Marc had a plan. At his day job at the New Zealand consulate in New York City (must remember to check this), Marc had been working on a project with concert promoters Live Nation. Marc asked them how much hypothetical money they would hypothetically guarantee to pay Carter for a one-off hypothetical show at Brixton Academy, regardless of whether we sold a single ticket. Live Nation gave Marc a figure that he knew wouldn't be anywhere near enough for me and Les to be interested. Marc then asked Live Nation how much we'd make if the gig was completely sold out. It was that considerably larger figure, that Marc told me and Les Live Nation would guarantee us, even if we didn't sell a single ticket.

BLOG . THE LOST ART OF KEEPING A SECRET 8/04/07
So, the secret is out. Carter are doing a gig at Brixton Academy on November 2nd. I can now stop telling everybody.

As soon as Brixton Academy was booked, I started to worry about ticket sales. What if the audience's thrill had been in the chase and wanting us to reform was enough. Now we'd reformed everyone would move on to hassling the Smiths or The Clash and we wouldn't sell any tickets. I wondered if we'd made a big mistake. Marc must have really been shitting himself. But Brixton sold out in four minutes or six and a half seconds or whatever. We added a second date at Glasgow Barrowlands, two weeks before Brixton. Glasgow didn't sell out quite as quickly but ignoring my fears that we were victims of the world's fastest backlash, Glasgow was soon close to being sold out. We could put Carter to one side for a few months and I could get back to my solo shizzle.

MY SOLO SHIZZLE

My next album, *A Humpty Dumpty Thing* was almost finished. It was a semi-conceptual record about a disillusioned man who works in an office in the centre of London. I'd written a long-short story called *Word Count* to go with the album. It was about a different man, also working in the centre of London but this time in the near future. I think you'd call the story dystopian. I just did. I'd later turn *Word Count* into a script for an as yet unmade movie. As yet unmade, optimism fans, as yet.

I recorded most of *A Humpty Dumpty Thing* at Earth Terminal studios but I also went down to Truro to work on a couple of the songs with some old friends, Kevin Downing and Tim McVay from The Family Cat. They both worked at Zebs, a drop-in centre and recording studio for young people in Cornwall. We recorded vocals with a dozen enthusiastic teenagers there, on the songs 'Pizza Boy' and 'Why Can't We Get Along?' The day before, I'd been in Devon visiting my sister. Her nine year-old son Jake was auditioning for a part in a musical and needed to learn a song. He chose Queen's 'Don't Stop me Now' and I was asked to help him with the song, because of my musical experience and skills (stop laughing at the back). Jake just couldn't seem to get the line 'like Lady Godiva' right. The words didn't mean anything to him and he'd learned them by their sound rather than meaning. In the same way all British children think the twelfth letter of the alphabet is ellermennopee. Ever since that day with Jake in Devon I've never been able to hear 'Don't Stop me Now', without singing along to the 'like Lady Godiva' bit as 'Daygee Gerdigaa'.[43]

Clinton USM, the Japanese Carter tribute band who flew over to Brixton three times to play at our aftershow parties, seemed to have learned the Carter songs in a similar onomatopoeic way. I'd like to see that bloke in the Irish bar in Berlin deconstruct their version of 'New Cross'.

Just a few days working on music with young people in Devon and Cornwall really inspired me. When I left the West Country to return home, it was with a feeling of optimism and hope for the future of humanity that lasted right up until the guard threw me off the train at Plymouth because I didn't have the correct ticket.

Whether I was recording my solo album, playing the occasional solo

---

43 My favourite Queen lyric is in the song 'Killer Queen'. When Freddie
    Mercury from Queen sings about gunpowder and gelatin. Unless the Killer
    Queen was making a poisoned trifle, I'm guessing Freddie meant gelignite.

gig or finishing my long-short story or working on my first novel, the impending Carter reunion was never far from my mind.

BLOG – A SECOND BITE OF THE CHERRY
22/04/07

I seem to have made a mockery of Andy Warhol's quarter of an hour fame theory by getting a bonus ten minutes. Somehow I'm not the same person I was the day before we announced the Carter reunion show. My girlfriend's sister asked me what it was like to be famous again. There was a nice piece in Time Out that mentioned Carter without the usual snide bracketed insult. I went to Athens for a solo acoustic gig and a big Greek promoter showed up. He was hoping to get a Carter show booked in Athens. When I got home there was another Carter gig offer among my emails, I expect more to follow. I feel guilty for turning them down. When I was drunk in Athens, for a brief cocktail and adrenalin fuelled moment I started to imagine getting on a big bus and going to Barcelona and Zagreb, to Berlin and Vienna and all those exotic places where Carter were well received before.

I was reading the Sunday papers today and when I saw the ads for gigs by Devo and other names from the past, I was almost disappointed that the Carter gig had sold out so fast. We'd saved a load of cash by cancelling all the intended advertising that we didn't need anymore. But then I thought that, aside from us and the audience, the world might never know we'd got back together at all. I suppose I thought I might have been able to use the oxygen of publicity to breathe life into my solo career and get me and my new album onto Jools Holland and the Mercury Music Prize podium. And maybe even get a book publishing deal too. But now nobody is going to believe me. Maybe we should take out a big ad in The Observer with the words SOLD OUT slapped across it.

I'm a natural worrier. I worry that after this is all over and everything goes back to normal, will it? Will it go back to normal? Were people coming to my solo gigs because they knew that one day I might do the Carter songs properly? Has the thrill of the chase now gone? What happens next? I know the logical thing to do is to play my summer festivals, finish recording my album, and look forward to a great winter and two legendary Carter gigs. I should just try and enjoy the ride. And make sure I get off the ride before it reaches the latter pages of my Carter autobiography.

In June it was time to find out how strictly enforced the supposed Glastonbury ban on Carter was. I was booked to play in the Left Field tent, the festival's political zone, where political speeches and debates mixed with pop music. I was on the bill as part of the Shelter Affordable Housing campaign. Joss Stone was the secret headliner and was responsible for one of the funniest moments in music I've ever witnessed.

It was so muddy at Glastonbury that year. In my blog I said, 'To get across quite how much it rained, at one point Team Jim Bob found themselves sheltering in the ambient trance tent.' Going to see anyone else play soon stopped being fun and I had to keep the team's dwindling spirits up by pointing out to them every time we trudged past the Pyramid stage that I had once headlined it, looking around us on the ground for any foam balls still left behind. I'd heard the balls were worth a bit of money on eBay.

In case you don't know, when Carter headlined Glastonbury (Carter headlined Glastonbury), we fired thousands of sponge balls into the audience with the name of our latest single 'Do Re Me, So Far So Good' printed on. We had planned to drop the balls from a helicopter but couldn't get permission from the Civil Aviation Authority. The same spoilsports who wouldn't let us fly a giant inflatable Brussel sprout above Battersea Power Station a few months earlier. At Glastonbury we had to fire our balls from two giant cannons at either side of the stage. But that's not why we were asked to leave.

There were no cannons or helicopters for my 2007 Glastonbury return. Just me and an acoustic guitar. We pitched our National Geographic tents and unpacked our National Geographic backpacks and made our way through a mile of thick brown soup to the Left Field stage and the backstage green room, where all the seats were taken up by various union leaders and their entourage. We stood in a corner. At least we were out of the rain.

Billy Bragg was in the green room. I used to know Billy. Carter had hidden from him in a cupboard at Wembley Arena because he wanted to talk to us about the war. We hid from Jonathan King in the same cupboard on the same day. We may have been childish idiots but we didn't discriminate. Obviously, Billy Bragg didn't recognise me and I had to face my usual dilemma of wanting to say hello but not wanting to have to explain who I was.

After about five minutes of eavesdropping on Bob Crow from RMT I noticed Marc was talking to Billy Bragg. After a while Billy came over and said hello. He told me he'd heard that Carter had just sold out five nights at Brixton Academy. He said he was going to have to split up and reform too. Five nights. Classic Marc Ollington.

After my gig I did a video interview for the Love Music Hate Racism people. I was attempting to make a very clever point, which I started with the words, "Everyone is a little bit racist". They stopped filming and thanked me before I managed to complete what would have been my very clever point and give any much-needed context for my almost proud sounding "Everyone is a little bit racist" declaration.

A little later, Joss Stone arrived backstage. She tested the 'we're all in it together' ethos of the Left Field stage, if not the whole festival. First a sofa was carried into the 'portable building' dressing room. Presumably the sofa had come from the green room and Bob Crow had to get up. For a transport union leader he didn't seem to like moving about much. Joss Stone's rider arrived and a load of teddy bears were brought to the dressing room. Mister Spoons says I've made this detail up but I definitely remember teddy bears. After two day's worth of bands traipsing in and out without removing their Wellingtons, the dressing room was just as muddy as the rest of the festival, but it did now have a settee, some soft toys and a huge rider in it. It looked like Pete Doherty's bedroom.

Joss Stone arrived with her team and me and Spoons went out front to watch her. The tent was pretty empty and it must have been soul destroying[44] for Joss.

Her band came on first. There were about a hundred of them. They were all fantastic musicians, horns and keys and guitars and a wall of backing vocalists etc. They started playing, establishing a groove. All good so far. And then the funny bit. The song reached its crescendo and the backing vocalists sang something like, "Here she is, Miss Jooooosss Stooonne!" and the band all turn to face the side of the stage. Nothing. No Joss Stone. Everyone in the band smiled awkwardly and then slipped back into the groove. Starting the song again, until it reaches the crescendo for the second time, "Here she is, Miss Joooosssss Stoooone!" Still nothing. No Joss Stone.

Marc Ollington was backstage and he later told us what was going on. While the band were playing the big introduction number, Joss Stone's manager, who was also her mum, wasn't happy about her client, who was also her daughter, having to walk barefoot through the mud to get to the stage. It wasn't until somebody made a long strip of carpet from flattened cardboard boxes that she could reach the stage without getting trench foot.

According to Marc, Joss Stone's fifteen minutes of vocal warm-ups consisted mostly of her repeating the words "To the left. To the left." Which is ironic, as just before she arrived in the Left Field tent, all the trade union stalls and the stalls set up to promote various political causes allegedly had to be removed.

I played the Left Field tent at Glastonbury twice. In 2007 (mud) and in 2008 (dust). In 2008 I was booked to play for half an hour, which was then cut down to twenty-five minutes, and then, just before I went onstage, because everything was overrunning, I was asked if I could maybe do a tight twenty. A similar situation in 1992 had led to us having a huge row with Michael Eavis and eventually being asked to leave.

By 2008 I'd either mellowed with age or I couldn't be arsed arguing

---

44   No pun etc

anymore. I obediently played my twenty minutes, rushing through the songs without talking so that I could fit in as many songs as possible. I feel a bit guilty for not making more of a protest. You could say, that like Joss Stone, I was going against everything the Left Field stage was supposed to be about.

LOOK AT US, WE REFORMED A BAND

In August we started rehearsing for the Carter gigs. We went to Antenna Studios in Crystal Palace. We'd rehearse for all the reunion gigs there. It was close to my house and unlike most other rehearsals studios, I didn't dread going there. I didn't feel the need to wait outside until Les arrived before I dared enter. Rehearsal studios can be as intimidating and unwelcoming as music shops for idiots who don't know an acoustic guitar might need a battery. Antenna was different. We'd often turn up and find the building was completely deserted. We could pretend we owned the place and just get on with it. Getting the amps out of the cage (sadly, rehearsal studios still keep their amplifiers in cages) we'd plug everything in and rehearse. There were no distractions. No pinball or fussball. There was a Coke machine but it didn't always work and a kitchen that we never used, but that was about it. In a blog around the time of our first rehearsal at Antenna I say that I hope we don't blow up their PA system. In the seven years we rehearsed there I think we blew up three. Florence from Florence and the Machine had, or perhaps still has, a space in the Antenna building. Mrs Jim Bob runs a craft stall in a market in the car park every Saturday. She sells some lovely one-off bags and purses and accepts both cash and cards.

We booked twelve regular sessions at Antenna. Every Monday, from the start of August until the first gig at the end of October. We could have had fewer rehearsals and packed them all into a shorter time period a bit closer to the gigs but we wanted it to feel as natural as possible when we stepped onstage. That's what jazz musicians do. They rehearse a lot, so they know the songs backwards. And then they play them backwards. Just before we got on the tour bus for Glasgow we had one day in a bigger, more intimidating studio nowhere near my house. But by then we knew the songs and it was really more like an expensive get together with the crew.

THE CREW

Many of the infamous Crazy Carter Crew from the old days were either busy or in prison but we did manage to track down enough of them to not have to resort to working with professionals.[45] Seriously though, we couldn't expect people to drop whatever they were doing just to do two gigs.

---

45   This is a joke. Of course the Crazy Carter Crew were professionals.

Pip, who was one of the original Crazy Carter Crew members, put together a suitably over the top light show and Mad Dog was there on the merch stall at Barrowlands. And Jon Beast was back of course. When Jon turned up in the dressing room in Glasgow on the afternoon of the gig, I think it was the first time I'd seen him since September 7th 1996 at the Sheffield Leadmill. It was the first full Carter gig as a six-piece and Jon had a charity stall at the venue, selling various band memorabilia and autographed gubbins he'd collected over the years. Jon had photocopied some old CARTER DRESSING ROOM signs and Wez refused to sign them because they weren't genuine. There was an atmosphere.

We'd kind of fallen out with Jon in the early nineteen nineties. I don't know exactly when it was or why. I think we just probably spent too much time together in the end and there was bound to be a clash of egos. Jon Beast was a nice place to visit but I wouldn't want to live there and I imagine the same could be said of me at the time. These days, obviously, I'm brilliant and fun and any time spent with me is never long enough. I'm like Center Parcs in that respect. Whatever the reason for us falling out with Jon Beast all those years ago was all forgotten and forgiven in 2007. Band reunions are a bit like funerals like that. I do remember feeling nervous about meeting Jon again after so long though. What if he was skinny?

Sometimes people remember the same things differently don't they. Personally, I remember Jon Beast used to walk onstage at the start of Carter gigs, fully clothed, occasionally lifting his shirt seductively, to reveal his belly. There was that one time we played a gig in the courtyard of a club in Zagreb. The venue was on the same street as the Presidential Palace where an important meeting was taking place to try and avert another war. The noise from our soundcheck was hampering the talks and a small troop of soldiers was sent to the venue to investigate. When they'd decided we were of no great threat to national security, all but two of the soldiers left. The two remaining men stood guard at the side of the stage for the whole gig. As they were carrying rifles, we told Jon to not say or do anything too provocative that might end up getting us shot. With hindsight we should have used reverse psychology and told him to go onstage and see if he could start a war. Jon introduced us wearing nothing but his trainers, his glasses and a paper Pepsi Cola cup taped over his accouterments that night. It was that one Croatian gig that Jon seemed to remember as the norm for every gig we'd ever played and when he introduced our triumphant return at the Glasgow Barrowlands, Jon walked onstage, wearing a Jock strap made out of gaffer tape, and with an apple shoved up his arse.

Before Jon arrived that afternoon, I went for a walk around the venue. I've done this at all the reunion shows. I like to get there too early and soak up the atmos. Sit in the dressing room and eat snacks. I go for walks. Say hello to the security, making full use of my Access All Areas pass by accessing all areas. I'd walk out into the auditorium, happy that I was playing somewhere that had one. If I saw a door I'd open it, if it led to a staircase I'd climb the stairs. I'd go up to the circle and sit down to watch everyone hard at work on the stage down below. I'd watch them climbing the lighting rig and one, two-ing into microphones. I'd visit the sound and lighting desks, the T-shirt stall and the bars.

When I went walking around Glasgow Barrowlands in 2007, Bob Dylan's 'Like a Rolling Stone' was playing on my iPod and I was overcome with a sense of absolute calm and invincibility. I became a huge fan of Bob Dylan that day. I could have cried. It was a feeling I'd get during the day at all the reunion shows that followed. I felt like I was King of the World. That first afternoon in Glasgow in particular though, there was something about the emptiness of that big sticky-floored room and knowing what was coming that moved me. The lights were being tested and white noise blasted through the speakers, like a giant clearing its throat. I was so acutely aware of the enormity of it all. The sound and the lights, the people hard at work, the booze in the dressing room, the sandwiches, the crisps and the nuts, and all the fruit we'd always leave behind. Everything was there because of me.[46] But the responsibility didn't feel like a burden. I felt totally in control. I'll never forget that feeling of power, a kind of benign arrogance. I imagine it's how Jesus must have felt a lot of the time. I wrote about a similar sensation of omnipotence in *Goodnight Jim Bob*.

> If the venue was empty I'd be retching with nerves but when it was
> packed, with the crowd not only in front of us but also behind us
> and on our side, I couldn't help but get mesmerised by the power.
> There were times when it was like we could have stopped the gig
> and led the audience out of the building and on into the centre of
> London, where we would march on the Houses of Parliament,
> burst through the doors and bring down the government.

After the Glasgow soundcheck, my ears were ringing like nobody's business. It was incredibly loud onstage. I worried that it might be too loud out front and I went to share my concerns with our front of house (FOH) sound dude (SD) Roly. On the way there, Ashley from The Frank & Walters told me our soundcheck was the loudest thing he'd ever heard. It suddenly felt like we'd won something and I immediately forgot any concerns I had about damaging my or anyone else's hearing. I forgot to

---

46   And the other bloke.

tell Roly to turn the volume down until two weeks later in Brixton. Sadly, the politically correct gone mad *Guinness World of Records* no longer have a 'Loudest Band in the World' category, for fear of promoting hearing loss, so you'll just have to take Ashley from The Franks & Walters' word for it.

BLOG - UNTITLED OR DATED

There I was, sitting in a green room in a transport museum in Coventry talking to Jason Donovon about the early nineteen nineties while I was being filmed by Channel 4 pretending to watch the Pigeon Detectives perform on TV. It was the night before Brixton. The second of the great comeback Carter concerts. On the drive up to the Midlands we had a phone call asking me to present an award on behalf of Shelter to the Best Newcomer at the UK Festival Awards a week later – when and where I'd be sitting on a table about six feet away from Michael Eavis and with that Pete from Big Brother bloke who can't help swearing. The Daily Mirror gossip columnists were on the phone, desperately (and unsuccessfully) trying to get onto the full Brixton Academy guest list: Russell Brand had just been added to the list (I don't think he showed up), along with Neil Tennant (who apparently did). It was like I'd won a be an indie pop star for a week competition.

What can I really say that hasn't already be said about that Brixton gig? The way everyone I've ever known in my entire musical life was at the aftershow party, that was nice. So many old friends who'd flown over from LA and Israel, Greece, Australia, USA, France, Germany, Poland, Austria, Sweden, all points on the Carter compass, just for the gig.

I liked it when Les came on for the encores dressed as 'Fruitbat', in his shorts and cycle cap and had his first beer for seven months served up on a silver tray. And seeing the Tom from Tom and Jerry glove puppet in the front row just like he would have been in 1991. I'm glad we could go away for so long and return to play two of our best ever shows, without it being embarrassing or sad, although we did make quite a few big men cry – including Jon Beast. Oh and we – or rather, you – broke the Brixton Academy bar record.

The Coventry television thing was, I believe, for a *Transmission* special on Channel Four. It was hosted by Steve Jones and filmed in the Motor museum. There were musical performances and interviews. My role on the show was to sit in the bar drinking. Viewers had to guess who I was. Story of my life.

The night after the Brixton Academy show I was exhausted. There'd been such a long build up and then all of a sudden it was over. I would normally deal with the comedown that seems to follow the bigger and more emotional gigs, by staying indoors, watching television and eating whatever rider leftovers I'd managed to fit into a carrier bag at one in the morning when we finally vacated the dressing room. Over the years, taking home the leftover sweets was one of the most rewarding parts of the show. Mrs Jim Bob would come equipped with bags for life and even a shopping list.

At some point during our rehearsals at Antenna I'd agreed to play at their Bonfire Night party the night after the Brixton gig. It seemed like a good idea in September, or at least one that I didn't need to think about yet. But the night after selling out Brixton Academy and drinking quite heavily, I was feeling fragile. I would have rather done pretty much anything else than another gig.

I walked up the road to Antenna and found that just like when we rehearsed there, there was nobody in charge. The laidback attitude and the whole having to get your own amps out of the cage and find a microphone and something to plug it into vibe, was less attractive in a gig situation. I found a small guitar amp under a table and plugged my guitar and a microphone into that. No sound engineer, no roadies, no rider, no Jon Beast with an apple up his backside. I'd say there was no light show but the 'stage' was in front of a window and there was a firework display going on throughout my set. If selling out Brixton Academy had put my head in the clouds, the following night had brought me right back down to Earth again.

IT'S A HUMPTY DUMPTY THING

I released my new solo album in between the two Carter gigs, like a government minister hiding a hospital closure between Royal weddings. Three weeks after our triumphant Brixton show, I bought a plastic Christmas tree and some fairy lights from Woolworths and I went on tour.

Just before the tour started the producers of *Later…With Jools Holland* had been in touch to ask if I could quickly get a band together to perform a couple of songs from my new solo album. It was exactly what I'd hoped might happen as a result of my raised profile after reforming Carter. With Chris T-T's help, I quickly assembled a band of musicians. Drummer Damo had played on the *Humpty Dumpty* album, as had Simon, Lindsey and trombonist Vicky. Chris's friend Johny Lamb played bass. Johny would appear on my next two records, *Goffam* and *What I Think About When I Think About You*. He lives in Cornwall, where in a world made of coincidences he works with former Carter manager Adrian Boss.

I booked a rehearsal and we worked hard on the songs. It sounded great. I couldn't wait to share it with the BBC2 viewers. I reassured a paranoid Chris T-T that Jools Holland wouldn't replace him on the piano. We waited for the call from the producers with details and dates.

Even at the height of our career, Carter had never been asked to appear on *Later…With Jools Holland*. We'd always believed it was because we used tapes and the programme had a 'live music only' policy. Either that or we really had been banned from the BBC because of the incident. Everyone uses tapes in their live shows now of course and the show has had no choice but to give in and adapt.

There was no call from the producers of *Later…With Jools Holland*. It turned out the performance we'd worked so hard on was only pencilled in. I was actually some sort of understudy, a last minute stand-in act, in case the Stereophonics got stuck in traffic or Seasick Steve broke another string. I'm sure I must have been annoyed about it at the time but it bothers me even more now. It feels like the show's producers were demonstrating their power and subsequently, my lack of it. Reforming Carter and selling out two big gigs in six and a half seconds didn't count for a thing.

Any Carter knock-on effect I might have hoped for on my solo tour didn't materialise either. Or rather it did but it was a different kind of knock-on effect. More like a knock-*off* effect. It was one of my most poorly attended tours. Reforming Carter had reset my solo career. I'd landed on a metaphorical snake and I was back at the flipping beginning of the board. Why would anyone need to go and see 'Shit acoustic Carter karaoke' when there was now the very real possibility of seeing the real thing?

I remember seeing a documentary about Mick Jagger. The film followed Mick around the world as he went to various recording studios, hotels and houses, while he worked on his latest solo album *Goddess in the Doorway*. The album must have cost a fortune to make. Mick put his all into the project, travelling long distances so that he could work with Bono and Pete Townshend and Lenny Kravitz. When it was released, the album received mixed reviews and made it to No. 44 in the UK album charts and No. 39 in the US charts. The following year, The Rolling Stones released a greatest hits double album. It went to No. 2 in both the US and the UK. One of the gigs they played to promote the album attracted an estimated audience of 490,000. Keith Richards called Mick's solo album *Dogshit in the Doorway*. Mick Jagger was very much being reminded where he was from.

I like Mick Jagger. And not just his music. He's one of my favourite people on Twitter and Instagram. There's such joy in the little videos he makes of himself dancing his tiny arse off and the photos of himself posing in front of bits of architecture all around the globe. He's always on his own in the pictures but he looks so happy.

You might be surprised that I like Mick Jagger or that I'm still a Rolling Stones fan, after being sued by them. But that whole Ruby Tuesday shenanigans had nothing to do with The Rolling Stones really. They didn't own the song anymore. And although I didn't like it when Mick said in a magazine that if they let us sing their words it set a dangerous precedent, nowadays I just like thinking about Mick Jagger having to listen to 'After the Watershed'. That he heard me singing his words and perhaps turned to Keith or Ron and said, "Who *is* this angry dude?" I'm certain Mick Jagger would have called me a dude. I love the idea that Mick Jagger called me a dude.

I hadn't spent such a huge fortune on my solo record and I could survive a few half empty club gigs. It wasn't the end of the world. It wasn't as if Les had called my new solo album *A Humpty Cunty Thing* or anything.

PRESS RELEASE – FEBRUARY 2008 –
CARTER USM Just Two More Times

It seems we'd got back in bed with Carter without realising just how comfortable that bed would be. Perfectly sprung with sumptuous upholstering, silk sheets, warm blankets and a chocolate on the pillow. So, after much thought and discussion the focus group has decided.

Carter The Unstoppable Sex Machine will play Birmingham Carling Academy on Friday 21st November Brixton Carling Academy on Saturday 22nd November

The 22nd is Jim Bob's birthday and for these two days, he and hopefully the audience will be partying like it's 1992.
Tickets go on sale on....
Jim Bob & Fruitbat

It was like opening a pop-up tent. There was no way that thing was going back in the bag without a fight. Even though we hadn't, and I stress, *hadn't*, at any point said the Glasgow and Brixton gigs would be the only gigs we would ever do – that was Jon Beast. At the Brixton Academy show he told the audience it was the last time they would ever see us play. Not for the first time in my life, I find myself issuing the disclaimer, "the words of Jon Fat Beast are not necessarily those of the band". Nevertheless, we felt like the one-off-chance-in-a-lifetime-ness of the gigs was somehow implied. We didn't want anyone feeling as though they'd been cheated. So we sent an email out to our mailing list and posted on the Carter Facebook page, asking the hypothetical question, if we did another gig, how would everyone feel about it?

The responses ranged from delight to disgust but the vast majority were very positive. As in, YES, do more gigs! We still had to want to do them ourselves of course. We could send out as many emails as we liked and post a hundred Facebook messages but in the end, it still came down to whether me and Les wanted to do more shows. As it happens, it turned out being Carter The Unstoppable Sex Machine again was incredibly moreish. The important thing would be to know when to stop.

Although I personally hate disappointing anyone or letting them down, I think pop stars should be allowed to be hypocrites by the way. I expect them to break their promises and go back on their word, to change their minds and their opinions, to say outrageous things and generally be arseholes. If John Lydon wants to advertise butter or appear on reality TV shows, that's up to him. Incidentally, in 2007 I was invited to a meeting with the makers of *Celebrity Big Brother*. I presume because they were considering asking me to be a contestant. I was going to go the meeting, just out of interest, to see what they'd offer me. But in the end I didn't go, because I was worried the offer was enough to make it worth my while and I'd end up ruining my life.

2007's *Celebrity Big Brother* would turn out to be a racism special. A particular shower of fuckwits I seem to recall. I'm guessing if I'd been on the show I would have been occupying the Donny Tourette from Towers of London role. If I had been on *Celebrity Big Brother* I would have been the quiet one in the corner. Everyone at home would have been looking at me and making the same joke, "I thought this was supposed to be *celebrity* Big Brother."

GOING INTO ADMINISTRATION

Once we'd decided to do more gigs, the hard work began. I believe it was Thomas Edison who said that genius was one percent inspiration and ninety-nine percent administration. Tom was bang right. There's a surprisingly large amount of admin involved in putting on a couple of gigs for two men and a tape machine every twelve months or so. The admin would begin in January, sometimes sooner, when we'd get together to decide whether or not there should be any gigs in the coming year. If we decided that the answer was yes, the email exchanges and further face-to-face meetings could begin. There'd be lots of questions. What should the theme of the shows be? Sometimes it would just be something to put at the top of the advert, like 'Norf and Sarf' in 2011. There was often only the one advert, as the gigs would sell out before we got the chance to properly advertise them. It's one of the reasons people are still surprised to find out we'd reformed at all. Other years, the theme was more than just a title, like when we played the first four albums for 'The Drum Machine Years' in 2009.

When we had a show theme we'd write the announcements and press releases and send out emails to the mailing list. Maybe we'd make a little promo video for Facebook. The tumbleweed teaser of 2014 was my favourite. We'd post the dates on social media and prepare for the questions. Why no Liverpool show? Come to the U.S. Will there be a full tour? Is Wez playing?

We'd make wish lists of who we'd like to have on as our special guests. Should we ask our contemporaries from the old days or a new band? Nature or nurture? Les was always more in favour of asking someone new but the more familiar bands from the same era as us always got people out of the pub and into the venue earlier. There were more pub meetings and more emails. Here's one Marc sent us in 2008 about our dressing room rider:

Begin forwarded message:

From: Marc Ollington <Marc⟋⟋⟋⟋⟋⟋⟋⟋⟋⟋⟋⟋⟋
Date: 9 September 2008 19:04:45 GMT+01:00
To: "Les Carter" <fruity⟋⟋⟋⟋⟋⟋⟋⟋⟋⟋⟋ "Jim" ⟋⟋⟋⟋⟋⟋⟋⟋⟋⟋⟋⟋
Subject: Carter rider

I have updated this slightly from last year. I have made Les' Kettle a priority and I have asked for some cheese and crackers. I have added gin and tonic for Jim.

Anything else?

There were aftershows to arrange and riders to be added to, always *added* to. We exchanged badly drawn T-shirt design ideas. The 2009 'Jim Bob's Birthday suit' T-shirt design, with its pretend shirt collar and tie was one of mine. It could only have been thought of as a good idea after a few drinks and I'm surprised it made it as far as the printing stage to be honest. It may have looked fine on paper but as soon as we printed the shirts we realised the pretend collar and tie were halfway down the wearer's chest. I don't think I always took the merchandise aspect of the band seriously enough.

As the gigs approached we'd exchange more emails. We'd sort out transport and crew hotels. Often these simple things didn't get resolved and in those first couple of years it would lead to some members of the crew and even the band having no way to get home from the venue and nowhere to stay afterwards. After the first Brixton gig a friend of Marc's took the T-shirt money home with them on the top deck of a bus. The thought of that still makes me feel physically sick. At least it was a friend of Marc's (not a euphemism) rather than Marc himself. As he would definitely have left the money on the bus.

We'd design a laminate and decide who should get one and it wouldn't matter anyway because Les would hand his around to all the people he'd forgotten to put on the guest list. Les would always forget to put somebody on the list. Usually his brother. The guest list would start earlier each year. In 2007 it was so full we had to turn tabloid journalists away. They must have thought we were trying to make ourselves appear more popular than we really were. A few years later the space on the guest list made us wonder if the game was up.

Every year we'd have to work out which email requests for photo passes were genuine and which were from blaggers who didn't even own a camera. It was only at the very last Carter gig that I found out the details of the photographers first three songs rule. I knew they were allowed in the pit to take photos for the first three songs and then they had to leave. But I didn't know they were escorted out of the pit and straight through the side exit of the venue. Gig photographers must have a very distorted, anticlimactical view of live music.

This email arrived from the *NME*.

I am writing a feature for NME called "Where Did All The Old Indie Bands Go". We are looking for classic bands of NME past who are still around and we'd love to give Carter USM a starring role!

Here we go again I thought. Another bullshit Where are they Now? piece. But for once I was wrong. It was actually a nice interview and led to a very positive piece. Rather than let it spoil my earlier cynical theory about there being no such thing as a genuine Where are they Now? piece, I've decided it's the exception that proves my, let's face it, brilliantly observed rule.

A few weeks before the gigs we'd make a shopping list. We'd stock up on batteries and new guitar leads and rolls of gaffer tape – we weren't about to let Jon Beast go onstage un-gaffered. We'd buy guitar picks and strings. If I had to name one thing I prefer about being an author to a musician it's that I don't have to change any guitar strings when I'm writing a novel. The fear of a string snapping while I'm winding it into tune is the same now as it was in 1974 when I first put a string on a guitar. And no matter how hard I try to stop it from happening, I've never managed to restring a guitar without stabbing my fingertip on the end of a string or finding one of the old lost bits of string by stepping on it in my bare feet later on.

Throughout a Carter gig year, Marc would spend ages working on elaborate budget spreadsheets, constantly updating and adjusting them. Marc put a lot of time and effort into his budget spreadsheets. I never read any of them.

We'd argue about what songs to play. Les would ask if we really had to play 'Sheriff Fatman' and I'd say yes. We'd print setlists, using bigger and bolder fonts every year. By 2014 I had three A4 pages worth and I still couldn't see what they said. I could have worn my glasses. But Carter didn't wear glasses. More than one year me and Les would disagree about that.

At some point I'd compile mixtapes. A CD to play when the doors opened and another for the guest bar. I made thirty minute changeover wind-up CDs to play before we went on and get the audience in the mood for what lay ahead. Senseless Things, the Sultans, Ned's, the Wonder Stuff, EMF, James. There was a terrible moment that became a wonderful moment when we played the Beautiful Days festival. We were waiting at the back of the stage ready to go on. 'Sit Down' by James was playing and the audience were singing along. And then there was a power cut. The festival was plunged into darkness and everyone stopped singing along. People ran around frantically backstage trying to fix the problem. Me and Fruitbat stood in the dark, I'd already started to panic, mentally working out which song to drop if we ran out of time. And then the power returned and the music restarted, exactly at the point in 'Sit Down' where it had stopped and everyone immediately carried on singing where they'd left off. It was as though time had stood still for everyone except me and Fruitbat.

I wore a white suit at Beautiful Days. It was the same one I'd worn at *Nerdstock* at Hammersmith Apollo two years before. Luckily none of the style magazines noticed I'd worn the same outfit twice. They would have crucified my thrift. I'd usually start thinking about what I was going to wear at the Carter shows before the tickets went on sale. Les would buy something on the afternoon of the gig. He has more of relaxed attitude to things than me. Les believes admin is a dish best served cold. He's very much last minute dot com.

In 2007, at the Barrowlands gig, I wore a red shirt and trousers with a matching belt and a black tie. I had really heavy steel toe-cap boots on and when I went off at the end of the set, I'd change clothes and come back for 'GI. Blues' wearing camouflage trousers and a green army shirt. The trouble was, I was so exhausted from the gig and the heavy boots, that I couldn't get the fucking things off.

At the Brixton show two weeks later, Les left the stage at the end of the last song and came back on dressed as 'Fruitbat', wearing shorts and a cycling cap. To get himself 1990s fit, he hadn't been drinking for six months. During the encore his first beer for half a year was delivered to him on a silver tray. Some might view this as a bit Elton John.

More than once, the Brixton show coincided with my birthday and a cake would be wheeled on for me on a hostess trolley. I was still surprised when it happened though.

For the years after 2007, there would be a special moment at the London shows. The special moment – gimmick if you like – might be something like the dancers who recreated the 'Let's Get Tattoos' video in 2012, or it might be other musicians joining us, like the string quartet who played on 'My Defeatist Attitude' in 2011 or Tom Hingley joining us for 'This is how it Feels' in 2012 at Brixton and Leeds. Two years in a row we came incredibly close to having Chris Barrie, dressed in full Rimmer costume, recreating the beginning of 'Surfin' USM' live on stage. Unfortunately something always prevented it from happening at the last minute. And I think it was Les who came up with the idea of having an actor dressed as a robber, come onstage during 'Glam Rock Cops' at the final 2014 gig. He would try to steal an amplifier and then a couple of coppers would come on and arrest him. We asked our friend Tim *Plunkett & Macleane* Connery if he knew any suitable actors. He misinterpreted our simple request and instead we ended up with a fully-staged and costumed five minute scene from *The Sweeney*, with police and thieves and a choreographed dancing police force.

In 2009, when we played the first four albums in full, we thought it would be great to have a real choir singing the opening song on *101 Damnations,* 'The Road to Domestos' ('Love Divine, All Loves Excelling' before we shamelessly re-badged it). Tim Connery's son Liam was in a popular chart-topping choir Libera. They'd sung for the Pope and Bill Clinton and had an entire episode of *Songs of Praise* devoted to them. We thought they needed to be brought down a peg or two by having five thousand people chanting you fat bastard at them. We hadn't realised quite how difficult it would be to organise.

First of all, we had to get permission from Lambeth Council. Marc filled in a long form about the nature of the performance and what Libera's role would be. As they wouldn't be on stage until 10pm, the council turned the permission request down, thinking it was too late for eleven-year old boys. They asked if we could move the gig to the afternoon. Marc took part in a phone meeting with four people at the council. He had to explain what gigs (not just our gig but *gigs* in general) were and why they had to take place in the evening. One person at the council wouldn't accept the show had to be so late. He said that he'd seen Mott the Hoople play a matinee performance in 1973.

Marc explained that the tickets had already been sold with an advertised 7pm start time. After the meeting, Lambeth council at last seemed fine with everything and then a week or two later Marc received a short email, asking him to urgently call them. Apparently, somebody had noticed the words 'Sex Machine' in the band's name. Marc had another meeting and was asked for details about the exact content of the gig. He had to promise there was no nudity and that it wasn't a sex show of any kind. Once again, they seemed fine with it all, until a day later when someone from the council committee found a YouTube video of Jon Beast pulling an apple out of his arse. The council also brought up the chanting of 'you fat bastard' that they'd seen on YouTube. In his third meeting with Lambeth council Marc had to explain that Jon was only the warm-up man and had simply got a bit carried away. Marc assured everyone there would be no nudity and the chanting was a one-off.

Two weeks later, Marc received official notification that we had permission for Libera to appear but as 'organiser' of the concert and the band's representative, Marc would need to be background-checked, to be sure he was okay to work with children and wasn't on the sex offenders register. Marc filled out more lengthy forms. He then had a meeting in person where he was asked if he had children of his own and how responsible he was and so on. The council seemed to think Marc was responsible enough and permission was finally granted.

We then had to get permission from Brixton Academy, because it was an over 14s only venue. The twenty-one boys (it may have been twenty-three. And I don't mean because we lost a couple or anything. It was just a long time ago) had to be chaperoned at all times. They weren't allowed to watch any of the rest of the show and had to be escorted out of the venue like photographers, as soon as they'd finished their two minute hymn. Jon Beast was on strict instructions to keep his distance. We'd forgotten what I said earlier about Jon being contrary. We should have used reverse psychology again and told him to take all his clothes off and run into their dressing room.

Libera were amazing. They were so good in fact, that during the soundcheck I thought they must be miming. They weren't. That short hymn was a nightmare to organise but it was one of the most moving moments of all the reunion gigs. When it ended and the machine guns signalled the start of 'Everytime a Churchbell Rings', Libera were supposed to walk off the stage. But they just stood there. Who knows what they were all thinking. The strobes, the noise, the crowd. It must have been confusing. In the end, Fruitbat waved his hands and shooed them off the stage, like a herd of sheep that had wandered onto his land from the adjacent field.

JIM BOB GOES TO HOLLYWOOD

The admin for 2008's Carter gigs was more complicated because Marc had gone to live and work in Los Angeles for a year and correspondence took place between two different time zones. While Marc was away, apart from when I played two nights at the 100 Club with the band I'd put together for the stupid Jools Holland show, my live solo career was on hold until he returned. I could have played gigs without him of course but, and this might be hard for you to believe if you've ever met Marc, the gigs were less fun without him.

While he was away I wrote the songs for *Goffam*, another semi concept album. This time about the fictitious city of Goffam, its corrupt police force and a group of cowardly failed superheroes hiding in a cave while the city burned. I started recording *Goffam* with Chris T-T and Johny Lamb and then in May, I just couldn't live another minute without Marc and so I went to LA. My family went with me and we stayed with Marc and Mrs Marc in their tiny bungalow in Santa Monica, on Euclid Street, coincidentally the same street where Frank Derrick's daughter Beth lived and where Frank would go to visit her in the second J.B. Morrison novel *Frank Derrick's Holiday of a Lifetime*.[47]

When we arrived in Santa Monica, Marc was waiting for us with a detailed itinerary of events. When I say itinerary, I do mean itinerary. Typed out and printed, with comically titled days. There were three

---

47 I don't like this title. I'd originally wanted to call it 'Frank Goes to Hollywood'. For a long time the book had no title. I made loads of lists. Titles that included 'Frank Derrick's Extra Ordinary Vacation', 'Euclid Holiday', 'The United States of Frank', 'Euclid Reunion', '13 Days on 13th Street' and 'American Heartwash'. The first Frank book 'The Extra Ordinary Life of Frank Derrick, Age 81' was originally called 'The 12 Days of Kelly Christmas' but it was thought the word Christmas would date the book, especially as it was published in June. I learned all about the importance of metadata and Amazon tags. Ideally the book's title should contain words or themes from other, hugely successful, vaguely similar books.
Hence, 'Age 81' was added to ensnare fans of 'The Hundred-Year-Old Man Who Climbed Out the Window and Disappeared'. Having Frank Derrick's name in the title and tagging the novel with words like 'old' and 'man' would trick readers of 'The Unlikely Pilgrimage of Harold Fry' into buying my book too. It works. Just look up Amazon reviews for films like 'Girl on *the* Train' and see how livid and or confused some reviewers are that they ended up watching a black and white silent film about a child who takes a steam train journey to Crewe. For what it's worth, and I hope it never comes to this, Frank Derrick could take Harold Fry and the one hundred-year-old Swedish dude with both his hands tied behind his back.

copies of Marc's itinerary. One for me, one for Mrs Jim Bob and another for our daughter, Jim Bob Junior.

On 'Hooray for Hollywood' day we went on a minibus tour of the stars' homes. We saw where the Fresh Prince lived and where (spoiler alert) The Osbournes only *pretended* to live. We visited Greystone Mansion and went to the cinema. All the things Frank Derrick would do in the future. Just like Frank, we went to the Griffith Park Observatory and the Cheesecake Factory. In *Frank Derrick's Holiday of a Lifetime*, Frank's granddaughter wins him an enormous Spider-Man toy at Universal Studios. I did that. I won that enormous plush superhero by throwing a ball through a hole at Universal Studios.

On 'Baywatch' day we rented pushbikes and cycled along the beaches – Venice, Santa Monica and Roy Rodgers – It was Hollywood hot but I'd covered myself in high-factor sun cream. Everywhere except for my hands. I spent the rest of the week looking like I was wearing red gloves.

On a day that's untitled on Marc's itinerary, the Jim Bob family left Santa Monica and went to stay in Los Feliz with some old friends Mark and Cerise. Cerise used to follow Carter around the UK in the very early days. We used to arrive at the venue and there would be Cerise, with her green army kitbag. A lot of the early Carter hardcore who followed us on tour, would end up working with us as part of the Crazy Carter Crew. They're all in the first book: Daz and Big Al, and Nick Ely who left the army to operate our onstage pyrotechnics. The Army should put that in the TV ads.

Cerise was now a movie producer. I'd given her a copy of my long short story *Word Count*, and to cut a long short story short, Cerise and her husband Mark (with a K) wanted to turn it into a film. They wanted me to write the script. As usual I had no idea what I was doing and had to Google my way through the whole process. But as we've already established, winging it wins you Tony Awards. Marc Ollington constantly tells me he has no idea what he's doing and is perpetually awaiting the day when he's found out. Pip, who used to do Carter's lights, confessed to me that when we'd played at Wembley Arena for the British Music Weekend it was the first time he'd ever touched a lighting desk. Pip now does lights for Radiohead and Oasis, Paul Weller and Boy George, among others. Almost all of the original Crazy Carter Crew members were unqualified for their jobs until they started doing those jobs. A bit of faith and making things up as you go along can get you a long way in life. Take away the miracles and Jesus is just a man with an idea, talking on a hill.

I wrote eight drafts of the script for the as yet unmade *Word Count* movie – as yet everybody, as yet – and I had a number of conference phone call meetings with Mark and Cerise and their production company partner Julie. I was definitely going to win an Oscar.

I stayed for three days at Mark and Cerise's house in the hills of Los Feliz and I knew without any doubt whatsoever that I was going to be a movie screenwriter. I was going to sell my house in Crystal Palace and move to LA. I'd sit in coffee shops in Silver Lake with all the other screenwriters, working on my next blockbuster and in the evening I'd drink Martinis at the Dresden Room while Marty and Elaine (as featured in the film *Swingers*) crooned Cole Porter songs while I sat and fantasy-cast my next movie (Edward Norton and Zooey Deschanel for the as yet unmade *Word Count*).

JIMMY PURSEY FROM SHAM 69

Back in England, where it was probably raining, after an uncomfortable flight with zero legroom and this annoying woman in front of me who kept pushing her seat back as far as it would go, I was already feeling less like a Hollywood screenwriter. I made my second solo appearance at Glastonbury (dust, tight twenty minutes) and then we started rehearsing for the latest Carter shows. As a nod to our perceived hypocrisy, or that of our spokesfatbastard Jon Beast, we'd called the shows 'Never Say Never Again'. We'd play James Bond themes between bands and I'd wear my dad's old tuxedo.

A third gig had been added. A secret show a few days before the Birmingham and Brixton Academy gigs, at Southampton Joiners. We were billed as Billy Boy and the Wild Bananas, the same nom de plume we'd used to play a secret gig for CND at the New Cross Venue in 1991. Billy Bragg was our secret special guest then. He'd obviously found us in that Wembley cupboard.

The name Billy Boy and the Wild Bananas came from two different brands of German condoms. They were part of Fruitbat's Condoms of the World collection and featured on the cover of 'The Only Living Boy in New Cross'. We had to put the singles in brown sleeves, otherwise Woolworths wouldn't stock them. What an incredibly twentieth century paragraph this is.

The Billy Boy and the Wild Bananas 2008 reunion gig was a tribute to Mint Burston. Mint used to promote at the Joiners and put Carter on there a number of times. The Southampton Joiners was very different then. It was the small side room of a pub that used to get so packed that we'd have to climb over the bar to get to the stage, sorry, 'stage', I don't think there was a stage as such. When I look at old YouTube videos of Carter gigs – something I do every morning, just before my five-mile run and my sauna – I'm always astounded at how chaotic some of those gigs were. It's hard to tell if there were any stages at any of the venues we played.

I watched a video of Sham 69 at Reading Festival (every morning, after my sauna and before my smashed avocado and brunch mojito) and then in the same week, I also saw some of the BBC's 2018 Reading coverage. Like those old Carter gigs, Sham 69 at Reading is chaotic. There are people all over the place. It looks like something out of *Game of Thrones*. In the more recent Reading TV coverage, I was surprised to see the audience separated into manageable groups with a big empty stripe in between them. I know it's for safety reasons but it looks less fun somehow.

When Carter first played Reading and Glastonbury, the divide between band and audience wasn't as vast as it is now. There were no television cameras and the pit didn't need to be so large to accommodate them. And there were no golden circles or VIP areas at venues either. I'm kind of glad I'm not successful enough to warrant a golden circle or a VIP area at any of my solo gigs. It's incredibly easy to get talked into these little compromises. We've come a long way from finding out about a gig in a newspaper, going to the Post Office, buying a postal order, sticking it in an envelope and hoping for the best. First come first served sounds like something from medieval times.

Anyway, in 2008, the Southampton Joiners was a much bigger venue than it was when Carter had last played there. The bar was in a separate room now and not only was there a stage, it was the highest stage in England. It was wide too. But it doesn't have any depth. It's a bit like playing on a high shelf or on the edge of a cliff. And with my aforementioned fear of heights, it was a struggle to not throw myself off. If I'd done that at any of my solo gigs at the Joiners, it would have been a disaster, because there wouldn't have been anyone there to catch me.

I don't want to make this all about the stage at the Joiners but the stage at the Joiners also slopes slightly downwards towards the audience. If I'd played in roller-skates I would have rolled off it like a snooker ball on a hill. It was like one of the stages in my Carter bad gig dreams.

My Carter bad gig dreams had stopped in 1997 but as soon as the reunion shows were announced, the dreams were back. Douglas Anthony, the lead character in *Word Count* (played by Edward Norton in the as yet unmade movie) doesn't remember his dreams and hates anyone who does.

> I could dream The Catcher In The Rye or The Brothers
> Karamazov, a new Holy Bible or another complete works of
> William Shakespeare and I'd wake up with nothing. I don't
> remember my dreams. If I have them at all.
>
> If you should ever meet me and we get to know each other well
> enough for you to feel it's time to tell me your dreams, don't
> bother. As soon as you start the sentence, "Hey Doug, I had this
> crazy dream last night," I will have already switched off and by
> the time you reach the end of the sentence you'll be talking to
> yourself.

Like Douglas Anthony, if I *do* have dreams, I very rarely remember them. Except for my Carter bad gig dreams that is. As soon as we got back together I was dreaming about sloping stages again. I was dreaming of microphone stands slipping down and strings breaking. I wouldn't be able to find the venue and when I arrived, late and flustered, I'd be inconsolably sad for some reason. And everyone at the venue would hate me. In my bad gig dreams I forgot the words to the songs and Fruitbat would insist on playing songs that were so new that I had to make the words up on the spot. And Fruitbat wouldn't seem to care about how disastrously the gig was going. He'd be drunk and laughing along with the roadies. And all the while, the audience was leaving in drones. Sorry, droves.

Marc Ollington refers to the songs that bands want to play but the audience is less keen on hearing, as 'toilet songs'. When Carter played 'And God Created Brixton' in 2008, Marc was convinced there would be such a mad rush for the toilets, it would cause a stampede, sparking the biggest riot in Brixton since the one we were on stage singing to a rapidly emptying venue about. In my Carter anxiety dreams every song in the set was a toilet song.

My last minute real gig nerves would start about a month before. I'd wake up in the morning – after a terrible dream – and the first thing I'd do was test my voice to see if it was still there. I'd make a falsetto 'ooh' sound and hope it wasn't just a squeak. I was so paranoid I was going to lose my voice that I'd start to lose my voice. That's what everyone kept telling me. It's psychosomatic Jim. You're imagining it and that's what's making you ill. I'd always get a cold in the week leading up to the gigs. Psychosomatic Jim, my friends would say, like they were qualified doctors and not just fed up with my hypochondria, my valetudinarianism and the way I always carried a thesaurus with me.

I realise there are people who'd see me losing my voice as a vast improvement to the band but – and I hope this isn't bigheaded – I think the majority of the audience at a Carter gig want to hear the words. Knowing that many of them would have taken time off work, booked hotels and babysitters and bought train and sometimes plane tickets to hear those words, didn't help.

That's the trouble with booking so few gigs and so far in advance. The long wait and the exclusivity really piles on the pressure. There's too much time for things to go wrong, for me to lose my voice or for Fruitbat to fall off his bike (1992) or hurt his back cleaning his bath (1995). Doing just two gigs in twelve months puts a weight of importance on them you wouldn't get from a three-week tour. It's like David St. Hubbins from Spinal Tap once said: 'There's too much fucking perspective.'

When I said before that I expected pop stars to let everyone down, I wasn't talking about me. I don't want to let anyone down. I didn't even go to the *Celebrity Big Brother* meeting remember. Just in case I ended up on the show and anyone thought less of me.

When mustn't the show go on? Is it when you're the band on the Titanic and the ship's just hit an iceberg, or when someone throws half a plastic cup of beer at you and it nearly hits you on the shoulder? I haven't cancelled many live shows in my career and even though there have been occasions when I've prayed we'd get a phone call informing us the venue had fallen into a sinkhole, so I could have a day off or avoid the shame of an empty gig, I don't like cancelling gigs. I hate letting people down.

On July 7th 2005 I was due to play at the Barfly in Camden. It was being filmed for a live DVD. Marc Ollington and Mister Spoons were at my house. We were loading up the car, getting ready to drive to the venue, when we heard the news about a series of explosions on London Underground, apparently caused by a power surge. There were further reports of transport chaos and so we decided to wait until we had more information before leaving, expecting nothing more serious at the time than getting stuck in horrendous traffic in the centre of town.

The news worsened and we learned that people had died in a series of terrorist attacks. After a while we realised we needed to make the decision whether or not to cancel my gig. It sounds incredibly self-centred and even crass that we were even thinking about something so trivial but we had to at least let people know.

I'd already decided anyway. I didn't want to do the gig. The promoter disagreed. He wanted the gig to go ahead. Using some sort of 'the terrorists would have won if we cancelled' hypothesis. He even suggested the atmosphere would be 'electric'.

We cancelled the gig. Or rather, we postponed it. That's another reason I hate cancelling gigs. Because they aren't really cancelled. They're postponed. I hate putting things off until later. What if I'm a different person when the rearranged date comes around? With the Carter gigs we probably would have had to wait months until an alternative date became available. And we'd have to offer people refunds. I don't want to give anyone the chance for second thoughts. Show is an incredibly fickle business. There's always somebody 'new' waiting in the wings, ready to climb over a chair and steal your thunder. I couldn't risk losing out to thunder thieves.

There have been a few occasions where I've completely lost my voice and we had no choice but to cancel gigs. In 1992 I had acute laryngitis.[48] I'd completely lost my voice and wasn't allowed to even attempt speech. A doctor told me I was in danger of permanently damaging my voice and having to learn how to sing all over again (shut up at the back). We were supposed to appear on *Top of the Pops* and we'd gone to the

---

48 See *Goodnight Jim Bob* for 'a cute laryngitis' joke.

television studio in the hopes that my voice would return in time. I had a steroid injection in my buttocks in Harley Street. I mean at a doctors in Harley Street of course. I don't want anyone thinking I store my bum in a special bum storage facility in the West End of London. I'm not Walt Disney. While we were at the *Top of the Pops* studio I had to communicate using written notes. At one point during the day, I passed Jimmy Nail from *Auf Wiedersehen Pet* on the stairs and showed him my piece of paper with HELLO written on it. Jimmy Nail looked at the note and then at me and he told me to fuck off. Once again, like that time the bloke in Newcastle was disappointed when I walked onstage and picked up a copy of my novel, it works best if you imagine Jimmy Nail is telling me to fuck off in a Geordie accent.

After almost a year of admin, bad dreams and psychologically pacing the room, the shows went ahead. I didn't lose my voice or fall off the stage and the audience didn't all go to the toilet during 'And God Created Brixton'. Here's the Brixton setlist from 2008.

SURFIN USM
2ND TO LAST WILL & TESTAMENT
RUBBISH
BILLY'S SMART CIRCUS
DO RE ME
MURDER MILE

WHILE YOU WERE OUT
THIS IS HOW IT FEELS

A SHELTERED LIFE
BLOODSPORT FOR ALL
GLAM ROCK COPS
LEAN ON ME
PAUPER'S GRAVE
LET'S GET TATTOOS

NEW CROSS
ANYTIME ANYPLACE ANYWHERE
AND GOD CREATED BRIXTON
AFTER THE WATERSHED
THE MUSIC THAT NOBODY LIKES
FALLING ON A BRUISE
THE FINAL COMEDOWN

ENCORE 1
SENILE DELINQUENT
HER SONG
PANIC
IMPOSSIBLE DREAM

ENCORE 2
FATMAN
G.I. BLUES

SEX PISTOLS MANCHESTER LESSER FREE TRADE HALL JUNE 1976

In 2009 Marc was back in the UK. The latest Carter shows, that were starting to feel as much a part of winter as putting a tree in the front room, were booked and on sale, and in springtime I went on a fourteen-date solo tour. Attendances were mixed. Some gigs were full, others not so. One particularly empty date was in Lincoln. There were either twelve or fourteen people in the audience. The number changes depending on who you speak to. And I have met a surprising amount of people who were at the Lincoln Library Bar on 23rd April 2009. Definitely more than twelve or fourteen. It's a bit like that Sex Pistols gig that everyone in Manchester went to. Or the other Sex Pistols gig at the 100 Club that the whole of London were at.

I was with Mister Spoons and Chris T-T when we arrived in Lincoln for the soundcheck. The venue was next to the University campus. I'd played in Lincoln twice before, both times with Carter. The first time, in 1989 is featured in *Goodnight Jim Bob*. I describe the venue as a 'scampi in the basket disco'. The film *Alien* was showing on TV screens during our set and more people were watching it than were watching us.

In 2009, as we started setting up for soundcheck, it became clear the sound engineer didn't really know what he was doing. I had to show him where to plug the leads in to the mixing desk. The blind leading the blind. The poor sod knew even less than me. He seemed incredibly flustered, like an actor who'd turned up for the first day on set to discover a horse waiting for him and remembering he'd lied on his CV. After a while he went outside for a cigarette. Fifteen minutes later it was obvious he wasn't coming back. I think when he realised how far out of his depth he was, he must have literally run away.

Between us we managed to get the PA working and finished the soundcheck. There were two supports that night. The promoter was on first and, ignoring the fact that that's cheating, let's focus on the other act. He was seventeen years old and full of self-confidence in a way that the music business would soon knock out of him. The promoter was very young too and I was embarrassed these two youngsters should witness just how unpopular I was in Lincoln, especially as they were both probably too young to be aware that I used to be way more famous in Lincoln. Even in 1989 when everyone was watching *Alien* while we were on.

Both support acts were better musicians than me. They must have thought I was a late starter or something. The seventeen year old did that annoying thing of slapping his guitar and playing it really fast. It was more like watching sport or a party trick than music. He was using loop pedals. He'd play a riff, sample it and then add another riff, maybe a bit of slap work, building up a sound, like a one-man band from the future. I remember he had a song that dissed the Brit School. My daughter used to go to the Brit School and I felt overly protective about that.

Almost a decade later, in 2018, I was on a short Australian tour with Pop Will Eat Itself. Every day on the drive from the airport, someone in the van would ask what such and such a mega venue we were passing was. It would either be a sports ground or a stadium, with a capacity of fifty or sixty thousand. Our Australian tour coincided with another UK artist's tour. He was playing at all these enormous venues, sometimes for more than one night. In Melbourne there was a huge stall set up in the middle of the city selling his T-shirts. He hadn't even arrived yet.

In Perth I asked our Australian tour manager about one of the huge venues we were driving past and realised it might be where Carter had played as part of the Big Day Out festival tour in 1993. I Googled it and sure enough it was the same venue. The capacity at Perth Oval had been expanded since 1993. The artist who was selling out Australia's biggest venues and those all over the world, held the record for the largest ever audience there. Thirty-two thousand people came to see him in 2015. In 2018 he played in Perth to a total of 114,031 people over two nights at the brand new Optus Stadium.

There were either twelve or fourteen people in the audience when he played in Lincoln. It changes depending on who you speak to. And I have met a surprising amount of people who were at the Lincoln Library Bar on 23rd April 2009. Definitely more than twelve or fourteen. It's a bit like that Sex Pistols gig that everyone in Manchester went to. Or the other Sex Pistols gig at the 100 Club that the whole of London were at. There definitely weren't as many as thirty-two thousand or one hundred and fourteen thousand people there, but rather than let that fact get to me, I find comfort in the knowledge that the twelve or fourteen people in the audience were all there to see me and not my support act with his loop pedals, fancy guitar playing and his songs dissing my daughter's school. My Ed Sheeran anecdote, ladies and gentlemen.

THE DRUM MACHINE YEARS

In 2011 we played the first four Carter albums in their entirety. *Post Historic Monsters* and *1992 The Love Album* at the Kentish Town Forum and *30 Something* and *101 Damnations* at Brixton Academy. Not only did we perform all the albums in their entirety, we also played the songs in the right order. This is the correct and as far as I'm concerned, the only way of playing albums in their entirety. Changing the order of the songs to make the live set flow better or so you don't have to start the show with your biggest hit and end on the ten minute experimental jazz instrumental the drummer wrote, is cheating.

Luckily for us, we used to order our album track listings as though they were set lists for gigs, so there weren't too many toilet songs or anti climaxes. A few of the songs had never been played live before and there were no backing tapes for those, or there'd been no need for backing tapes. For the sparse and acoustic 'Being Here' from *Post Historic Monsters*, Carter producer Simon Painter played piano and Fruitbat played double bass. Luckily, by reunion year three we'd finally nailed organising transport home for the band and Fruitbat didn't have to take the double bass back on the bus.

I've just remembered something. I was on a night bus once and a man got on carrying a double bass. There were no vacant seats and he stood in the buggy and wheelchair area. After a few stops another man got on, also carrying a double bass. He too had to stand in the buggy and wheelchair area. If one of the men had been me, I would probably have awkwardly acknowledged our amusing coincidence with a nod and then pretended the next bus stop was mine and got off. The two double bass players on the night bus were normal human beings though and with one definite and obvious thing in common, they chatted for the whole journey. They talked about where they'd both been, at a concert or a music lesson. They probably exchanged phone numbers and became friends for life that night, playing double bass at one another's weddings. Maybe they formed a band with two double bass players. Like an acoustic Ned's Atomic Dustbin.[49]

One song from *Post Historic Monsters* I didn't manage to get right at the Kentish Town Forum was 'Evil'. It's only got about two chords but so many words, including a long passage from *The Snow Queen*, read at a ridiculous Eminem tempo in the middle. There was no way I

---

49   At the time of writing, Jonn and Rat from Ned's Atomic Dustbin are doing gigs as Ned's Acoustic Dustbin. Sadly not with two double bass players.

was ever going to remember all the words, so I had to resort to using a music stand. I know. Music stands have no place in punk rock. I've noticed, presumably because all the bands are so ancient now and their memories are going, that a lot of singers today are using music stands at their gigs. Even John Lydon had one on his recent dates with Public Image Ltd. I can allow him the butter advert and even forgive the pro Nigel Farage nonsense but Johnny Rotten? Using a music stand onstage? He'll be wanting a chair next.

Unfortunately, a music stand was the only way I had any chance of getting 'Evil' right. It didn't matter in the end, because without wearing glasses and with fifty million strobes going off (and on and off and on) I couldn't read the sheet of paper on the music stand anyway. The only other time I can remember playing 'Evil' live was in 2014. On that occasion we asked Rory from The Frank & Walters to play my guitar parts (D), leaving my hands free to hold the copy of *The Snow Queen* I'd bought to read the words from. I still fucked it up.

We called the two 2009 gigs 'The Drum Machine Years'. Both shows were recorded and burned onto CD, packaged up and available to buy as soon as the gigs were over. The thought that whatever we played at those two gigs, warts and all, 'Evil' and all, would be available to buy before I'd even had my post show aperitif, would only add to the pressure to play well and for nothing to go wrong. My bad gig dreams that year were off the scale.

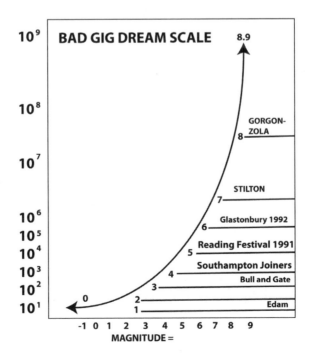

Following the second 'Drum Machine Years' gig there was an after show at Jamm, half a mile up the Brixton road from the Academy. I sang 'Angelstrike!' with Chris T-T and the Hoodrats but I was so drunk that I couldn't remember the words. What I really needed was a music stand. When the ringing in my ears died down to its normal high-pitched whistle, I started to wonder: what next?

BLOG – 9/12/09

The day after the Brixton Academy show I had an incredibly stiff neck, bruised knees, pains in my stomach and a lump on my forehead from when my guitar
attacked me full in the face during 'A Perfect Day to Drop the Bomb'. It was of course worth it.

I don't know whether or where or how, when etc we'll do more Carter shows. My personal feeling as the gigs were approaching was that I felt like I might have a nervous breakdown and couldn't bear the thought of doing it all again. Then pretty much as soon as the final chord of 'Rent' was played at Brixton on Saturday I was already wondering about Christmas 2010.

TELLY SAVALAS

2010 was a fallow year. To give the farm and the village a chance to recover, there would be no Carter gigs. I'd finished my first novel *Storage Stories* and there were three thousand copies in my house. To get rid of a few and to save my marriage, I went on a UK tour. I sang solo and Carter songs (slightly more of the latter with every passing year) and I read passages from the book. I'd bought a tiny projector and a screen to project some of the seventy-three drawings from the book onto. At my solo gigs, whenever I play 'Sheriff Fatman' I notice little red lights coming on in the audience, as people start videoing. For some reason, on the *Storage Stories* tour, the camera phones seemed to light up every time this picture appeared on the screen behind me.

It's not even one of the seventy-three drawings in *Storage Stories*. It's the punchline to a bit about Iggy Pop being told the rules and the etiquette for playing golf. The drawings that are in *Storage Stories* were the work of the novel's unnamed narrator, whose digital camera had been dismantled by his friend Carl and so he had to resort to his 'rubbish drawings'. In my next book *Driving Jarvis Ham*, I blame my lack of drawing skills

on Jarvis. The book's narrator (unnamed again[50]) finds Jarvis's drawings, along with photographs, letters and newspaper clippings, in an old shoebox inside this large brown suitcase:

For my third novel, there was no one in the story to blame the pictures on. My literary agent[51] and my editor both suggested removing a few. The writing is strong enough on its own Jim, my editor said. Let's get rid of just a couple of pictures. The wristwatch for instance, could go.

And the calculator.

I agreed that neither picture particularly added anything to the story and removed them. In the next draft the 'Lift out of Order' sign would go and also two of the charity calendars and Groucho Marx saying 'And it's not just the rainbow trout.'

And it's not just the rainbow trout.

Maybe you could reuse the pictures in a future

---

50 Dave Eggers's advice to his friend who doesn't want to read about real people, to 'Pretend it's fiction' works the other way round as well. If readers don't want to read my first two novels as fiction, as I've cleverly not named the narrators, people can pretend the books are autobiographical. *Storage Stories* did of course start out as a semi-fictional autobiographical account of what happened to me in the years after the break-up of Carter. In 2013 I had a number of meetings with scriptwriter Matt Sinclair. We were going to try and turn *Storage Stories* into a TV series. At some stage in the process Matt's agent suggested it might work if I was to 'star' in the show as myself, working in a self-storage warehouse after the break-up of the band. It would be a bit like *Curb Your Enthusiasm*. I love the idea but it would never really work because of the reformation. And I don't mean the 16th-century religious challenge to papal authority initiated by Martin Luther and leading to the Thirty Years War. I'm talking about the reformation of Carter The Unstoppable Sex Machine for our two annual live shows. I should point out that the television version of *Storage Stories* is as yet unmade. That's *as yet*.
51 I had a literary agent. I was a proper author now. I'd come a long way as a writer. *Goodnight Jim Bob* for instance, contains three incorrect uses of the word 'less'. I'd never allow that to happen now.

memoir Jim, my editor said. To illustrate how I talked you into removing the drawings from your Frank Derrick novel. Nothing is wasted, isn't that what you said Jim? This exact conversation definitely happened. I remember it word for word.

One by one the *Frank Derrick* drawings were removed, until it was agreed I should leave just the one picture of Frank's stone-faced cat Bill at the end of the story. And then, do you know what Jim, my editor said, without all the other pictures don't you think the drawing of Bill looks a little out of place? Maybe lose the cat as well. Here's Bill, shortly after receiving the bad news:

When *Storage Stories* was published, I was asked to write a 'top ten' piece for *The Guardian*. They rejected my 'Top 10 novels by musicians' and so I wrote about my 'Top 10 Illustrated Books for Adults'.

I always wanted to have illustrations in my own novel. Maybe just a couple of graphs and a picture of the building where the book is set, and I knew there'd be a drawing of a job ad at the start of the book. Then I added more and more pictures and they became an integral part of the story and the way it's told – I couldn't imagine the book now without them. My drawing skills are pretty limited, but luckily the main character in my novel – the one who's drawing the pictures in the story – turned out to be somebody with limited drawing skills too.

I also said this:

I have mild OCD. One of the symptoms is that when I read a book I often have to read each sentence two or even four times before I feel I can move onto the next one without thinking one of my loved ones will die in a plane crash. Big fat doorstops of text are a daunting prospect. The 560,000 words in your copy of 'War and Peace' could be as many as two and half million for me. I like short chapters, big titles and even gaps of empty page. I think this might be one of the reasons why I like books with illustrations in. A picture between chapters, mid paragraph or even sentence takes my OCD addled mind off all the re-reading nonsense and I can get to the end of a book a lot more efficiently. As Telly Savalas once said, "A picture paints a thousand words." That's three pages closer to the end of War and Peace.

I don't have OCD. Not mild or otherwise. But I wasn't lying exactly. I was just ignorant of what Obsessive Compulsive Order was at the time, or how serious and debilitating a condition it could be. I imagine it's infuriating if you do suffer from OCD and you have to constantly listen to people like me referring to my need to keep the forks on the correct side of the drawer or having to read a sentence twice before being able to turn a page, as being 'a bit OCD'. The thing I said about having to read sentences over and over again was true however. But it isn't OCD. It's more of an inconvenience than anything else.

In the dressing room before a gig, I'll repeatedly touch the ceiling and the walls and the edges of doorframes and the corners of tables. I'll move bits of the rider around and check my guitar picks are all facing the right way up in my pocket. I'll touch the mirror and the wall again, the ceiling, the wall, establishing the chosen point where I should touch each and returning to that point on the ceiling, the wall, the mirror, the table. As show-time approaches, the regularity and intensity of these nervous touching tics will increase. I'll count the number of times I touch things. It will have to be a certain number but not always the same number and invariably one more than that. And when I pass that number by I'll have to move on to the next number, in my own higgledy-piggledy version of Prime. I do the same thing at home. Most often, when I'm about to leave the house or go to bed, especially if I'm going somewhere new or to do something important, either out or in bed, like to sleep. Perchance to dream – ay, there's the rub, for in this sleep of death what dreams may come when we have shuffled off this mortal coil, must give us pause. There's the respect that makes calamity of so long life.

I used to have a friend who couldn't cross the road without pausing halfway to bend over and touch the ground. No matter how fast or heavy the traffic was moving or how great the risk to his life, he simply had to do it. It's not impossible for me to get stuck in a rut when touching a doorframe on the way out of the house an ever-increasing number of times. I've missed buses and trains before because of it. But I've never missed a gig because I'm too busy touching the corner of a dressing room mirror. I am always professional. Some might call me a hero. But it's not OCD.

When I sent my 'Top 10 Illustrated Books for Adults' piece to *The Guardian* they did seem particularly pleased that I had an anxiety disorder. I do wonder if they would have rejected my great article if I hadn't opened it with my 'mild OCD' declaration. Without it it's just another list of stuff. My 'mild OCD' made me more interesting. Being 'from Carter' didn't quite cut it for *The Guardian* in the way that being unable to turn the page of a book did. It was my TV cop idiosyncrasy.

Hey. I haven't dropped a famous name for a bit. So here's a picture of actor Mathew Horne. Seen here, standing between me and Andrew Collins, at the launch party for *Storage Stories*. I wasn't happy with my double chin so I've given myself a beard and a pirate eye patch. Also in the photo are Bransby (seated and reading) and just behind me, leaning slightly forward, is Adrian Todd Zuniga, co-creator and MC of Literary Death Match, the scene of my Kaiser Chiefs faux pas. I'm not sure who that is with one hand on Andrew's shoulder and his other doing Winston Churchill bunny rabbit ears. Let's pretend it's James Corden.

Behind Adrian Todd Zuniga and not quite in the photo, is Martin White. Martin came to the *Storage Stories* launch party with Danielle Ward. I'd met Martin the year before when he was musical director for *Nine Lessons and Carols for Godless People*. Martin had already made one of my dreams come true when I got to sing with his orchestra (not a euphemism). Another dream come true would be when I recorded an album with the same orchestra. Apart from *Jim Bob Sings Again*, a collection of old solo and Carter songs recorded with just Chris T-T's piano accompaniment, I haven't made an album since *What I Think About When I Think About You*. Once you've recorded with an orchestra, it's difficult to go back to guitars. That's my motto.

I'd met Danielle Ward in 2009 when me and Les were guests on Dave Gorman's show on Absolute Radio. Martin and Danielle were Dave's co hosts.[52] Danielle's cultural review 'Ward's Weekly Word' was always

---

52 I've talked a lot about celebrity Carter fans. Dave Gorman is possibly the only celebrity Jim's Super Stereoworld fan.

my favourite bit of the show. Danielle created and hosts the podcast *Do the Right Thing*, which I've appeared on twice. Once on the pilot and the second time as the 'Ask the Expert', expert. Angelos Epithemiou was one of the panel members that time and I found out that he – or his creator, Dan Renton Skinner – stage dived (stage dove?) at a Carter gig at the Astoria and nobody caught him.

In 2010 Martin and Danielle wrote a musical. They were taking it up to the Edinburgh Festival and they asked me if I'd like to be in it. With no Carter gigs, admin or rehearsals, and with time on my hands, my jazz hands, I decided to go back to my roots.

MUSICAL THEATRE 2 – JIM BOB'S FRINGE

When people ask me if I want to do things these days, my first thought is often, how can I politely and diplomatically say no? I've become incredibly lazy and unadventurous. But in 2010, the fire in my belly hadn't quite gone out, and there was no Netflix or Amazon Prime, so when Martin and Danielle asked me to appear in their new musical, even though it was so far from anything I had planned to do and such a long way out of my comfort zone, and for such a long period of time, I said yes.

As it happened, I'd been thinking about putting a version of my *Storage Stories* live show on at the Edinburgh Fringe. Just a few months earlier, me and Chris T-T had been for a pub meeting with MJ Hibbett and Steve Hewitt. MJ and Steve were taking their show *Dinosaur Planet* up to Edinburgh and me and Chris were thinking there might be a way of pooling the resources of our three shows, *Dinosaur Planet, Storage Stories – Storage Songs* (as it was called) and a Chris T-T show. After the meeting, the admin involved in putting a show on at the Edinburgh Fringe and the house sharing I'd need to do scared the hell out of me and I immediately changed my mind about going.

The last time I went to the Edinburgh Festival was in 1971. I was ten years old and I went with my dad. My parents were separated. It's what the Carter song 'Good Grief Charlie Brown' is about. All that stuff in the lyrics about sending ten shillings as we had arranged. My dad used to send me a ten shilling note every week or two, sometimes a postal order. My dad died in 1996 when Carter were in the middle of recording songs for *A World Without Dave*. I hadn't seen him or heard from him for a number of years and it was weird being the one who had to arrange his funeral. His coffin was carried into the crematorium by the singer from 999, remember. Not that I'm trying to take the credit for that. With the help of my cousin, who had seen my dad more recently than I had, we cleared out his Battersea flat. The fact my dad had been living just six miles from me all the time I hadn't seen him was a surprise. I'm not sure where I thought he lived. Timbuktu? Afghanistan? He didn't have a lot of stuff in his flat. We didn't need to hire a van. There were a few small bits of furniture my dad had made out of what looked like wood he'd taken out of a skip. He used to be a carpenter.

My cousin told me my dad had collected press clippings of Carter:

photos and interviews from the music papers. But we couldn't find a single one. His flat had the look of a man who knew he was going to die and was clearing everything up before he went. One thing he had kept was a large collection of his flattened cigar boxes. He'd died from lung cancer. It was hard not to find that weirdly poetic. I wrote 'You Can't Take it With You' about my dad and what he hadn't left behind. I kept his glasses for a while and his tuxedo suit. It smelled of cigar smoke. I wore the jacket at Brixton Academy in 2008. Halfway through the gig, in the middle of 'Good Grief Charlie Brown', I put my hand in the pocket and found a photograph of me and Les inside a folded up *NME* review of *30 Something*. Not really. We didn't play 'Good Grief Charlie Brown' in 2008. But the jacket did smell of cigar smoke.

In 1971 my dad was living in his old hometown of Edinburgh and he took me there for a holiday with him. It was the first time I'd ever been on a plane. I remember it far too well. It was a British Airways flight. I know it was 1971 because my dad told me that if I was eleven, rather than ten, he would have had to pay more for my seat on the plane. I don't know if that was true or not, if British Airways charged more for their seats once passengers were eleven years old, but it's a piece of knowledge that's been stuck in my brain ever since.

My dad was born in Edinburgh in 1925 – don't worry, this isn't that tedious two hundred page skippable bit about my ancestors that all music autobiographies begin with. I'm not trying to sneak it in halfway through when you least expect it. But my dad was born in Edinburgh in 1925. He would meet my mum there about thirty years later, when he was the stage manager at a theatre she was performing at, presumably with the Four in a Chord. There's a bit in *Goodnight Jim Bob* about one time when the Four in a Chord appeared in Edinburgh and my mum's sister had tonsillitis and she had to mime. Maybe it was that time.

I just did a quick search online to see who was performing at the Edinburgh Festival in 1971. The most famous person I found was Robin Williams. He made his Edinburgh debut in a production of *The Taming of the Shrew*. I'd love to be able to say that me and my dad were in the audience. I even contemplated saying that we were. Who's going to dispute it? But I've lied enough already.

I remember me and my dad went to the castle in 1971 for the Military Tattoo. I ate haggis and Edinburgh rock and climbed up Arthur's Seat and we stayed at my aunt's flat. She had one of those Trimphones. I remember that more than anything. At the time it seemed incredibly futuristic. It looked like something out of *Thunderbirds* or *Captain Scarlet*.

Every time I went back to Edinburgh after 1971, it was for gigs: five with Carter and twice on my own. I was never there for very long and as usual I didn't get to sightsee. The thought of spending a whole month in the land of my father appealed to me. It would be a challenge of course. My acting experience mainly consisted of miming in my own promo videos and playing a shoplifting policeman in the video for Little Man Tate's House Party at Boothy's video.

Team Jim Bob – me, Marc and Mister Spoons – went up to Sheffield in 2005 to DJ at Little Man Tate's Christmas party. The band were Carter fans. 'Sheriff Fatman' was their intro music. According to my blog, at the Christmas party we played Fratellis, Nirvana and Girls Aloud records and Spoons wore a policeman's helmet. Me and Marc wore trilbies. We also played the Arctic Monkeys because there was a sort of friendly local rivalry between them and Little Man Tate and we thought it would annoy the audience. There was a rumour going around that year that I wrote the Arctic Monkeys lyrics, as Alex Turner from the Arctic Monkeys was thought to be too young to have used some of the references in his songs. Whenever I was asked if it was true in interviews I always said that I couldn't comment on it, hoping that would confirm that it must be true, or at least keep the rumour going for a little longer. You've got to take publicity opportunities when you can.

Sometimes I think how my life could have been different if I'd listened to my English teacher. When I was fifteen or sixteen she told me she didn't think school was really right for me. She wanted to arrange an audition at the Italia Conti drama school. I don't know why I didn't take up the offer. Lack of confidence maybe, or because I was far more interested in smoking and girls and punk rock. I did agree that school wasn't for me though and I left as soon as possible. I started work in the advertising company I mentioned earlier. In the building where the *Never Mind the Buzzcocks* pilot would later be recorded and where Theon Greyjoy, the only living son and heir of Lord Balon Greyjoy of the Iron Islands, and younger brother of Yara Greyjoy, would tell his dad Keith off for not letting me get a word in edgewise.

How different would my life have been if I'd gone to drama school? I could have been in *Game of Thrones* with Alfie Allen and Julian Glover, the actor who reads the audiobook of *The Extra Ordinary Life of Frank Derrick*. If I was an actor I could have read my own audiobook.[53] I could have appeared in *Casualty* or *The Bill* or even in *Grange Hill*. I would have been star-struck just looking in the mirror every day. I remember how excited me and Les were when Carter were on *Top of the Pops* and we were told that some of the cast from *Grange Hill* wanted to meet us. I was way more excited than I ever would have been about meeting someone from a band.

---

53 I am the voice of the *Driving Jarvis Ham* audiobook. It took almost three days and was exhausting to listen to my own voice for so long. Shut up at the back.

In 2011 I was asked to choose my favourite opening, middle and end movie scenes of all time, for the film-based live comedy show *Richard Sandling's Perfect Movie*. I picked *Carlito's Way*, *One Flew Over the Cuckoo's Nest* and *Butch Cassidy and the Sundance Kid*. On a cold day in March, in two upstairs rooms at the Railway Hotel pub in Southend, me and Richard Sandling recreated those three iconic movie moments. I played a dying Carlito on a gurney in *Carlito's Way*, Randle McMurphy in the Juicy Fruit scene from *One Flew Over the Cuckoo's Nest* and Butch Cassidy in an almost identical and precise recreation of the 'Blaze of Glory' scene from the end of *Butch Cassidy and the Sundance Kid*. I'm not suggesting I was better in those roles than Al Pacino, Jack Nicholson or Paul Newman. That's for the Academy of Motion Picture Arts and Sciences in Beverly Hills, California to decide. But I enjoyed it immensely.

The finished film clips were shown on a screen in front of an audience in the upstairs room of a different pub in London's West End. Before the films, comedian Nick Helm did some movie related stand-up. He talked about favourite films, asking members of the audience what theirs were. Marc was with me that night and because I was due to take part in the show, I was sitting on the front row. I have only one rule in life and that's never sit on the front row at a comedy gig with Marc Ollington. He will *always* interact with the performers. Whether he's invited to or not. When Nick Helm asked Marc what his favourite film of all time was, without hesitation, Marc said, "*Mickey Blue Eyes*." This isn't Marc being ironic or clever or trying to annoy Nick Helm. *Mickey Blue Eyes* is his favourite film of all time. Apart from anything, it stars Marc's favourite actor of all time, Hugh Grant. Anyway, Nick Helm called him a cunt. Twice.

In 2010, when Martin White and Danielle Ward asked me to be in their Edinburgh musical, apart from when I was a shoplifting cop in the Little Man Tate, my acting experience still consisted almost entirely of lip-synching in my own promo videos. Sometimes I'd have to do something other than mime, like in the 'Glam Rock Cops' video where I was in a room being questioned by the police or when I was rolling around on a bed in the 'Lenny and Terence' promo. In the video for 'The Young Offender's Mum', when I had to interact with a prison officer, played by the lovely Stephen Lewis, any acting I'm doing is simply me trying to disguise what's going through my mind: "Oh my God. It's Blakey from *On the Buses*."

In Carter's most epic promo video: 'The Impossible Dream', even though I ride a horse, wield a sword, look through a telescope and wave at a hot air balloon (God I miss the 1990s), I'm still miming along with my own song. In Martin and Danielle's musical I'd be singing songs I hadn't written. And singing other people's songs isn't as easy as singing your own. It's one of the reasons I very rarely do karaoke (Three times: 'Green, Green Grass of Home' in a Japanese karaoke bar in Sydney, 'Everybody's Talkin'' as a duet with Les in a pub in Croydon, and thirdly, every solo gig I've done in the past four years with my 'Shit acoustic Carter karaoke' act.) The thing is, if you aren't a professional singer and you manage a half decent karaoke performance, everyone thinks you're amazing. If singing is your job and you don't hit all the notes or you sing slightly off key, everyone's writing stiff letters to *Watchdog*. And apart from the songs, I would have to learn lines. I feel sick just thinking about it.

Fruitbat, incidentally, hated having to act in Carter videos. "I'm not an actor. I'm a musician", he always used to say when he was asked to do anything other than mime playing guitar. If you'd seen the outtakes of him pretending to drive a car in the 'Glam Rock Cops' video, you might take issue with Fruitbat's modesty.[54] As he turned the steering wheel from hard left to hard right and back again, if the car wasn't fixed to the back of a flatbed truck, we would have been careering across traffic, smashing into parked cars and pedestrians. It was quite the performance. But he really didn't enjoy the process. Directors had to find a way to use Fruitbat's difficulty.[55] That's why, in the video for 'The Impossible Dream', he spends a lot of his time onscreen, playing with his Gameboy (possibly a euphemism).

Martin White emailed me the script for *Gutted: A Revenger's Musical*. It's the story of a girl named Sorrow (all the characters in *Gutted* were named after David Bowie songs) who witnesses the brutal murder of her parents when she's seven years old. Fifteen years later she finds the man responsible. She plans to marry him and kill all his family. *Gutted* is described on Danielle Ward's website as 'The perfect combination of jazz hands and inappropriate violence' and also, 'Glee meets The Texas Chainsaw Massacre with bells on (NB The show does not include bells)'

---

54 'Fruitbat's Modesty'. A perfume for the modern woman. I'm looking for £250,000 for a 40% stake in the company.

55 'Fruitbat's Difficulty'. An aftershave for men. Two hundred grand for a 50/50 share of the profits.

THE CAST
(See if you can name all the Bowie songs)

Director – Chris George
Mr Bewlay (and all his relatives) – Colin Hoult
Sorrow – Helen George
The Vicar – Michael Legge
Mrs Station – Margaret Cabourn-Smith
Jean – Sara Pascoe
Joe – Ben Bailey Smith
Mr Wendy – Humphrey Ker
Redd – David Reed
Kook – Thom Tuck
Buddy Stardust – Jim Bob (from Carter USM)
Iris – Lizzie Roper
Andy – Jim Bob again
Rosalyn – Lizzie Roper
Chorus – Fiona Stephenson and Daniel Tawse
Piano – Martin White
Bass – Danielle Ward
Guitar – Graeme Mearns
Drums – Ali Murray

At first I was asked to play the vicar. I started practising my vicar voices: Derek Nimmo, the Vicar of Dibley, the Reverend Lovejoy from *The Simpsons*, and Dick Emery, just so I could shoehorn this anecdote into a book one day:

In 1968 my mum took me to see *Cinderella* at the Streatham Odeon. It started Dick Emery and Joe Brown. I remember Joe Brown played about a gazillion different musical instruments. When I was eight that blew my mind. Now I'd probably walk out because I thought he was showing off. After the show, we went backstage to meet Dick Emery, who was a friend of my mum's (not a euphemism). Because I was only eight I can't remember much about meeting Dick Emery. Even though I did seem to have remembered more about it than most of the things that have happened a hell of a lot more recently.

Just as I'd perfected my inner vicar, Frank Skinner pulled out of *Gutted* and I was asked if I'd like to take his place in the role of washed-up wedding singer called Buddy Stardust. For some people, the thought of me replacing Frank Skinner in a comedy musical probably sounds as bad an idea as when Carter were allegedly on stand-by at Reading Festival in 1992, to replace Public Enemy on the Saturday and Nirvana on the Sunday, in case either should pull out at the last minute. The story about us being backstage all weekend with our amps and guitars, ready to step in if required, is one I've heard so often since, that I've started to believe it might actually be true.

I switched roles to faded wedding singer, leaving Martin and Danielle needing to find someone else to play the vicar. Michael Legge's angry Northern Irish clergyman was way, way better than any of my uptight and posh, toothy Englishmen would have been. It also meant I got to meet Michael Legge. If you filmed me and Michael during our month in Edinburgh and you edited the film into a montage and slowed it down, with a soft focus filter over the top and some French pastoral pop music underneath, you might think we were in love. I've just remembered, there's a fourth time I've performed karaoke.

Anyway, I had fewer lines to learn as Buddy Stardust and 'faded wedding singer' didn't seem quite so far outside my comfort zone. Possibly even a glimpse into my future. I would also be playing Sorrow's dead dad, Andy. But it was only for one scene and just the one song. How hard could it possibly be?

UNCHOREOGRAPHABLE SEX MACHINE

It turns out I'm not as good a dancer as I thought I was. I'm not suggesting I'd ever considered myself as some sort of Michael Jackson figure but until the *Gutted* rehearsals, I hadn't realised I was more like Ann Widdecombe. I've always struggled with the simplest of direction when it comes to movement. The physiotherapist who treated my frozen shoulder recently just couldn't seem to get me to make my arm go limp for example. No matter how hard I tried (maybe I was trying too hard) my arm would not play dead.

I find the most basic of instructions very hard to follow. Left-right-left-right, feet together, step to the side, hands up, face the front, do-si-do. My brain can't process the information fast enough. By the time my left leg knows what to do everyone else in the room is six moves ahead of me. They're all doing the Hokey Cokey while I'm still shaking it all about.

In *Gutted* there was a song called 'Kill Him'. It was a duet between Sorrow's ghost father played by me and her ghost mother, played by Lizzie Roper. The song was complicated enough already. It was the 'Evil' of the musical. I'd sing a line then Lizzie would sing the next line, then it would be my turn then, just as a pattern was established, it would be my turn again. There was dialogue in between choruses as well. And dance moves. For me it was like rubbing my belly and patting my head while solving a Rubik's cube. Blindfolded. On a tightrope. In a hurry. If I ever got the whole song right – words, dialogue and dance moves – it felt like a real achievement.

There were three weeks of London rehearsals for *Gutted* and a couple of performances at the Riverside Studios in Hammersmith before we went to Edinburgh for the whole of August. Getting the tube to Liverpool Street and walking to the rehearsal space, above an art gallery off London's trendy or impoverished – depending on your circumstances – Brick Lane, every morning, was the closest I'd been to having a regular job for a very long time.

The rehearsal day would start with a warm-up. I'd never warmed up for anything in my life. I've always approached everything very much cold, or at least at room temperature. At first I felt incredibly self-conscious running around in circles and jumping up and down on the spot and so on but it turned out to be a good way to get rid of some of my excess inhibitions. And I had a lot of those.

As I think we've established, I'm not the most self-confident person in the world and everyone else in *Gutted* seemed to already know each another. But they were all very welcoming. Margaret Cabourn-Smith was especially nice to me when I turned up at the first rehearsal. She knew about my previous life and even used to be a bit of a Carter fan. Although, not as much as she was a Wonder Stuff fan. It's possible Margaret was just being nice so that I could introduce her to Miles Hunt.

While I was writing this, the actor Mark Wahlberg (perhaps most famous for posting a couple of bouncers outside a backstage toilet at the 1991 *Smash Hits Poll Winners Party*, to stop anyone else except him from using the toilet) revealed his strict daily routine while he prepared for a movie. He may have been playing a big old joke on us, because it certainly reads like that but who knows. Mark Wahlberg's day apparently began at 2.45 am with a prayer, followed by a 3.15 breakfast, a series of workouts and showers, a game of golf, some high protein snacks and cryo-chamber recovery treatment. After a few meetings and more showers, more snacks and another workout, and after picking the kids up from school (not a euphemism), Marky Wahlberg was back in bed by 7.30 pm.

Here's the daily routine of the actor Jim Bob, also coincidentally most famous for something that happened at the 1991 *Smash Hits Poll Winners Party*.

I wake up in my massively overpriced one bedroom Edinburgh flat, less than two minutes walk from the Assembly Rooms, and the Ballroom venue where *Gutted* was playing every night in August 2010 except for Tuesdays. I make myself breakfast in my tiny kitchen, probably toast, usually Marmite. I watch the news. *Gutted* isn't on until 11.15 pm and there's a lot of daytime to kill. I was going to write a novel in this time but it soon becomes obvious that was never going to happen.

I go for a stroll around Edinburgh. I walk up Calton Hill. I'd been there with my dad when I was ten. I walk down the Royal Mile to the Scottish Parliament building and look up at Arthur's Seat. I think about climbing it. I have a memory of doing that when I was ten. It looks too steep for a ten year old. It definitely is for a faded forty-something wedding singer.

I walk to the Scottish National Gallery and the Scottish Gallery of Modern Art and to Stockbridge, where I walk along the banks of the Water of Leith. As far as the place that looks a bit like Spain or Italy. There's a Caffè Nero in Stockbridge. There's another one on Infirmary Street. It's next door to Blackwells book shop. I have a browse of the books. I bump into Richard Herring and Andrew Collins in Nero's, planning their *Collings and Herrin* podcast. They both have shows on at the festival. Almost everyone in *Gutted* except for me is also appearing in their own show. I go and see them all. One afternoon I sing 'Cartoon Dad' halfway through Michael Legge and Robin Ince's *Pointless Anger, Righteous Ire* show. They call me the Elaine Paige or Barbara Dickson to their *Two Ronnies*.

I'm in the middle of the biggest arts festival in the world and after a couple of weeks I'm desperate to escape it. I have a spicy bean burger upstairs in the Burger King where it could be February or June. There's little evidence there that the city has been taken over. I begin to resent all the visitors clogging up my dad's hometown. I show my resentment by refusing to take any flyers for improvised musicals or satirical puppet shows that I'd politely accepted at the start of the month.

I do a bit of afternoon food shopping at the Sainsbury's Local or the bigger Marks and Spencer's on Princes Street and I go back to my flat and watch TV. There are only five or six channels and nothing is on. I end up watching *Celebrity Masterchef* for the first and only time in my life. Inspired, I cook my latest microwave meal for one, in my one bedroom flat for one.

I have a shower. I wash my hair every day because of all the gel I'm using to slick it back as Buddy Stardust. At eight pm I start pacing my tiny flat. I touch tabletops and windowsills. I don't want to go over and over my lines or the words to the songs because I surely know them by now, but my brain has other ideas. My brain will never allow me to go 'off book'.[56]

Sometime after ten pm, feeling like having an early night and going to bed, I walk slowly to the theatre. I do my best to not always be the first to arrive but I almost always am. When the rest of the cast have arrived I'll put on the fat suit and curly wig. Colin Hoult is playing all six members of the Bewley family. To maintain the illusion that it's actually six different actors, during the opening number, other cast members disguise themselves as the four characters Colin isn't currently playing. I'm the double for Bob Bewley. He's large, gluttonous and South African. Luckily I don't have to do the accent.

Before the show begins my microphone is stuck to my face. There are many technical issues for the musical. The majority of them are microphone related. At first there aren't enough microphones for the whole cast. I don't get one for the opening song for the first few dates. At the time that seems mad to me but I don't say anything. No one would have heard me anyway, because I didn't have a microphone. I'd say I was reminded of my horrendous experience at Latitude festival but that

---

56 Theatre term. Going off book in rehearsals means the actors can no longer hold or look at a script and must rely on their memories and having actually learned their lines.

hasn't happened yet. When more mics arrive, the sticky tape to hold them in place isn't very sticky and my microphone constantly falls off.

Richard Herring's show is on before us at the same venue. I see him every night but I don't thank him for roasting the lyrics to 'Sheriff Fatman' for my birthday because that hasn't happened yet either. Richard comes off stage and after some frantic stage set alteration, we go on. Or *up*, as they say in stand up comedy and theatre. That's the main difference between theatre or comedy and rock and roll. We go on stage and they go up. Someone hands me my stunt sausage prop and the show begins.

After the first song I change out of the fat suit and into my Buddy Stardust costume. Some nights I think I'm not going to make it in time. Sometimes I can't get my shoelaces undone or the fat trousers off. It's like changing out of a wetsuit in the transition stage of a triathlon. I enjoy performing the Buddy Stardust song 'The Ballad of Rancid Mortimer'. I think it improves with each performance. I only totally balls it up once and there are no dance moves to worry about. And I get to use a handheld microphone so I don't need to worry about not being heard or the microphone falling off. I like the audience reaction when I sing the last chorus.

> She married that man
> Became his wife
> Not long were they wed
> When she bought a Stanley knife
> Cut his father's cock off, then forced it down his gob
> Smashed in both his children, with a snooker ball in a sock
> Stitched uncle's mouth to his own bumhole, disembowelled his
> favourite niece
> Left the man in ruins, God let them rest in pieces

One night when I walk onstage, I swear I hear someone in the audience chant a very quiet 'you fat bastard'. I hadn't been bigheaded enough to consider that might happen. It was the tiniest glimpse into the life of what it's like for someone from *Harry Potter* or *Game of Thrones* when they take on a role in a West End play and the audience scream every time they appear. It doesn't happen again. I'm both relieved and disappointed.

Apart from the microphones, the other main technical issue is the door at the back of the stage. I have to make two entrances through it every night and it gets stuck every time. It doesn't really function very well as a door and I grow to hate it.

After Buddy Stardust finishes his song I change into my dead dad Andy costume. My stage wife, Lizzie Roper, does my make up and we perform the world's most difficult song, 'Kill Him'. After that I change back into the Buddy costume for the last song and the bows and applause and plaudits and shit.

And then we go to the bar. Every single night for a month, I drink Heineken and gin and tonic until we get thrown out at three in the morning. I go back to my one bedroom flat and try to sleep while all the drunks outside my window shout at each other.

There were moments that would upset this regular routine. Tuesdays for example were days off. I didn't need to think about the performance ahead and I could relax. One Tuesday I went to see Dan le Sac Vs Scroobius Pip with Michael Legge. I mean of course that me and Michael were in the audience. It's not a hip hop/stand up comedy crossover trio. That was the night Scroobius Pip sang "Carter USM – Just a band" and it was really thrilling for me. But not quite as thrilling as when Pip dedicated a song to the cast of *Gutted*. My allegiances had shifted. I was very much now Jim Bob from *Gutted*.

On another Tuesday night off, Martin and Danielle's *Karaoke Circus* was in town at the Spiegeltent in Princes Street Gardens. Members of the audience and stand up comedians would sing popular songs, backed by the live *Karaoke Circus band*. I hadn't planned on getting anywhere near the stage but I'd been to the pub with Michael Legge and I was pretty drunk when we arrived and one thing led to another thing and somehow me and Michael ended up 'singing' 'Common People'. It's a song I thought I knew all the words to, until I had to sing them that night. There was a BBC *Watchdog* episode dedicated to it.

I'm glad I said yes to being in a musical. I made some great new friends, who like most of my great new friends I never ever see or speak to. Sometimes I do see one of them on television. Helen George in *Call the Midwife* for example, or Ben Bailey Smith in *Law and Order: UK*. Sara Pascoe hosting *Live at the Apollo*. But they never seem to hear me when I call out hello from my sofa.

When it was all over, just like when I came away from *Jammin'* thinking I was about to start a career in radio light entertainment, and after *Dick Whittington* when I thought I'd be writing music for the theatre, or when I returned from Hollywood believing I was going to be a movie screenwriter, after *Gutted* I expected the phone would be ringing off the hook with offers from West End musical producers. The phone never rang.

I felt like I was part of a gang when I was in *Gutted*, in a way that I hadn't since the heady days of Jim's Super Stereoworld. After a month in Edinburgh, I was sure we were the hardest gang, in all of show business. I felt part of something unique to only us. We'd been through something that no one outside of our group would ever understand. Like when people come out of *Big Brother* or *I'm a Celebrity Get me out of Here* and they bang on about the experience, as though they'd just fought in the Vietnam War together.

There were bad times in *Gutted*. But they only made us stronger. On a night that would be known as 'Black Saturday', absolutely everything that could have gone wrong, went wrong. It started at the very beginning of the show when the 'body' that falls from the roof onto the stage didn't fall. Because of health and because of safety, we all had to vacate the stage until the body was recovered. We left the stage and the audience started leaving too. It was like one of my Carter bad gig dreams. Loads of other things went wrong that night and an emergency meeting was called in the bar afterwards. It ended in tears and a massive row, with fists banged on tables and so on. After surviving Black Saturday, the bond between us was even stronger. Not quite Vietnam War veterans – maybe Volkswagen Beetle owners.

I learned a lot about myself while I was in *Gutted*. I know I could never live on my own for a start. Standing on the platform and watching the train leaving Edinburgh Waverley station, taking Mrs Jim Bob and our daughter back to London after visiting me for a couple of days, before returning to my one bedroom, massively overpriced one bedroom flat to watch *Celebrity Masterchef* on my own, may have been the loneliest I've ever felt in my entire life.

BLOG. 30.8.10.

It was the final performance of Gutted last night and I'm missing everyone already. Even John the racist dog. I haven't felt like this since I left school. I should have got everyone to sign my shirt and throw eggs and flour at me. To take my mind off it I've been tidying the flat I've spent the past month in. I've eaten whatever food is left over so I don't have to throw it away. My last supper consisted of crumpets, cheese, Starburst, cheesy wotsits and a Penguin biscuit. Beat that Jesus. I've just ironed the tablecloth - I washed it because it had a curry stain on it - and I'm having a cup of the tea Mister Spoons left behind after his visit the other day. I don't drink tea.

I've changed.

I think the moment I knew I'd changed was the day after the Gutted wrap party when I remembered how at another party the night before, 'Don't Go Breaking My Heart' was played and the male cast members had stood in a line on one side of the room and sang the Elton John parts, while the female members of the cast faced them on the other side of the room and sang Kiki Dee's bits. I was Elton John and I was loving it.

Tomorrow I get the train back to London, stopping at Rejection,
Disappointment, Backstabbing Central and Shattered Dreams
Parkway. I'm going to have a lie down and a bath. After that, I
really have no idea.

When *Gutted* was over I felt a bit lost. I was confused about who I was
and what I should do next. All I could think of was doing more of the
same thing that had left me feeling so lost and confused. On the train
back to King's Cross, I was already planning my next Edinburgh show. It
was going to be called *Jim Bob from Carter* and would open with a tweet
about how I'd just found the cure for cancer.

TINKER TAILOR SOLDIER CARTER

In January 2011 we had our first Carter meeting of the year. It was earlier than usual. My last minute nerves would begin sooner every year. 2012's first meeting would be in 2011. Venues have to be booked up so far in advance now, especially for the dates closer to Christmas and those at the weekends. And we were sure the Carter gigs needed to be at weekends. At our age and presumably that of our audience, every week night is a school night, regardless of whether or not you have kids.

The first meeting would mainly be about deciding whether or not to actually do any more gigs. It may have seemed like a foregone conclusion (see footnote #31) but there were always doubts. We'd meet up in a pub and ask ourselves the same set of questions: Were we still popular enough to sell out the big venues? Could we make it interesting and exciting for everyone involved? Did we want to do it? What should Jim wear? I wonder if those inaugural meetings had been held anywhere other than the pub, I wonder if we would have kept going so long.

We'd get drunk and agree to booking more gigs. We'd start brainstorming ideas for what we'd call the gigs and how we could make them different somehow. In 2011 the best we could come up with was playing one gig in Manchester and another in London, and calling them 'Norf and Sarf'. We used images of Bet Lynch and Barbara Windsor on the artwork for the ad.

Dennis @Snafflebold_Den69 . 5m London isn't South. What about Portsmouth? #youfatbastards

In 2011, like every Carter reunion year before, one of the first things we'd do was meet up with our lighting designer. It was Pip in the first few years and then Nic Lights (actual name, huge coincidence) when Pip had other commitments.[57] We'd challenge them to come up with a bigger and better show than the previous one. In 2010 Fruitbat had gone to live in Folkestone (not a euphemism). Nic Lights lived in Norwich and I was still in Crystal Palace. We looked for somewhere in the middle to meet up and would end up having all of our subsequent lighting meetings in Paul, a patisserie restaurant inside St Pancras station. It wasn't really a restaurant as such. Paul had no walls or doors or windows. It was just a counter, a few tables and chairs and presumably a man named Paul.

---

57 If there isn't a Commitments tribute band called The Other Commitments I will be very surprised.

JIM BOB FROM CARTER

Having our lighting meetings in a busy London station made them seem very John le Carré. It was as though we didn't trust one another and had to meet in plain sight, where there were plenty of people about. Every year, over coffee and croissants or maybe a pain au chocolat, Nic would reach the same conclusion about how to make the latest Carter shows better: more lights.

The need for a huge light show was the main reason we only played three festivals. We had a lot of other offers but they were all for afternoon or early evening slots. A proper Carter show needs lights and lights need darkness. I'm glad we stuck to our guns (whatever that means). When Bearded Theory, one of the three festivals we did play, posted videos of the 2014 main stages online, the video thumbnails of all the other acts looked fairly conventional: musicians, amps, drum kits and so on. The thumbnail for the Carter video was just a rectangle of white light. I like that.

In the summer of 2011 Carter played two festivals. Beautiful Days in Devon and Eden Fest, a small boutique festival in Mister Spoons's back garden in Beckenham. Eden Fest takes place every August with a lot of fallow years off to allow the lawn to recover and because a couple of bits of the decking were coming loose next to the garden shed. Mister Spoons's neighbours (Mister Forks directly to the left and next to him, Mister Knives) must have wondered what was going on when they looked out of their windows and saw twenty bare-chested and beer-bellied Crystal Palace fans, dancing to 'Sheriff Fatman'. There's a frightening video of that moment online, that I suggest you don't look for. Imagine a reunion of the cast of the 1963 *Lord of the Flies* movie, with all the actors now in their fifties or sixties, re-enacting the scene where the boys steal Piggy's glasses before pushing a boulder off a cliff and killing him. That was Eden Fest 2011.

A week later we headlined Saturday night at Beautiful Days, a festival set up and managed by The Levellers. In the afternoon of the day we were due to play, we were hanging around backstage when I saw Mark from The Levellers. I thought I should go over and say hello. Ordinarily I would have been so wary of not being recognised that I would never have risked it. But with the context of us both being backstage at a festival Mark ran and I was headlining, I was more confident than usual he would recognise me. I waited for my moment. There were a lot of people keen to speak to Mark. A queue had formed. I patiently waited my turn and when I saw a gap I made my move. Hello Mark, I said and you can probably guess the rest.

Do you remember when I said that Jon Beast was a nice place to visit but I wouldn't want to live there and that we'd parted ways in the nineteen nineties because of a clash of egos? I'm afraid history would repeat itself at Beautiful Days and it would be our last show with Jon.

There was no announcement about it – and I've just realised the irony of that. At our next gig at Manchester Academy, we came onstage to 'Two Little Boys' by Rolf Harris.[58] Every year a few people on Facebook would ask if Jon would be at the latest shows and both us and Jon avoided answering. I think people presumed he was ill. Jon was always saying he was ill. I suppose that's why we didn't take much notice when he really was. We didn't see each other after Beautiful Days and then three years later Jon passed away. We set up an online fund to pay for his funeral and very quickly it raised £6,000. There were donations from Jon's friends and from fans and musicians who he'd worked with.

I was interviewed by a newspaper just after Jon died. I talked about him affectionately for fifteen minutes. I told the paper how loved he was and about all the times he'd made me laugh and how he'd almost got us shot in Croatia and about how his amazing light shows had changed Carter forever. How I used to watch him from the stage and it looked like he was 'playing' the lighting desk, really getting into it, throwing his hands up and punching the air when he timed a cue perfectly. I talked about how Jon first started touring with us and how he wasn't actually invited but just turned up at the start of the tour and didn't leave. Apart from doing our lights and introducing us he also sold the shirts on that tour. He bought a load of toilet rolls and wrote CARTER USM on them and sold those too. I mentioned the long conversations I'd had with Jon late into the night on tour buses and about our shared love of books and films, and how, although he was never technically part of the band, he was very much part of the legend.

After a quarter of an hour of me eulogising and praising Jon, I realised I was making him out to be too perfect. He wasn't a saint, even though he did support Southampton.[59] For a bit of balance I added that Jon could also be a massive pain in the arse. That was how the newspaper opened their interview with me. They put that sentence first for anyone who didn't read any further, those were my very first thoughts on the death of my friend. Possibly my only thoughts: 'Mr Morrison referred to Jon as a "massive pain in the arse."'

---

58 Rolf Harris, *Jim'll Fix It*. Bloody hell. Maybe the authorities should use my choice of intro music as some sort of *Minority Report* prediction app.

59 The book's second football footnote. The nickname of Southampton FC is the Saints.

STAVROS FLATLEY FROM BRITAIN'S GOT TALENT

A week after Beautiful Days I played another festival. This time solo. I was on before Miles Hunt and Erica Nockalls from The Wonder Stuff, on the second stage. Collaboration festival had a capacity of about five thousand but when we arrived in the afternoon the site looked deserted. We thought it must have just opened or perhaps there'd been a bomb scare or something was on television. There were a lot of fed up looking stallholders there, almost one per customer. I imagine they were expecting a few more people. Everything was there for the audience. Where were they? A hog had been even more needlessly slaughtered than usual and those people who sell kangaroo burgers had murdered Skippy in vain. Everything you'd expect at a modern music festival was there. Plenty of bars and food stalls, a fun fair and a kids area, a bouncy castle, clean toilets and Stavros Flatley from *Britain's Got Talent* on the main stage. They turned out to be the biggest draw of the day. It was the one time anyone really left the camping area and entered the arena. Apart from when Toploader came on and we left.[60]

Here's the bounced cheque:

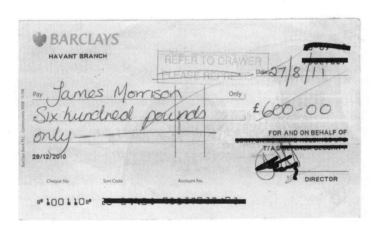

---

60   Those two events are not necessarily connected.

PREVIOUSLY, ON JIM BOB FROM CARTER

Following the break-up of his band Carter The Unstoppable Sex Machine, Jim Bob has written, recorded and released a number of records under different names. He has toured the UK and Europe, either on his own or with his disco-pop-punk group Jim's Super Stereoworld. Jim has been to Hollywood, where he thought he was going to be a movie screenwriter, and to Edinburgh, where he hoped to become the next Michael Crawford (Ooh Betty). Jim Bob (AKA Jim, James Robert Morrison, J.R., J.B. Morrison) has written two songs for a pantomime – oh no he hasn't![61] – and had two novels published, which may be why he's started referring to himself in the third person. In 2007, ten years after their break up, Carter The Unstoppable Sex Machine got back together. So far they've played twelve gigs.

It is now 2012. Jim has just finished a solo tour of the UK, where he played songs from his solo records, his Carter back catalogue and also reading (out loud) from his second novel *Driving Jarvis Ham* (with varying degrees of success – Exeter, Glasgow, Brighton etc – and the opposite of success – Carlisle, where anyone who wasn't at home watching the UEFA Champions League Final, had arrived at the gig drunk. Perhaps disappointed by the promise of the misleadingly disproportionate size of the Carter logo in relation to the words 'Jim' and 'Bob' on the poster stuck to the door of the venue, every time Jim tried to read to them, they do their best to put him off by fat shaming Jim and questioning the marital status of his parents. And then they stole all the books and CDs from the merch stall).

Summer of 2012. The London Olympics are about to start. Jim is at home waiting for the Opening ceremony, worrying about ticket sales for that year's Carter gigs. Although sales are going well enough, there is less of the urgency that there was in 2007 or the panic buying of 2008. Even though the gigs are almost sold out, Jim can't help focusing on that word: 'almost'. He is concerned that the inevitability of there being more Carter gigs has led to audience complacency. He tries to convey this with an analogy: Carter gigs are like London Underground trains. There's no need to rush to catch them. There'll be another one along in a minute.

With his thoughts of impending failure keeping him awake at night or haunting him in his sleep, with ever worsening gig dreams, Jim goes

---

61   Oh yes he has.

in search of ways to make any future Carter live shows different or better than the last. Like the Olympics opening ceremony, with its thirty-two Mary Poppinses and the Queen jumping out of a helicopter, and not like the closing ceremony, a video of Boris Johnson not being able to do his jacket up properly. One Sunday afternoon, Jim attends a TED talk on the topic of heritage acts and how to maintain their popularity and longevity.

THE REFORMED ACT. RULE OF FIVE – A TED Talk by Colin G Larmton

Slide #1
YEAR ONE. The audience never thought they'd get the chance to see the band live again. Tickets fly out of the door.

Slide #2
YEAR TWO. The first year's shows were so amazing that everyone who went wants to go again. Those who missed out meanwhile, don't want to miss out twice. Tickets don't even wait for the door to open. They just fly straight through it.

Slide #3
YEAR THREE. Year two's shows were still great and well worth going a third time but there is less urgency to buy tickets. The novelty has worn off slightly and beenreplaced by a feeling that this might be a regular occurrence. There's a sense that there might be further opportunities to go again. Although tickets do sell out, more advertising is needed. Ironically, this increased marketing leads to a higher profile for the band. The previous years' gigs had sold out so quickly that anyone without tickets didn't notice the band had reformed in the first place.

Slide #4
YEAR FOUR. Again, the shows still sell out but nowhere near as fast as year one, two or even the more sluggish year three. Even more advertising will be needed. Perhaps a special guest, almost as big as the main act will be added to the bill, towards the end of the campaign to shift those final stubborn couple of hundred tickets.

Slide #5
YEAR FIVE. Unless the band have taken at least one year off in the first five years, to avoid 'excitement fatigue', they will now be 30% less popular than they were in year one.

Slide #6. A picture of Chris Tarrant.
There are a few *Who Wants to be a Millionaire* style lifelines that

may prolong the phenomenal success of year one and thus delay the potential disappointment of year five. If any of the gig years coincide with significant anniversaries for instance, it's worth mentioning. Anniversaries traditionally happen every five or ten years but bands may choose to adopt a more punk rock duodecimal system and play their anniversary shows every six or twelve years. A prime numbered anniversary system, with gigs celebrating events every second, third, fifth, seventh, eleventh, nineteenth, twenty-third year and so is not advised.

Greatest Hits shows or special nights where albums are played in their entirety can keep the band and audience interested. The second option is a popular idea, invented in 2005 by Jim Bob from Carter, during his three nights at the Water Rats in England. If the band in question's records are 'all killer no filler' however, this may lead to them performing exactly the same songs, merely in a different order.Unfortunately, without a time machine, it's not possible to go back and make the albums not quite so brilliant. Hopefully everyone will be too drunk to notice.

Thank you.

APPLAUSE

ARTISTS OR ENTERTAINERS?

Colin G Larmton is an anagram of Marc Ollington and there was no TED Talk. I based it on an email from Marc about why an all day indie gig I was appearing at, wasn't selling as well in its third year as it had in its first. Marc used the five years of Carter reunion shows to illustrate his theory:

Year One – Big
Year Two – Bigger. Because the year before was ace and those who missed out want in
Year Three – Back to big, because it's still great but fatigue is setting in for some
Year Four – The decline starts
Year Five – If you haven't taken a break then you are now 30% less popular than year one

I should say that Marc has a lot of theories and I don't know how accurately or fact-based his 30% figure is. But it was certainly true that by our fifth year of playing reunion shows, the gigs were taking longer to sell out. When we had our first meeting after those 2012 shows and had to decide whether or not to play more shows, either in 2013, or perhaps ever again, we were less certain about what our decision should be than we'd ever been before. Usually, we'd meet up not long after the November gigs. Our ears would still be ringing and the memory of the gigs would be fresh in our minds and hearts. It was like going food shopping when you're hungry and ending up with a trolley full of crisps and doughnuts. Of course we were going to do more gigs.

Years ago, we used to say in interviews that as soon as Carter stopped being fun we would split the band up. But it did stop being fun and yet we carried on. I don't know if we didn't have the nerve to stop or we lacked the benefit of hindsight, or maybe we still thought it was worth soldiering on a bit longer. Perhaps we just forgot our promise to quit when we weren't enjoying it.

Lack of enjoyment wasn't an issue with the reformed version of the band. The gigs had been some of the best ever. And I mean *ever* ever. Not just in the five years since we'd reformed. I enjoyed every single one of those gigs. Regardless of how long it took to sell the tickets and how anxious it made me feel. Any last minute nerves, tedious admin and disagreements about set lists were instantly forgotten as soon as we stepped onstage. I know all bands say they have the best audience in the world. The difference with Carter though, is that it's true. Of course we wanted to carry on. We just needed to shake things up a little.

We looked for other *Who Wants to be a Millionaire* style lifelines that weren't included in Colin G Larmton's TED Talk – I've just remembered there was no TED Talk and Colin G Larmton doesn't exist. We'd already played our first four albums in their entirety (and in the right order) and in 2012 we'd gone back to basics in Leeds and Brixton with our 'All The Hits & Classics' shows. We talked about playing the other four albums in their entirety, joking that we might have to do it at the Brixton Windmill rather than the Academy. A B-sides show was mentioned and a gig where we performed all of our cover versions was suggested. We even seriously considered putting on a Carter weekend at a holiday camp. We were going to call it 'All Yesterday's Parties'. But the logistics involved in such an event were frightening and we sensibly shelved the idea. The Shiiine Weekender in Minehead is quite similar to what we had in mind. I can only imagine how hard that must be to organise. I played the Shiiine Weekender in 2017 and Fruitbat will have done it with Abdoujaparov by the time this book is published. For the sake of the story, I hope nothing too anecdotal happened while he was there.

One other logical way to extend the life of a reformed band is to release new material. Fruitbat wanted us to do that after the first two years of gigs. I think he was worried we would be seen as the entertainment at everyone's annual office Christmas party. Judging by comments on social media there did seem to be a demand for new Carter songs. It actually annoyed me a bit when I was told I really needed to write something about the state of the world. Because I felt that was exactly what I had been doing, with albums like *Angelstrike!* and *A Humpty Dumpty Thing*. It was the same voice singing the words, written by the same person after all. Fruitbat was even playing guitar on some of the tracks. All that was missing was the name over the door.

And what if there wasn't really a demand for new Carter material? Three people having a passionate conversation on Facebook can seem like a thousand. What if we released a new album and nobody bought it or actually wanted to hear any of the songs? What if we then played them live and everyone went to the toilet? Why can't we just carry on playing the hits? I asked Les. I love playing the hits.

As an experiment, Les emailed me a couple of instrumental pieces of music. It was one of the ways we used to write songs. Les would give me cassette tapes with a few tunes on. Usually consisting of a drum machine, a bass line and a synth melody and I'd write some lyrics. Nine times out of ten I'd mistake Les's intended choruses for the verses and his verse for choruses. Maybe the magic lay in that misinterpretation.

I sat at home with Les's latest instrumentals. I la la'd and ba ba ba'd along, waiting for inspiration to strike. I didn't know what songs on a new Carter record should even be about. There wasn't a lot left for us to fix. We'd already ended war and racism the first time around, and there was no more inner city violence because of 'Midnight on the Murder Mile' and 'The Taking of Peckham 123'. The far right were a thing of the past because we wrote 'The Music That Nobody Likes', and when was the last time you heard of a dodgy landlord? What, in the idyllic utopia of 2009, was left for a band like Carter to sing about? I remembered the promise I'd made to myself that I wouldn't write any songs unless I had something to write about. Was it worth getting myself mugged again for the sake of a new Carter album?

I couldn't even use puns anymore. Social media had ruined that for me. If Twitter had been around in 1989, titles like 'Twenty Four Minutes From Tulse Hill' or 'The Taking of Peckham 123' would have already been tweeted and retweeted hundreds of times. I'm sure I can't have been the first person to come up with 'The Only Living Boy in New Cross'. It's just that in 1992, the only way to share your wordplay was to form an electro punk pop band and get a record deal.

And it wasn't just the lyrics that were an issue with any new Carter material. What would a twentieth century band like Carter The Unstoppable Sex Machine sound like in 2009? I didn't want us to sound like a Carter tribute act. I tried but I couldn't seem to write anything to Fruitbat's tunes.

To be honest I suspect he may have been holding back his best stuff for his own records. I know I would have done the same. It's one of the reasons I've written so few songs since I started writing books. If I think of a good line or idea, I'd rather use it in a novel than in a song. I used to be able to do both but I can't seem to multitask anymore. That's why I haven't written a new song since 2013. I wish I was still artistically ambidextrous but my creative plumbing only flows in one direction at a time these days. I can't have a shower when someone's doing the washing up. All I can do is make these lame analogies.

We took another year off in 2013. We'd return to the subject of whether or not to play more Carter gigs at the end of the year. I concentrated on editing my first novel as J.B. Morrison and recorded an album with an orchestra. At some point I accidentally became a semi-regular guest on a Saturday night political talk show on LBC, currently home to shock jock Nigel Farage. DJ Nigel wasn't at LBC when I was a guest. I don't know how I would have dealt with it if I came into close proximity with him. What if somebody introduced us?

More recently I was on Iain Lee's show on talk RADIO.[64] When I arrived at the radio station, the show before Iain's was almost over. When we went into the studio, Iain Lee introduced me to the previous show's presenter. I think I shook his hand. Iain told him I was in a band called Carter The Unstoppable Sex Machine and the other presenter said he wasn't aware of our work but he would definitely look us up. I wonder if he did. Maybe he went home and searched for us on Spotify and listened to 'Sheriff Fatman' or 'The Only Living Boy in New Cross'. Perhaps he liked what he heard and before he knew it, he'd stayed up all night, working his way through the entire Carter back catalogue.

And then, still wanting more, he listened to my solo albums too and then downloaded my 'Frank Derrick' novels from Amazon. He very quickly became my biggest fan, seeking out everything I'd ever created. He read *Goodnight Jim Bob* in one breathless sitting and when he heard there was to be a sequel, he could barely wait to read it. When it was published he rushed out and bought a copy. He read the new book, laughing out loud on public transport and not caring whether anyone saw him. He was almost at the end of the book and already feeling sad that it would all soon be over. He wanted it to go on forever. He started reading this chapter and the paragraph you're reading now. And he got to the sentence that ends with me, his favourite artist of all time, saying that when we'd been introduced at talk RADIO, I wish I'd told George Galloway that I really didn't like him. How that would make George Galloway feel is how I felt when Thom Yorke blanked me in Paris and when Mari Wilson gave me a bad review on 6 Music.

When I was discussing the news and current affairs on LBC, it was a bit like the time in the green room at Bloomsbury Theatre with Professors Cox and Dawkins. I was never the smartest person in the room. The other guest would usually be a respected political editor or commentator and I'd do my best to not sound too out of my depth. I'd watch the news before leaving my house and think about what I might say, so as not to sound like a halfwit. I didn't even agree with some of the things I said. Peter Tatchell was on with me one night and I hardly said anything. I agreed with everything he was saying and there didn't seem much point me adding to it. I was saying so little that Peter Tatchell had to ask me for my opinion. I think he felt guilty for monopolising the show. It reminded

---

64 It was Iain Lee who was instrumental in the publishing of this book actually. Before I went on his show he read and enjoyed *Goodnight Jim Bob*, and when he learned it was no longer available he hassled Cherry Red to reprint. At the time I was thinking about self-publishing a sequel (this sequel) and Cherry Red offered to print both books.

me of the time Keith Allen's son told his dad off for not letting me get a word in on *Never Mind the Buzzcocks*.[65]

More than hating being so out of my depth, I really didn't like leaving my house so late on a Saturday night, to get the tube to Leicester Square and back to talk to taxi drivers. One night while I was waiting to go into LBC, I looked through the window of Classic FM, which was in the same building, and saw Alex James from Blur presenting his weekly show.

I reviewed the newspapers on Sky News once. It was incredibly early in the morning. They sent a car for me at five am and I was supposed to read the huge pile of newspapers on the back seat on the way to the television studio. If I read in cars I get carsick, so I waited until I was in the green room and quickly read the pile of papers there. I probably wasn't as prepared as I could have been. I remember someone on Twitter afterwards being incredulous that a singer from an indie band should be reviewing the newspapers on a serious television channel. Three years later, the same person could have tuned into LBC and heard me mumbling incoherently about news and current affairs. Furious, they switched to Classic FM, only to find the bass player from Blur introducing Beethoven's *Symphony No. 5*. They must have thought it was the end of days.

I've been on Sky News twice. In 2010 I was asked to give my opinion on 'Whether the current political climate would give birth to a new wave of artistic protest.' I had a stinking cold at the time and I didn't really care whether the current political climate would give birth to a new wave of artistic protest or not. Laurie Penny was the other guest and when I was introduced, they played a bit of the 'Glam Rock Cops' video. She laughed, as though it was a comedy video. It wasn't even the bit where Les was 'driving' the car.

By the way, I was promised a fee for both my Sky News appearances and I didn't receive either of them. I've had to take my payment from Rupert Murdoch in National Geographic tents and tote bags and by stealing copies of *The Sun* and *The Times* and throwing them in a river.

In the summer of 2013 I stood on a table in a fish restaurant and read from *Driving Jarvis Ham* and *Goodnight Jim Bob*. I was interviewed about my novels on stage in a theatre in Folkestone to an audience of about twelve people. May have been fourteen. Fruitbat was there. I was paid in English wine and locally produced chocolates. I played one full-length gig in November. At Bush Hall in Shepherd's Bush, where I was backed by the Mystery Fax Machine Orchestra. We played *What I Think*

---

65 Of course, I wasn't really reminded of the time I was on *Never Mind the Buzzcocks*. This is just a plot device to help the flow of the story. Which I've now ruined with this footnote.

About When I Think About You in its entirety. And then it was time to make a decision. Should we play more Carter gigs or not? We couldn't take yet another year off and I for one didn't want the indecision and uncertainty hanging over everything else I did. So, not wanting to remain in limbo like a boyband on a bullshit hiatus we had to make a decision. It was time, in the immortal words of the Queen Mother, to shit or get off the pot. I think we decided just before Christmas.

■THE UNSTOPPABLE SEX MACHINE■

Carter The Unstoppable Sex Machine play their last ever show at Brixton Academy on November 22nd 2014
Tickets on sale 9am 20th February 2014
From www.gigsandtours.com

'All good things must come to an end' – Geoffrey Chaucer

These bittersweet announcements are always difficult.
Let's start with a quote. Let's blame it on Chaucer, old Geoffrey C with his silly glass half full all good things being destined to end theory.

Here goes.

On November 22nd this year at Brixton Academy a very good thing will sadly come to an end when we play our final ever Carter the Unstoppable Sex Machine live show. I say 'sadly' but the sad element will come afterwards. On the 22nd we're going to have a big party. We're going to celebrate all the fantastic Carter shows that have taken place since we got back together in 2007. Those first two 'one off' shows in 2007 that completely blew us away and made us desperate to do more. The Drum Machine Years gigs where we played the first four albums from start to finish, even 'Evil', which I completely fucked up. There was the incredible Beautiful Days festival, the Glasgow King Tuts benefit show, all of them, all of the reunion gigs have been amazing. I'm sure other bands say it but we genuinely have got the best audience in the world.

That's you that is. It wouldn't just not be the same without you it would be rubbish. Join us for one last time this November. Come and meet old friends, make new ones, dance yourself lame and sing yourself hoarse. Let's go out on a high that makes Richard Branson's Virgin Galactic project seem subterranean by comparison. Have a bloody good laugh, shed a tear, raise a glass or two and let's see if we can break the venue's bar record one more time before we go.

Jim Bob x

www.carterusm.co.uk

GOING NUCLEAR

On 12th February 2014 we posted a video on Facebook, of a tumbleweed, rolling down a deserted dirt road and the date '23rd November'. It confused a few people. It was supposed to represent the emptiness of the future after Carter The Unstoppable Sex Machine had gone. The intro music of 'The Final Comedown' played over the video. Two days later, on Steve Lamacq's show on 6 Music, I made things a bit clearer and announced our last ever gig would be at Brixton Academy on 22nd November 2014 (my birthday again). I told Steve we wanted to 'stop while it's really good – like *Fawlty Towers*.'

We called the gig 'The Last Tango in Brixton'. Tickets went on sale at 9 am on 21st February and half a second later they were all gone. We looked into adding a second date but the Academy was fully booked and so we added a show at Shepherd's Bush Empire on the day before, when I'd be a whole year younger. It sold out before we had a chance to properly announce it.

In previous years we'd talked about 'The Nuclear Option'. I don't know how serious we were but we used to say that if ticket sales were ever so bad that we were going to have to close the balcony, move to a smaller venue, or even cancel the gig, we would go nuclear. We'd announce that it was our last ever show. We couldn't think of a better advert for a product than to remove it from sale. We knew however, that we could only use the nuclear option once. I'm sure Dennis wasn't alone in thinking we'd been announcing a series of farewell performances and hypocritical comeback gigs, every year since 2007. Why should this latest one be any different? But honestly Dennis, we hadn't claimed any of the gigs between 2007 and 2014 were our last. That was Jon Beast. If we ever went nuclear, we knew there could be no going back. No tongue-in-cheek 'never say never again' nonsense. We renamed our last two shows *The Final Comedown*. A victory worth sharing.

We had one last lighting meeting at St Pancras station – I was going to miss Paul and his patisseries – and rehearsals started not long after that. We now had a third gig, at Bearded Theory in May. The festival had been trying to book us for a few years and in 2014 they sent us such a nice detailed proposal about why we should play, it seemed rude not to accept.

On June 5th *The Extra Ordinary Life of Frank Derrick* was published. There was a launch party at my favourite bookshop, the Bookseller Crow in Crystal Palace and on June 7th I made my third *Literary Death Match* appearance, this time as part of Stoke Newington Literary Festival. I made it through to the final but lost to Jessie Burton in a game of literary charades. Jessie's novel *The Miniaturist* went on to win *Waterstone's Book of the Year*. If I'd been better at charades my novel would have been book of the year. I think that's how it works. I went to a pub afterwards. Stewart Lee was there. I'd met him a couple of times before but if he didn't recognise me, I wasn't going to put myself through the humiliation of reintroducing myself. He didn't recognise me.

On 26th June I was back at the Bookseller Crow, reading from *Frank Derrick* as part of the Crystal Palace Overground festival and in July I struggled to be heard above the sound of Dutch techno, Billy Bragg and whatever was going on inside the 'Noisy Toys' tent at Latitude festival. I had to wait until August and a small tent at Wilderness festival, before I would stop feeling ashamed with myself for letting a few 'difficulties' so easily defeat me.

On July 27th Jon Beast died. The gigs in November immediately took on a whole new meaning and significance. They would now also be a memorial to Beast. We didn't know exactly how we'd pay tribute to him until a week before the first show.

In September me and Fruitbat were back at Antenna rehearsing, this time for our final comedown but also for a fourth gig, to be broadcast live on the Steve Lamacq show on 6 Music. The gig would be recorded at the BBC's Maida Vale Studios, less than half a mile away from where Fruitbat once lived. We'd gone back there in 1990, after the NME party where I'd tried to decapitate Fruitbat with my guitar. I'd later smashed that 12-string acoustic in the street outside his house.

I met Damon Albarn from Blur for the first time at a party at Les's in Maida Vale. He was still Damon from Seymour at the time. He was very drunk and he told me how hugely famous his band were going to be. When I was interviewed for the pop pages of either *The Sun* or *The Daily Mirror*, I made the same mistake I'd repeat years later when being interviewed about Jon Beast. I finished my lengthy praise for Damon Albarn and for Blur by adding that I knew Damon when he was a drunken idiot. That was the headline: 'Jim Bob from Carter says Damon from Blur is a drunken idiot', or words to that effect. If anything, it was Damon from Seymour who was the drunken idiot.

Maida Vale Studios is currently on the historic buildings death list. There's a campaign and a petition to save the building and its eighty-four years of musical history from being knocked down or turned into apartments or a posh hotel, like The Astoria and the Harlow Square and the Bull and Gate and so many other iconic venues. If and when the Maida Vale Studios do close, we can at least be proud that sixty minutes of those eighty-four historic years belonged to Carter and the two hundred people in the audience who'd registered to be included in a draw for tickets. There were apparently more ticket applications for us than for any other previous band or event at Maida Vale Studios.

I didn't know how many people were listening at home, or in their cars, the shower or wherever. At least a billion I reckon. When Carter broke up in 1997 it hadn't been big news. When we played our final show at GuilFest, two thirds of the band didn't even know it was our last gig. I'm not sure our audience even minded there wouldn't be any more gigs. I don't think a helpline had to be set up for distraught Carter fans in 1997. In 2014 our break up was far more public.

Tom Hingley sang 'This is How it Feels' with us at Maida Vale. He did at a couple of gigs too. Marc Ollington wanted to try and get the singers from every Carter cover version to join us onstage at our final Brixton Academy show. Imagine if we could have pulled that off. Pete Shelley from the Buzzcocks, Marc Almond from Soft Cell, Neil Tennant from The Pet Shop Boys, Billy Idol from Generation X, Paul Weller from The Jam, Micky Dolenz from The Monkees, David Essex, Elvis Costello, Björk… If we had been cheeky enough to ask and one by one they said no, my self-esteem would never have survived such a kicking.

Leading up to the Maida Vale gig, I'd been really worried about performing without a light show. What if everyone saw us onstage, in the altogether, just me and Les with no lighting other than a 6 Music logo in a small box behind us, and they realised Carter The Unstoppable Sex Machine had been an optical illusion? Imagine being exposed as frauds so close to the end? Just as we'd almost got away with it. My fears weren't realised of course. I always forget about the songs. The songs are actually pretty good. Even without lighting. It's easy to forget that. When I'm asked in interviews why I think Carter became so big the first time round, as though it must have been an accident or some flukish piece of luck, I used to either say that I had no idea or that it was just a timing thing. I'd say we were what people happened to be looking for at that moment in time. Recently though, I've realised it's simpler than that. We were good. That's why we were so successful. Nothing more mysterious than that. Carter were a good band with good songs. We released the Maida Vale session as the album, *Hello, Good Evening, Welcome, and Goodbye,* I wrote this in the sleeve notes:

> Steve had spoken to me a few times about a Maida Vale session
> to coincide with one of our almost annual reunion shows and
> it was great to finally get the chance to do it. I think everyone
> (me definitely) was surprised by the huge demand for tickets. It
> was apparently the largest ever for a 6Music Maida Vale show,
> which hopefully isn't something that they tell every band. It was

nice to end on a bigger bang than we had the first time around. Steve Lamacq helped make this happen. Steve is great. It was a risk I'm sure. I was expecting the audience to start chanting 'You fat bastard' as soon as the red light was switched on. But everyone politely waited until it was announced that we were off air before effing and jeffing and you fat bastarding like nobody's business and I was sort of proud that we'd all grown up a little. Like some sort of up-himself actor type I'm frightened of my own performances and so have never listened to this recording. I am reliably informed that it is superb. I really hope you enjoy it.

PS: Whenever Steve Lamacq plays a Carter song on the radio, three or four people on Twitter get disproportionately upset about it. I can only imagine what a whole uninterrupted hour of Carter must have done to them. Hashtag schadenfreude

Those three or four disgruntled people on Twitter must have wondered what the hell was going on that week. Two days after the Maida Vale gig we got to choose two hours of Carter related music on the Tom Robinson show. It must have seemed like we'd taken over the radio station.

Earlier in the afternoon, before going into 6 Music, I went to the nearby Phoenix pub to catch some of *All Day Edinburgh*, a whole day of stand up comedy, organised by my musical theatre lover Michael Legge and featuring a ton of acts from that year's Edinburgh Fringe. In 2010, I sang a couple of songs at *All Day Edinburgh*. It was the day after my surprise fünftieth birthday and I'd never felt so hungover or sick. After I played, Paul Sinha had commented on social media that he'd just seen a bloke do a great version of Carter's 'The Only Living Boy in New Cross'. I really need to get myself a name badge.

In 2014, I was standing at the bar in the Phoenix pub. Nick Helm was onstage and I was reminiscing with myself about the time he'd called Marc Ollington a cunt for saying *Micky Blue Eyes* was his all time favourite film, when Al Murray came over to get a drink. He was close enough for me to tap him on the shoulder and say hello. I'd met Al more than once before and surely he'd know who I was.[66] The moment passed of course and Al was on stage before I managed to say anything.

An hour or so later, at 6 Music, I had planned to tell Tom Robinson how me and Derek Chin – Mister X from the imaginary – and therefore the best – version of The Ballpoints, used to go to a lot of Tom Robinson Band gigs when we were teenagers. They were the best ever gigs for crowd sing-alongs. I still know all the words to 'Glad to be Gay' and 'Martin'. I didn't tell Tom Robinson any of that. I also neglected to tell him how proud I'd felt when he once read out the lyrics from my song

66 I think I'd be letting everyone down if I didn't say that I almost didn't recognise Al Murray. What with him being on the wrong side of the bar and all.

'Mrs Fucking MacMurphy' on the radio and described them as "immortal poetry".

Among the songs me and Les chose to play on Tom's show were 'Panic' (The Smiths), 'Goodbye Ruby Tuesday' (The Rolling Stones) and 'The Only Living Boy in New York' by Simon & Garfunkel. We played records by Pop Will Eat Itself and EMF, Senseless Things, The Family Cat and the Sultans of Ping. We played some of the music that had influenced the band: LL Cool J and Ian Dury and the Blockheads and Gilbert O'Sullivan, just like we had twenty-four years earlier when we were last allowed to choose the records for an alternative music radio station. We played 'Don't Dictate' by Penetration, who we'd toured with in the early days and 'Anyone Can Play Guitar' by Radiohead, even though Thom Yorke once blanked me. There used to be a rumour that, because 'Anyone Can Play Guitar' had the same chords as 'Do Re Me, So Far So Good' and because it mentions Jim Morrison, it must be about Carter.

We played 'Sufragette City' on Tom Robinson's show. A few years after we sampled a bit of the song on 'Surfin' USM', somebody who worked for David Bowie's accountant heard it and then found out we'd also sampled 'This ain't rock 'n' roll' on 'A Perfect Day to Drop the Bomb'. They grassed us up and we were on the brink of another legal copyright battle, when David Bowie intervened and stopped it. I was probably quite nonchalant about that at the time, but now the thought of David Bowie even knowing who we were, let alone being so decent to us, is up there with Mick Jagger calling me a dude that time. Also, I really wouldn't have minded having Bowie/Morrison/Carter on the songwriting credits on our records.

We also played 'Words That Say' by Mega City Four on the Tom Robinson show. If I think about the awful sadness of losing Wiz and how that tragedy would bring Carter back together, I can't properly express my ambiguous mix of emotions.

After two hours on the radio with Tom Robinson, during which listeners tweeted their song recommendations and their messages of good luck for the upcoming final gigs, including one from Phillip Schofield,[67] me and Fruitbat left the building. The same autograph hunters and collectors who'd ignored me when I was with Brett Anderson were waiting outside. When they asked us to sign all their stuff I told them to fuck off. Not really. I signed everything. And gladly. I loved being

---

67 In 2018 somebody posted a video of TV's Holly Willoughby singing along to a video of Carter's version of 'The Impossible Dream' playing on her phone. At the end of the video, whoever is filming Holly Willoughby turns the camera onto the person sitting next to her. Poor old Phillip has a look on his face that suggests it's not the first time he's been teased in this way.

famous again.

Twelve days later, Johnny Cash's 'The Beast in Me' played through the PA at Shepherd's Bush Empire, followed by 'You're the One for me Fatty', as thirteen topless men wearing Jon Beast masks walked onto the stage. Behind the masks were our manager, the show's promoter, Les's brother Bam Bam, Daz and Mad Dog from the original Crazy Carter Crew, members of The Frank & Walters and the Sultans of Ping and Mister Spoons and a couple of his friends. They each had a large letter written on their chests and when they stood in a line onstage, together they spelled out 'YOU FAT BASTARD'. And then the voice of Jon Beast, the ghost of our Christmases past, filled the room with his 1991 introduction from the *In Bed With Carter* live video. (I've omitted the line about people from Wales but for anyone who remembers it and is offended, I should point out that Jon was at least partially from Wales).

> Good evening Shepherd's Bush
> I thought you'd be a bit fucking louder than this
> You fat what?
> Oh it's so lovely to have so many friends here tonight
> Well, if you don't want to sex it up I do
> I think it's come to that time
> Time to sex it up a little bit
> Please put your hands together
> For the best kick-arse rock 'n' roll band in the whole goddam world...
> Carter The Unstoppable Sex Machine!

At the end of 'G.I. Blues' in Brixton the next night, I didn't want to leave the stage. I couldn't think of a better place to be or a nicer bunch of people to be there with. The five thousand or so in the audience and the fifty or so that it took to get two men and their tape machine onto the stage. And that's not including all the security and bar staff. We (you) broke the bar record at Brixton again. It would remain ours for four years, until April 2018 when The Streets played.

I knew I'd probably feel confused by it all in the morning. Not knowing what to do with myself. The tumbleweed in that video was me. The comedown would surely be huge this time. I wanted to stay on the stage for just a bit longer. I needed to bask in the heat of the moment before it was gone forever. It had all been quite successful really. Our second go at being Carter. And it could just have easily been a disaster. What if we'd built it and they *didn't* come? What if we'd sent out the email in 2008, asking people if they wanted us to do more gigs and everyone had said no? As I often say at the end of a particularly successful gig, "I think we got away with it." Two days after leaving the stage at Brixton

Academy, while I was still – to paraphrase my old friend Bono – stuck in the moment I didn't want to get out of, I tried putting my thoughts into words.

It's Monday now. The ringing in my ears might be permanent. I feel a bit weird. There's a guitar strap burn mark on my neck. If I close my eyes I swear I can see strobes. My calves hurt. I think that's more as a result of going up and down the stairs between the dressing rooms and the stage than anything else. I'm expecting the final comedown that we advertised to hit me any minute now. I'll be like Phil Daniels going back to work after the bank holiday bag of pills, the court appearance with Sting and the you know what with Lesley Ash in the alleyway. It's lucky that I'm self-employed or I'd end up telling my boss to stuff the franking machine right up his arse.

There is so much to be proud of from the past 7 or 8 years (I can't count). This year was the same but more. There were the usual bar takings records but also a 'most applications to be in a live audience at Maida Vale' record. The 480 crowd surfers at Brixton. The sold out aftershow party at Jamm. The trending on Twitter. So much love on Facebook. Being in a position to put Mrs Jim Bob in a reserved seat next to Cillian Murphy.

Ordinarily Carter gigs pass relatively unnoticed by the outside world. There isn't the need for any advertising and we don't tend to do any interviews. This time though there were people in the forest when the tree fell (I'm an author, I can say things like that now).

The Maida Vale session and the two hours choosing songs with Tom Robinson, the bit in the Guardian and the Independent. The trending on Twitter. Enough stuff on Facebook to make the cats and the terrorists envious. Even a good luck message from Phillip Schofield. The BBC4 music documentary makers would have had to have been in a 28 Days Later style coma (as portrayed so brilliantly by the gorgeous Cillian Murphy) to have not noticed.

I know it probably seems a bit daft to stop something that is so wonderful and so thrilling and fun and rewarding but it's also great to be able to stop while it still is all of those things. In spite of all the tears – seeing skinhead men crying is incredibly infectious – the weekend was I think, truly joyous. Perhaps happy endings aren't just for fairy tales and massage parlours.

Regrets, I have a few. We never did get Chris Barrie to come onstage dressed as Rimmer to do a live introduction to 'Surfin' USM'. We'd agreed it with him two years in a row but something always prevented it from happening at the last minute and anyway, this year thirteen Jon Beasts seemed a more fitting introduction. And those white Doctor Marten's look a bit like clown shoes in photos. That's it. Not a few regrets, but two. Two regrets.

Me and Les have made a lot of friends as a result of being

in this band. Many of them worked with us and were there this weekend, both backstage and out front, Crazy Carter Crew past and present but always Crazy Carter Crew. Perhaps that's true for the audience too. I honestly couldn't imagine a better audience than the Carter audience. The same life membership status goes for me and Les. Even though it will say on Wikipedia that we're 'former members of Carter', we will still always be Jim Bob and Fruitbat from Carter. We'll just be doing other things.

DOING OTHER THINGS

So that's where I am now. Doing other things. I'm still writing books. This one obviously, but I've also written two more novels, both as yet unpublished, as yet baby, as yet. Both the Frank Derricks did really well. *The Extra Ordinary Life* e-book, in particular was up at the top of the Amazon charts more than once. It was good to see Frank battling it out with Bridget Jones for the top spot.

Text-to-Speech: Enabled ☑

X-Ray: Enabled ☑

Word Wise: Enabled

Enhanced Typesetting: Enabled ☑

Average Customer Review: ★★★★☆ ☑ (474 customer reviews)

Amazon Bestsellers Rank: #5 Paid in Kindle Store (See Top 100 Paid in Kindle Store)

#1 in Books > Fiction > **Humour**

#1 in Kindle Store > Books > **Humour**

#1 in Kindle Store > Books > Literature & Fiction > Humour & Satire > **Literary Humour**

Would you like to **give feedback on images** or **tell us about a lower price?**

More About the Authors
Discover books, learn about writers, and more.

Jim Bob

J.B Morrison

In 2015, I, or rather Frank, won an award. The 'Best Older Person's Character in a Book, Film, TV or Radio Drama', beating Sir Derek Jacobi and Sir Ian McKellen, and yet, still no knighthood for either Frank or for me. Sir Jim Bob from Carter has a nice ring to it too. I'd turn such a vulgar gong down of course. Publicly though. There's no such thing as bad publicity. And it is always nice to be asked. The Frank Derrick novels have been translated into French, Italian, German, Japanese, Turkish, Czech and Dutch. I can't begin to tell you how thrilling that was for me. I loved seeing all the different covers and learning each new language so that I could proof read them all.

Almost two years after the last Carter gig at Brixton, I opened my guitar case again. I wasn't sure my guitar would even be inside and I half-expected a whisper of moths or a single white dove to fly out. At five twenty-five on the afternoon of the 1st October 2016, 'Alone Again (Naturally)' by Gilbert O'Sullivan played, and I walked onstage at Indie Daze, an all-day festival at the Kentish Town Forum. The audience sang along with every word. I felt like they'd been expecting me. Two months later, I went on my most successful-ever solo tour. The majority of the dates sold out in advance and half had to be moved to larger venues – and all without a single Carter logo on the posters.

In March 2018, two thousand people came to see me play a sold-out Shepherd's Bush Empire. My manager Marc Ollington, who loves a statistic, told me I was four hundred people more popular than Carter were in 1997, when we'd struggled to sell 1600 tickets for a gig at the Astoria.

It had taken me twenty-one years but I had bounced back.

I still haven't written a new song since 2013. But now that I've nearly finished writing this, perhaps the songs will come flooding out of me. It's not really up to me though, remember, it's up to my muse.

Dennis *@Snafflebold_Den69 . 1m Muse are shit. Get Carter back together. #Youfatbastard*

Ah Dennis. My nemesis. My Dennisis. I thought I'd be able to escape you in the epilogue. Since you ask though, I think it was about a year after our last ever gig when the offers to re-reform started arriving. Every year there are more. Anniversaries come and go. Opportunities are missed. Twenty years since we formed, ten since we reformed. Twenty-five years since the release of *30 Something*, twenty-five years since our legendary Reading festival appearance. We don't dismiss the offers immediately. We allow ourselves to first imagine what it would be like to play just one more gig, wondering if we could still manage it at our age, without making old fools of ourselves. And then we politely decline. Just thinking about all the administration and the anxiety dreams, all the stress and the worry, and the knowledge that a couple of hours of music can completely dominate the whole year leading up to them and disrupt the one that follows. I have to admit it's tempting.

ACKNOWLEDGEMENTS

Thanks to Jacqueline for putting up with a writer when they're writing and for not killing them, even when they're referring to themselves in the third person in the acknowledgements. Thank you to Holly, to Marc, Neil, Les, Chris and Tim for reading and liking the first draft and realising the importance of telling me that. Thanks to my literary agent Nicola Barr. Thank you Richard Anderson and Adam Velasco and everyone at Cherry Red. Thank you to Paul Heneker for making me look acceptable in photographs. Thanks to Mark Reynolds for the drawings and Nathan Eighty for the book's design. Huge thanks to everyone I've mentioned in this book and all the many others who aren't in it but really should be. There are so many people I've worked with over the years that if I start naming them now I'm bound to forget somebody and that would be awful. All the hand-holders and designated drivers, without whom I'd never have left the house. Ben Lambert, Pete Allinson and Salvatore Alessi, Adrian Boss, Matthew Woolliscroft and Sam Carter spring to mind. As do Phil McDaniel, Ben Murray and Johny Lamb, Richard Crockford, Pip Rhodes and Ramie Coyle. Cathy Nero, everyone who works at the Brixton Academy for instance, and all the other venues I've appeared at in the past ten or whatever years. Thanks to the boy who punched me in the face. I hope you've grown up into a more rounded adult. Perhaps once day you'll find the cure for cancer. Thanks to Andrew Collins, to Steve Lamacq, Michael Legge and Robin Ince. Thank you Isy Suttie. Thanks Danielle Ward and Martin White for taking me so far out of my comfort zone I almost didn't want to come back. Thank you Iain Lee and Katherine Boyle. Thanks Herve for introducing me to Juliette Binoche and the Frank & Walters for bringing Cillian Murphy into the story. Thanks to Scott Pack and Natasha Harding, to Emma Ollington and Derek Fraser. Thank you Cerise and Mark. Thanks Jason Bootle. Thank you Jonathan, Justine and Karen at the Bookseller Crow. Thank you Fuzz Townshend and Tom Robinson. Thanks Dave Gorman and Chris Addison. I must not forget my sister Becca and her amazing kids, Addison, Madeline and Jake. Thank you James Garratt, James Kazeze and Tim Ten Yen. You see, there are just so many people. These are just a few. Crissi, Rifa and Sue Spoons. Everyone in Gutted – the cast and creatives. Thank you to The Mystery Fax Machine Orchestra. Thanks Kevin Downing and Tim McVay, Kate Rizzo and John Facundo, and of course, Dennis. I love you all.

ABOUT THE AUTHOR

This book is about the author.

ENCORES

JIM BOB FROM CARTER LIVE

These are the live dates I have a record of having played since *Goodnight Jim Bob On the Road with Carter the Unstoppable Sex Machine* was published. There will be errors and omissions.

1999

July 26 London Jim's Super Stereoworld debut at Pandamonium, the Bull and Gate, Kentish Town
Aug 29 Reading Festival NME Stage (JSSW)
Aug 30 Leeds Festival NME Stage (JSSW)
Sep 2 Camden Falcon (JSSW)
Oct 21 Camden Barfly 'Camdemonium' (JSSW)
Oct 22 Tunbridge Wells Forum (JSSW) The penny drops that I'm not quite so famous anymore
Oct 23 Bedford Esquires (JSSW) The penny drops again
Oct 24 Colchester Arts Centre (JSSW) And once more
Nov 4 Leicester Charlotte (JSSW)
Nov 5 Glasgow Cathouse (JSSW)
Nov 6 York Fibbers (As Australian JSSW even though we were billed on the blackboard outside as Carter The Unstoppable Sex Machine)
Nov 11 Sheffield Uni (JSSW)
Nov 12 Liverpool Lomax (JSSW)
Nov 13 Bristol Fiddler (JSSW)
Nov 18 Southampton Joiners (JSSW)
Nov 19 Birmingham Fleece and Firkin (JSSW)
Nov 20 Derby Victoria Inn (JSSW) Hid in a cupboard because Man Utd were playing Derby
Nov 22 Norwich Arts Centre (JSSW) My birthday with cigars, champagne, Absinth and a loud hailer
Nov 24 Manchester Roadhouse (JSSW)
Dec 11 Highbury Garage (JSSW)

2000

Feb 18 LA2 (JSSW) with My Life Story
March 31 Feltham Somewhere (JSSW)
April 29 Aldershot West End Centre (JSSW)
July 22 King's Cross Water Rats (JSSW)

Dec 2 King's Cross Water Rats (JSSW) 'Uncle Bob's Wedding
Reception' club
Dec 15 Kentish Town Forum (JSSW) supporting The Wonder Stuff
(Booed by some of the audience)

2001

March 27 Camden Barfly (JSSW) 'World Tour in a Day'
April 14 Played guitar with Abdoujaparov, as we all will eventually
June 7 Southampton Joiners (JSSW)
June 8 Aldershot West End Centre (JSSW)
June 9 Cardiff Barfly (JSSW)
June 14 Charing Cross Road Barfly at 144 (JSSW)
18 Aug DJ at the Who's the Daddy Now? club at Brixton Windmill
Sep 15 Harlow Square WTDN tour (JSSW)
Sep 16 Leeds New Roscoe WTDN tour (JSSW)
Sep 17 Leicester Charlotte WTDN tour (JSSW)
Sep 18 Hull Adelphi WTDN tour (JSSW)
Sep 19 Glasgow Garage WTDN tour (JSSW)
Sep 20 Portsmouth Wedgewood WTDN tour (JSSW)
Sep 21 London Mean Fiddler WTDN tour (JSSW)
Sep 24 Covent Garden the Spot (Solo supporting the Invisibles)
Dec 12 Northampton Roadmender WTDN tour (JSSW)
Dec 13 Glasgow King Tut's WTDN tour (JSSW)
Dec 14 London Astoria WTDN tour (JSSW) (with the Teen City Rockers
on backing vocals)

2002

Jan 14 Camden Jazz Café (acoustic Jim and Les)
Feb 16 Kentish Town Bull and Gate (JSSW)
March 8 Hartlepool (Solo Jim Bob)
March 18 King Tut's (Solo Jim Bob)
March 20 Bedford Balham with Bransby (Solo Jim Bob)
March 21 Sheffield Hallam Uni (JSSW) Special guest was Chris T-T
March 22 Highbury Garage (JSSW)
June 5 Islington Hope and Anchor Goodnight Jim Bob club night 1
(Jim Bob solo)
July 3 Islington Hope and Anchor Goodnight Jim Bob club night 2
(Jim Bob solo)
July 24 Brighton Concorde 2 (JSSW)
July 25 Leeds Joseph's Well (JSSW)
July 27 Harlow Square (JSSW)
Aug 7 Islington Hope and Anchor Goodnight Jim Bob club night 2
(Jim Bob solo)

Aug 3 Betsy Trotwood (JR gig) met Louis Eliot
Oct 23 London Acousticism (Jim Bob solo)
Nov 5 Peterborough WTDN tour (JSSW)
Nov 6 Leicester Charlotte WTDN tour (JSSW)
Nov 7 Harlow Square WTDN tour (JSSW)
Nov 8 Glasgow King Tut's WTDN tour (JSSW)
Nov 9 Dundee WTDN tour (JSSW)
Nov 10 Newcastle Trillions WTDN tour (JSSW)
Nov 11 Liverpool not the Cavern WTDN tour (JSSW)
Nov 12 York Fibbers WTDN tour (JSSW)
Nov 13 Leeds Roscoe WTDN tour (JSSW)
Nov 14 Worcester Marrs Bar WTDN tour (JSSW)
Nov 15 Mean Fiddler WTDN tour (JSSW)
Nov 14 Dec Welwyn Garden City cinema (JSSW)

2003

May 15th Rotterdam (NL) Rotown. (Jim Bob solo) with Louis Eliot
May 16th DenBosch (NL) R2. (Jim Bob solo) with Louis Eliot
May 23rd Edinburgh Bannermans (Jim Bob solo)
May 24th Glasgow Nice 'n' Sleazys (Jim Bob solo)
May 25th Leicester The Shed (Jim Bob solo)
May 26th Worcester Marrs Bar (Jim Bob solo)
May 27th Wigan The Collective Venue @ The Tavern (Jim Bob solo)
May 28th Sheffield Casbah (Jim Bob solo)
May 29th Brentwood White Hart (Jim Bob solo)
May 30th London Borderline. (Jim Bob solo) Special guests: Uncle
Fruity (Fruitbat) and Seymour from Miss Black America
Oct 16th Birmingham Glee Club (Jim Bob solo)
Oct 17th Glasgow 13th Note Café (Jim Bob solo)
Oct 18th Frome St John's Hall (Jim Bob solo)
Oct 19th Winchester Railway (Jim Bob solo)
Oct 22nd Northampton The Soundhaus (Jim Bob solo)
Oct 23rd London Lock 17 (Formerly Dingwalls, now Dingwalls again)
(Jim Bob solo)
Oct 24th Worcester Marrs Bar (Jim Bob solo)
Oct 25th Ivybridge Rugby Club (Jim Bob solo)
Oct 26th Cheltenham Playhouse Theatre (Jim Bob solo)
Oct 28th Manchester Night & Day (Jim Bob solo)
Oct 29th Nottingham Maze (Jim Bob solo)
Oct 30th Sheffield Casbah (Jim Bob solo)

2004

Jan 23 Sung a song at the Kentish Town Bull and Gate as part of Les's

Tommi and Chris musical
May 8 Berlin Magnet (Jim Bob solo)
May 12 Bristol (Jim Bob solo)
May 13 Cambridge Man on the Moon (Jim Bob solo)
May 14 Joiners (Jim Bob solo)
May 15 Reading (Jim Bob solo)
May 16 Hastings (Jim Bob solo)
May 19 Exeter Cavern (Jim Bob solo)
May 20 Leeds Joseph's Well (Jim Bob solo)
May 21 Glasgow 13th Note (Jim Bob solo)
May 22 Aberdeen (Jim Bob solo)
May 25 Liverpool Academy (Jim Bob solo)
May 26 Some other Academy somewhere (Jim Bob solo)
May 27 Islington Academy (Jim Bob solo, with Art Brut and Chris T-T)
Oct 1 Time for Change at the London 'Marquee' (Jim Bob solo)
Oct 23 *Angelstrike!* listening and release party upstairs in a
Battersea pub
Nov 8 *Jamming* airs on BBC Radio 2
Nov 14 Brighton Concorde 2 Strummerville gig (Jim Bob solo)
Nov 23 Sheffield Boardwalk (Jim Bob solo)
Nov 24 Glasgow King Tut's (Jim Bob solo)
Nov 25 Birmingham Glee Club (Jim Bob solo)
Nov 26 Hartlepool Studio (Jim Bob solo)
Nov 30 Cambridge APU SU Bar (Jim Bob solo)
Dec 1 Portsmouth Edge of Wedge (Jim Bob solo)
Dec 2 Bloomsbury Theatre (Jim Bob solo)

2005

Jan 19 Athens (Jim Bob solo)
Feb 20 Brixton Windmill Tsunami benefit with Abdoujaparov (Jim Bob
solo)
April 17 Partnered Andrew Collins on his 6 Music radio show. The
start and end of my radio career
April 23 London Pleasure Unit (Jim Bob solo)
May 4 BBC 6 Music Jim Bob Tom Robinson radio session
May 6 Berlin (Jim Bob solo)
May 9 Ebay gig at Carl's house (Jim Bob solo)
May 10 Bristol Prom (Jim Bob solo)
May 11 Birmingham Academy 3 (Jim Bob solo)
May 12 Leeds Joseph's Well (Jim Bob solo)
May 13 Glasgow 13th Note (Jim Bob solo)
May 17 King's Cross Water Rats (Jim Bob solo)
May 18 King's Cross Water Rats (Jim Bob solo)

May 19 King's Cross Water Rats (Jim Bob solo and JSSW reunion)
June 4 Gracetonbury at Brixton Windmill (Jim Bob solo)
July 3 Walsall (Jim Bob solo)
July 7 POSTPONED Barfly DVD gig (Jim Bob solo)
Sep 14 Rescheduled Barfly DVD GIG (Jim Bob solo)
Oct 8 Berlin (Jim Bob solo)
Oct 14 Bedford the Angel (Jim Bob solo)
Dec 7 Islington Academy Christmas School Concert (Jim Bob solo with full school band)
Dec 16 Brixton Jamm Urban 75 (Jim Bob solo)
Dec 17 Dublin the Village supporting the Sultans. Lost my voice (Jim Bob solo)
Dec 18 Belfast Spring and Airbrake (Jim Bob solo) Even less voice

2006

March 15 Bath Cellar Bar (Jim Bob solo)
March 16 Brighton Komedia (Jim Bob solo)
March 17 Wolves Little Civic (Jim Bob solo)
March 22 Leicester Charlotte (Jim Bob solo)
March 23 Sheffield Boardwalk (Jim Bob solo)
March 24 Hull Adelphi (Jim Bob solo)
March 25 Hastings Brass Monkey (Jim Bob solo)
March 29 Winchester Tower Arts (Jim Bob solo)
March 30 Shepherd's Bush Bush Hall (Jim Bob solo)
April 20 Wimbledon Library (Jim Bob reading and solo)
June 3 Strawberry Fair festival (Jim Bob solo)
June 8 Nottingham Social (Jim Bob solo)
June 17 Brixton Windmill Jim Bob (Jim Bob solo)
June 23 Bolton Festival Dog and Partridge (Jim Bob solo)
July 6 Team Jim Bob dressed up as coppers to appear in the Little Man Tate promo video for 'Boothby's Party'
July 7 Somewhere beginning with B (Jim Bob solo)
Aug 13 Battersea Barge (Jim Bob solo)
Sep 15 Cambridge Man on Moon (Jim Bob solo)
Sep 17 Portsmouth Edge of the Wedge (Jim Bob solo)
Sep 18 Bristol Prom (Jim Bob solo)
Sep 19 Mixing Tin Leeds (Jim Bob solo)
Sep 20 Glasgow 13th Note (Jim Bob solo)
Sep 21 Worcester Marrs Bar (Jim Bob solo)
Sep 22 Number 15 Bolton (Jim Bob solo)
Sep 26 Sheffield Boardwalk (Jim Bob solo)
Sep 27 Birmingham (Jim Bob solo)
Sep 28 Barfly ? (Jim Bob solo)

Sep 29 Barfly? (Jim Bob solo, backed by Subliminal Girls/Abdou supergroup)
Oct 6 Isle of Man (Jim Bob solo)
Oct 7 Isle of Man (Jim Bob solo)
Nov 11 The Lord Mayor's Show
Dec 5 Opening night of Dick Whittington and His Cat.
Dec 22 Little Man Tate Sheffield Team Jim Bob as superstar DJs

2007

Feb 1 Manchester Bierkellar Anti racism gig with Jason Manford (Jim Bob solo)
March 4 4 for Wiz (Carter USM)
April 18 Athens (Jim Bob solo)
May 25 Libraries Aloud Richmond (Jim Bob solo)
June 12 Islington Academy supporting CUD (Jim Bob solo)
June 22 Glastonbury Left Field (Jim Bob solo)
July 22 Yeovil In the Park (Jim Bob solo)
Oct 15 6 Music Live session (Carter USM)
Oct 20 Glasgow Barrowlands (Carter USM)
Nov 1 Transmission Channel 4 Coventry motor museum just sit there and drink and hope someone recognises me
Nov 2 Carter Brixton Academy (Carter USM)
Nov 3 Antenna Studios Crustal Palace (Jim Bob solo)
Nov 27 Bath Cellar Bar (Jim Bob solo)
Nov 28 Truro Cuckoo Bar (Jim Bob solo)
Nov 30 Edinburgh Cabaret Voltaire (Jim Bob solo)
Dec 1 Preston the Adelphi (Jim Bob solo)
Dec 2 York Certificate 18 (Jim Bob solo)
Dec 5 Southend Riga Music bar (Jim Bob solo)
Dec 6 Wolves Little Civic (Jim Bob solo)
Dec 7 Cambridge Man in the Moon (Jim Bob solo)

2008

Feb 6 Portsmouth (Jim Bob solo)
Feb 7 Manchester (Jim Bob solo)
Feb 8 Wolves Little Civic (Jim Bob solo)
April 9 London 100 Club (Jim Bob solo with band)
April 10 London 100 (Jim Bob solo with band)
May 31 Brixton Windmill Gracetonbury (Jim Bob solo)
June 28 Glastonbury Left Field (Jim Bob solo)
Sep 8 London Lexapalooza (Jim Bob solo)
Oct 8 Camden Dingwalls Cherry Red Party (Jim Bob solo)
Nov 17 Southampton Joiners tribute to Mint (Carter USM)

Nov 21 Birmingham Academy (Carter USM)
Nov 22 Brixton Academy (Carter USM)
Dec 4 Cambridge (Solo Jim Bob)
Dec 12 Brixton Windmill Jim Bob (Solo Jim Bob)

2009

Jan 11 Brighton Midwinter Picnic (Solo Jim Bob)
March 13 12 Bar (Solo Jim Bob) supporting Milk Kan
April 14 Portsmouth Cellar Bar (Solo Jim Bob)
April 15 Bristol Thunderbolt (Solo Jim Bob)
April 16 Welwyn Garden City Green Room (Solo Jim Bob)
April 17 Birmingham Victoria (Solo Jim Bob)
April 18 Newbury Arlington Arts Centre (Solo Jim Bob)
April 19 Winchester Railway (Solo Jim Bob)
April 22 Glastonbury Rugby club (Solo Jim Bob)
April 23 Lincoln library Bar (Solo Jim Bob) Supported by Ed Sheeran
April 24 Lancaster Yorkshire House (Solo Jim Bob)
April 25 York Fibbers (Solo Jim Bob)
April 26 Coatbridge Georgian Hotel (Solo Jim Bob)
April 29 Cannock the Uxbridge (Solo Jim Bob)
April 30 Manchester Lass O'Gowrie (Solo Jim Bob)
May 2 London Borderline (Solo Jim Bob)
July 18 Kev and Lousie's wedding in Cornwall sang two songs with
Dean Leggett from Jamie Wednesday and BOB
Sep 1 Camden Head (Solo Jim Bob with Chris T-T on piano)
Sep 3 Stourbridge Jim Bob (Solo Jim Bob)
Sep 4 Glasgow 13th Note (Solo Jim Bob)
Sep 5 Norwich Marquee (Solo Jim Bob)
Sep 6 Milton Keynes (Solo Jim Bob)
Sep 17 Charity gig at Brixton Windmill for Emmaus (Solo Jim Bob)
Nov 13 Kentish Town Forum The Drum Machine Years (Carter USM)
Nov 14 Brixton Academy The Drum Machine Years (Carter USM)
Dec 17 ?? Supporting the Wonder Stuff (Solo Jim Bob)
Dec 18, 19 Bloomsbury Theatre 9 Lessons and Carols for Godless
People (Solo Jim Bob)
Dec 20 Hammersmith Apollo Nerdstock (Solo Jim Bob with huge
orchestra. On the telly)

2010

March 29 Bloomsbury Theatre Robin Ince's Book club
May 4 Storage Stories Launch party
May 5 Literary Death Match (Book reading. Kaiser Chiefs incident)
May 11 Bury Fringe (Solo Jim Bob)

May 12 Manchester Night and Day (Solo Jim Bob)
May 13 Leeds the Well (Solo Jim Bob)
May 14 York Fibbers (Solo Jim Bob)
May 15 Dundee Doghouse (Solo Jim Bob)
May 16 Glasgow where? (Solo Jim Bob)
May 18 Easteney Cellars (Solo Jim Bob)
May 19 Upstairs at Highbury Garage (Solo Jim Bob)
May 20 Upstairs at Highbury Garage (Solo Jim Bob)
May 21 Bristol Tunnels (Solo Jim Bob)
May 22 Brighton West Hill Hall (Solo Jim Bob)
May 23 Poole (Solo Jim Bob)
May 26 Birmingham Hare and Hounds (Solo Jim Bob)
May 27 Portsmouth (Solo Jim Bob)
May 28 Guildford Boilerroom (Solo Jim Bob)
June 2 Walter Henry's Orchard hotel Bideford (Book reading and (Solo Jim Bob)
June 4 Crystal Palace Bookseller Crow event (Book reading and (Solo Jim Bob)
July 3 Brockwell Park Lido Café Mark Steel's 50th (Solo Jim Bob)
July 16-18 Latitude Angelstrike! with Orchestra and reading *Storage Stories* in literature tent
July 24 Port Eliot Fest (Solo Jim Bob)
July 26 Gutted preview Hammersmith Riverside
July 27 Gutted preview Hammersmith Riverside
August 4 -29 Gutted. Edinburgh Fringe Festival Assembly Ballroom. Not Tuesdays.
Sep 15 Kentish Town Bull and Gate (Solo Jim Bob)
Sep 25 Sundown festival at Village green fest (Solo Jim Bob)
Nov 24 Dingwalls (Solo Jim Bob) as part of 'Gutted Fest'
Dec 5 Storytellers (Book reading)
Dec 15 9 Lessons and Carols for Godless People (Solo Jim Bob)
Dec 17 Bookseller Crow Christmas party (With Phil Jupitus and Laura Dockrill) (Solo Jim Bob and reading)
Dec 19 and 21 9 Lessons (Solo Jim Bob)
Dec 19 Sky News early morning (Jim Bob reviews the newspapers)

2011

Jan 31 Leicester Square Theatre Gutted with an orchestra at
March 3 Leicester Square Theatre Gutted with an orchestra at
March 18 Literary Death Match for Red Nose Day (Judging)
March 22 Perfect Movie screening
May 16 Mister Blue Sky airs on BBC Radio 4. Theme music career begins and ends

June 4 Brixton Windmill Glastonwick (Solo Jim Bob)
June 7 Eastbourne The Lamb with Isy Suttie (Solo Jim Bob)
June 16 Brighton Koresh musical with the Indelicates. Jim Bob sings a song
Aug 14 Eden Fest (Carter USM)
Aug 20 Devon Beautiful Days (Carter USM)
Aug 27 Collaboration Festival (Solo Jim Bob)
Aug 31 Athens (Solo Jim Bob)
Sept 3,4 End of the Road Fest (Solo Jim Bob) Musical comedy career begins and ends
Oct 9 Words and Music Festival supporting Miles Hunt and Erica (Solo Jim Bob and book reading)
Oct 27 Wood Green, Big Green Bookshop empty (Book reading and solo Jim Bob)
Nov 18 Manchester Academy (Carter USM)
Nov 19 Brixton Academy (Carter USM)
Dec 21 and 22 Bloomsbury Theatre 9 Lessons (Solo Jim Bob)

2012

Jan 27 Birmingham Supporting Jesus Jones (Solo Jim Bob)
Jan 28 Islington Academy Supporting Jesus Jones (Solo Jim Bob)
March 11 Islington Pleasance Theatre 'Storytellers' (Book reading)
May 10 Jarvis Ham published. Launch party at Bookseller Crow
May 17 Nottingham the Greyhound (Solo Jim Bob)
May 18 Reading Velocity (Solo Jim Bob)
May 19 Carlisle (Solo Jim Bob)
May 22 Birmingham Hare and Hounds (Solo Jim Bob)
May 24 Exeter Cavern (Solo Jim Bob)
May 25 Wakefield the Hop (Solo Jim Bob)
May 26 Newcastle Legends (Solo Jim Bob)
May 27 Glasgow Old Hairdressers (Solo Jim Bob)
May 29 Southampton (Solo Jim Bob)
May 30 Bristol Thunderbolt (Solo Jim Bob)
June 1 Folkestone Googies (Solo Jim Bob)
June 2 Brighton West Hill Hall (Solo Jim Bob)
June 3 Portsmouth Edge of Wedge Café bar (Solo Jim Bob)
June 5 Leicester Fire Bug (Solo Jim Bob)
June 6 Newport Pagnell (Solo Jim Bob)
June 7 Cambridge (Solo Jim Bob)
June 8 Bedford Esquires (Solo Jim Bob)
June 9 London Borderline (Solo Jim Bob)
June 16 Three songs at C Palace Overground (Solo Jim Bob 4 songs)
June 23 Brixton Windmill Gracetonbury (Solo Jim Bob)

June 26 Do the Right Thing podcast (Guest)
Aug 17 Green Man Festival (Book reading)
Sept 15 Brockwell Park Country Fair (Book reading)
Nov 8 Glasgow King Tut's for charity (Carter USM)
Nov 9 Leeds Academy (Carter USM)
Nov 10 Brixton Academy (Carter USM)
Nov 20 Peckham Book fest (Book reading)
Dec 18 and 19 Bloomsbury Theatre 9 Lessons (Solo Jim Bob)
Dec 29 Cork with F and Walters (Solo Jim Bob)

2013

April 6 Islington Union Chapel (Solo Jim Bob)
April 21 Highgate Boogaloo with Mystery Fax Machine Orchestra (Solo Jim Bob)
May 11 Surrey Heath Literary Festival (Book reading)
June 15 LBC (Jim Bob reviews the news and politics of the day)
July 16 Ringwood book event in fish restaurant (Book reading)
Oct 12 Wood Green Lit Fest (Book reading and interview)
Nov 24 Folkestone book fest (Book reading and interview) Paid in English wine and chocolates.
Nov 30 Shepherd's Bush Hall Bush Hall (Solo Jim Bob with the Mystery Fax Machine Orchestra)

2014

Feb 4 A few songs at Pointless Anger (Jim Bob solo)
May 23 Bearded Theory (Carter USM)
June 7 Literary Death Match (Contestant)
June 26 Bookseller Crow with Will Wiles (Book reading)
July 18 Latitude Festival (Reading gig without amplification)
Aug 8 Wilderness Festival (Book reading)
Nov 7 Live at Maida Vale (Carter USM)
Nov 21 Shepherd's Bush Empire (Carter USM)
Nov 22 Brixton Academy (Carter USM final show)

2015

July 18 Curious Arts Festival (Book interview in comedy tent with Simon Evans)
July 30 Independent Age Big Tea (Book reading)
Aug 1 Port Eliot (Book interview)
Sep 7 Brixton Bookjam (Book reading)
Dec 20 Warwick Wild Boar (Book reading)

2016

Oct 1 Indie Daze Kentish Town Forum (Solo Jim Bob)
Nov 24 Leeds Brudenell Social Club Games Room (Solo Jim Bob)
Nov 25 Middlesbrough Westgarth Social Club (Solo Jim Bob)
Nov 26 Manchester Deaf Institute (Solo Jim Bob)
Nov 27 Devizes The Lamb (Solo Jim Bob)
Nov 29 Cambridge The Portland Arms (Solo Jim Bob)
Nov 30 Leicester Musician (Solo Jim Bob)
Dec 01 Darwen Library Theatre (Solo Jim Bob)
Dec 02 Glasgow Stereo (Solo Jim Bob)
Dec 03 Birmingham Mama Roux's (Solo Jim Bob)
Dec 04 Reading Purple Turtle (Solo Jim Bob)
Dec 06 Cardiff Globe (Solo Jim Bob)
Dec 07 Bristol The Thunderbolt (Solo Jim Bob)
Dec 08 Brighton The Haunt (Solo Jim Bob)
Dec 09 London The 100 Club (Solo Jim Bob)

2017

March 24 The North Sea Shiiine on Cruise from Hull to Rotterdam
(Solo Jim Bob)
May 12 Brighton BOAT Theatre (Solo Jim Bob)
May 27 Manchester Gigantic all-dayer (Solo Jim Bob)
May 28 Norwich Indie all-dayer (Solo Jim Bob)
July 14 Reading Readipop festival (Solo Jim Bob)
July 30 Leicester Simon Says festival (Solo Jim Bob)
Aug 12 Elton, Peterborough Green Meadows festival (Solo Jim Bob)
Sept 9 Croydon Literary festival, the David Lean cinema (Jim Bob
talks)
Nov 10 Minehead Butlin's Shine Weekender (Solo Jim Bob)
Dec 9 Dogfest (Solo Jim Bob) Fruitbat joins Jim onstage for 'Sheriff
Fatman'

2018

March 8 Brisbane Triffid supporting PWEI (Solo Jim Bob)
March 9 Melbourne Max Watts supporting PWEI (Solo Jim Bob)
March 10 Sydney Factory Theatre supporting PWEI (Solo Jim Bob)
March 11 Perth Rosemount Hotel supporting PWEI (Solo Jim Bob)
March 24 Shepherd's Bush Empire (Solo Jim Bob)
Sep 8 Birmingham Shine All dayer (Solo Jim Bob)
Nov 27 A boat moored next to the Thames Launch part for Carter box
set (Solo Jim Bob)

2019

March 23 Shepherd's Bush Empire (Solo Jim Bob)

JIM BOB FROM CARTER – PHYSICAL PRODUCTS

MUSIC

1999 Bonkers in the Nut – Jim's Super Stereoworld single (7-inch vinyl and CD) Fierce Panda
Tracks: Bonkers in the Nut. You're my Mate (and I like you). Rock 'n' Roll Relay Race (CD version only)

1999 Could U B the 1 I Waited 4 – Jim's Super Stereoworld single (7-inch vinyl and CD) Fierce Panda
Tracks: CD – Could you B the 1 I waited 4. World of Disco (DJ Feltpen & Bubblegum 'Disco-train' Mix). Put your lips together and blow.
7 inch vinyl – Could you B the 1 I waited 4. Put your lips together and Blow. Jim's Super Stereoworld signs to Fierce Panda

2001 Jim's Super Stereoworld the album CD Musicblitz
Tracks: Bonkers In The Nut. Greetings Earthlings (We Come In Peace). Pear Shaped World. Superslob. The Happiest Man Alive. Could U B The 1 I Waited 4. 1000 Feet Above The Earth. A Bad Day. The King Is Dead. My Name Is John (And I Want You Back). When You're Gone (parts 1 & 2). Touchy Feely

2001 J.R. – James Robert Morrison album CD The Ten Forty Sound
Tracks: Good Hair Day. I Lost My Baby To The Arms Race. A New Man In The Morning. Freestyle (Jump In The Water Jim). One Too many. Dead Dead Dead. Being From Mars. A Time To kill. Carry On Alone. Coming Back 4 More. Cinderella reversed. So Long Farewell (Auf Wiedersehen Goodbye). Everything Is Going To Be Alright

2002 In a Big Flash Car on a Saturday Night – Jim's Super Stereoworld mini album CD The Ten Forty Sound
Tracks: Heads Will Rock. Young Dumb (And Full Of Fun). Big Flash Car. Jim's Mobile Disco. Hey Kenny. Mission Control. Candy Floss. Tight Pants. Happier Times

2002 Bubblegum – Jim's Super Stereoworld single CD The Ten Forty Sound

Tracks: Bubblegum. Hair Metal. Young Dumb & Full of Fun (album version). 1st Time Caller (Long Time Listener)

2003 Goodnight Jim Bob – Jim Bob album CD The Ten Forty Sound
Tracks: Fathers against Handguns. Cruel. He. Krakatoa! In the Future All this will be Yours. When you were my woman. War is the new Rock 'n' Roll. Julie's Secret. I'm all Alone (and Everything Sucks). Cool. Come Outside. You Can't Take It With You

2004 Angelstrike! – Jim Bob album CD The Ten Forty Sound
Tracks: 4 Angels. Come on Smart Bomb! Victim. Closure. 55 Cards. The Revenge of the School Bullied. The Children's Terrorism Workshop. Georgie's Marvellous Medicine. Obsessive Compulsive. Tongue Tied. Ray of Light. The Hippies were Right. We have the Technology. My Face Your Arse. Soulmates. Feral Kids. Angelstrike!

2005 Dumb and Dumber – Jim Bob single CD The Ten Forty Sound
Tracks: Dumb and Dumber. Fresh Kills. Song for my Friends. Victim (original demo version with drums and stuff)

2005 Jim Bob Live From London DVD Cherry Red Records
Tracks: Everything Is Going To Be Alright. Come On Smart Bomb! Victim. Sealed With A Glasgow Kiss. Everytime A Churchbell Rings. Fresh Kills. Georgie's Marvellous Medicine. Glam Rock Cops. Obsessive Compulsive. Tongue Tied. Ray Of Light. A Prince In A Pauper's Grave. The Revenge Of The School Bullied. Girls Can Keep A Secret. The Only Living Boy In New Cross. Angelstrike! Bloodsport For All. Falling On A Bruise. The Final Comedown. Back To School. Pear Shaped World. The Music That Nobody Likes. Touchy Feely. GI Blues

2006 School – Jim Bob album CD Cherry Red Records
*Tracks: The First Big big Concert for the Orchestra. Back to School. Special Wants and Special Needs. Hanging Around. Mrs F*****g MacMurphy (Teaches Good Technology). Storm in the Staff Room. Taking care of the Caretaker. School Wars. ASBOmania! The Headmaster's Song. The Mufty Day Riots. The School is not the Building (It's the Children)*

2006 The Best of Jim Bob – Jim Bob album CD Cherry Red Records
Tracks: Dumb and Dumber. Candy Floss. Victim. A Bad Day. Young, Dumb and Full of Fun. The Mufty Day Riots. You Can't Take it With You. Coming Back 4 More. Mrs Fucking MacMurphy. Come on Smart Bomb! Cinderella Reversed. In the Future all this will be Yours. Back to School. My Name is John (And I Want You Back). Jim's Mobile Disco.

Angelstrike! Touchy Feely

Brucie Bonus Second CD
Tracks: Welcome To Jim's Super Stereoworld. The Queen Visits Stereoworld. Mission Control (Here Comes Trouble Remix). Miss Stereoworld. Stereothumpin'. Jim's Mobile Disco (Chemical Cosh Remix). Partyworld. Dear Jim. Happier Times (JR unreleased b-side). So Long Farewell (JR unreleased single mix). Song For My Friends (slow version)

2007 Battling the Bottle – Jim Bob single CD Download only
Tracks: Battling the Bottle (Fighting the Flab, at War with the World). The Wheels on the Bus. Another Day In The Office (acoustic version)

2007 A Humpty Dumpty Thing – Jim Bob album CD (with free long short story 'Word Count') Cherry Red Records
Tracks: All The King's Horses Cartoon Dad. Every Day When I Come Home I Expect To Find You Gone. God's Blog. Robin, Patrik And Chris. Another Day At The Office. The Carousel. This Phoney War. Pizza Boy. Battling The Bottle (Fighting The Flab, At War With The World). Why Can't We Get Along? From This Moment. The I Can't Face The World Today Blues

2009 Goffam – Jim Bob album CD The Ten Forty Sound
Tracks: The Golden Years of Lonely Old Dears. Goffam. Support the Gofffam Cops. Goffam's Secret Millionaire. The Man Behind the Counter of the Science Fiction Superstore. Teenage Body Count. Lonely Cop. One Small Step For Man. Architect Architect. Our Heroes. Superhero Midlife Crisis. Not Far From Here

2009 Our Heroes download only single The Ten Forty Sound
Tracks: Our Heroes. Radio Goffam

2012 Day Job EP – Jim Bob EP free download with 'Driving Jarvis Ham' novel
Tracks: The Tesco Riots. The Lonely Dictator. The Ghost of Christmas Boring. Bands

2013 What I think About When I Think About You – Jim Bob album CD The Ten Forty Sound
Tracks: Dream Come True. Hands Free. Monster in a Tracksuit. Seventeen. My New Walk. Breaking News. Your Ghost. Blood on Your Shoes. You Yourself and You. Coach A: Seat 21. What I Think About

2016 Jim Bob Sings Again album – Jim Bob Accompanied on piano by Chris
T-T album CD The Ten Forty Sound
Tracks: Cartoon Dad. A Bad Day. Johnny Cash. Our Heroes. A Prince in a Pauper's Grave. Victim   Glam Rock Cops. Come on Smart Bomb! The Carousel. Falling on a Bruise. You Can't Take it With You

BOOKS

2004 Goodnight Jim Bob – On the Road with Carter The Unstoppable Sex Machine
Jim Bob autobiography Published by Cherry Red Books

2007 Word Count
Jim Bob long short story as part of the sleeve for 'A Humpty Dumpty Thing'

2010 Storage Stories
Jim Bob novel Published by Ten Forty Books

2012 Driving Jarvis Ham
Jim Bob novel Published by The Friday Project/Harper Collins

2014 The Extra Ordinary Life of Frank Derrick, Age 81
J.B. Morrison novel Published by Pan Macmillan

2015 Frank Derrick's Holiday of a Lifetime
J.B. Morrison novel Published by Pan Macmillan

2019 Jim Bob from Carter – In the Shadow of my Former Self
Jim Bob memoir Published by Cherry Red Books

CARTER USM DRESSING ROOM RIDER NOVEMBER 2008

72 x Premium Bottled Lager (Becks/Budvar – NOT Stella / Red Stripe)
2 x Bottles of white wine (Chardonnay)
2 x Bottles of decent Red
2 x Bottles of good champagne
1 x Bottle of Smirnoff vodka
12 x Cans of Red Bull
1 x Bottle of Jack Daniels
1 x Bottle of good quality gin + 4 bottles of tonic.
24 Cans Coke
6 Cans Diet Coke
12 Cans various soft drinks
8 Cartons of various fruit juices
24 Bottles of still water
8 Bottles of fizzy water

Crisps and snacks, peanuts etc.
Fruit Bowl with apples, bananas, grapes, oranges etc.
A range of Sandwiches (vegetarian)
Cheese and crackers
Tea, coffee, milk, sugar and sweeteners
Peppermint Tea
Kettle, Mugs, cups, saucers, tea spoons, sharp knife
Wine Glasses, plastic cups, bottle openers, napkins
Ice
4 x Hand towels
8 x Large towels

N.B Please can there be a kettle in the Carter dressing room at all times. This should not be shared with the stage crew. Les likes his tea!

MISTER SPOONS'S - A HUMPTY DUMPTY THING STUDIO MENU

2012 PRE CARTER SET WINDUP TUNES

Jim's invaluable pocket diaries.

Some of the BBC passes Jim forgot to return to reception on the way out of the building.

Team Jim Bob on 'holiday' at Center Parcs 2014.

Incredibly hungover Jim Bob and annoyingly not so hungover Marc with the wonderful promoter and cocktail wizard Makis in Athens.

USM's Clinton and Carter at the Brixton Academy after party at Jamm 2011.

Jamie Wednesday reform on a Cub Scouts campsite in Cornwall. Jim and Dean Leggett play
'White Horses' at Kevin and Louise Downing's wedding July 2009.

Jim (I was never the smartest person in the room) Bob, with Dara Ó Briain and Dr Ben Goldacre in a Hammersmith pub. after 'Nerdstock 2009.

Jim Bob teaches Fruitbat, Doctor Ben Lambert and Chris T-T how to play air guitar during the sessions for 'School', while engineer Lewis Childs does the actual real world work.

Jim considers his new career as a Hollywood screenwriter in a garden in Los Feliz.

Jim pretends to sleep in the back of the car while Marc and Mr Spoons talk about Doctor Who in the front on the 'Goffam' tour 2009.

Creative Team

Written by **Mark Ravenhill**
Songs by **Jim Bob, Anthony Drewe, Antony Dunn, Justin Edwards, Howard Goodall, Charles Hart, Kit Hesketh-Harvey, Dillie Keane, Issy van Randwyck, Mark Ravenhill, George Stiles, Sarah Travis**
Directed by **Edward Hall**
Musical Direction and Musical Arrangements by **Sarah Travis**
Designed by **Michael Howells**
Lighting by **Ben Ormerod**
Sound by **Matt McKenzie**
Choreographer **Emma Tunmore**
Movement Director **Toby Sedgwick**
Fight Director **Alasdair Monteith**
Production Manager **Simon Bourne**
Associate Director **Tom Daley**
Costume Supervisor **Jane Dickerson**
Associate Fight Director **Neil Blake**
Produced by **Andrew Collier**

14

Cast in order of appearance

Fairy BowBells **Debbie Chazen**
King Rat **Nickolas Grace**
Port, the ship's First Mate **Toby Sedgwick**
Lemon, the ship's Second Mate **Miles Jupp**
Totally Lazy Jack **Danny Worters**
Alderman Fitzwarren **Sam Kelly**
Sarah the Cook **Roger Lloyd Pack**
Alice Fitzwarren **Caroline Sheen**
Dick Whittington **Summer Strallen**
Tommy the Cat **Derek Elroy** (Fight Captain)
The Sultan of Morocco **Mel Slaky**

Ensemble

Shaun Henson (Dance Captain)
Chloe Campbell
Robin Colyer
Christopher Hawes
Zoe-Leone Gappy
Natasha Lewis
Sean Parkins
Joanne Sandi

Band

Keyboards **Sarah Travis**
Percussion **Steve Vintner** (until 9 Dec), **Rob Millett** (from 11 Dec)
Bass and Guitar **Steve Rossell**
Flute, Clarinet and Saxophone **Emma Fowler**
Trumpet **Richard Hammond**

Children's Ensemble

Blue Team
Mert Avci (Peter)
Paris Fosuhene
Christie Halsey
Tate Miller
Anna Murray
Harry Price

Green Team
Megan Ford
Daniel Gross
Hollie McKinlay
Chaquille Osborne (Peter)
Ella Scotland
Biancha Szynal

All the children appearing in Dick Whittington are students at the Italia Conti Academy of Theatre Arts

Team Jim Bob take a break from the road in a Costa coffee (not as good as Caffé Nero) in 2016.

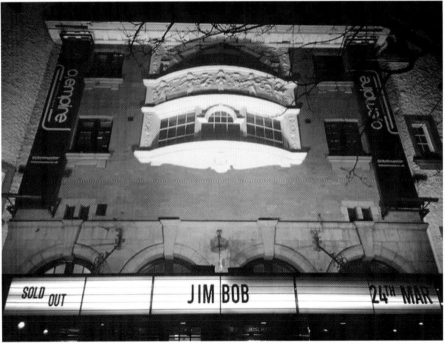

Other titles available from

Please visit **www.cherryredbooks.co.uk** for further info and mail order

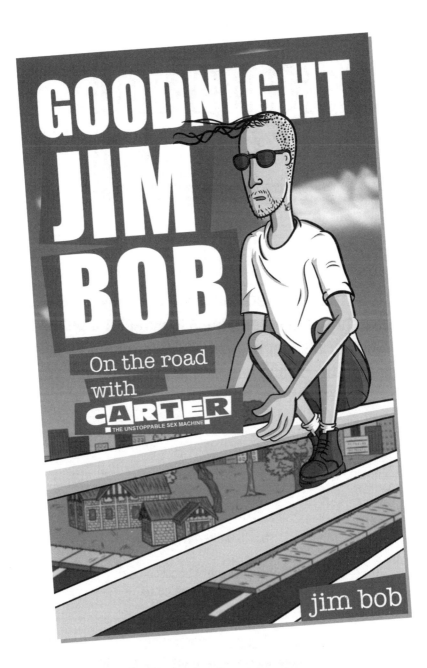

ALSO AVAILABLE!

Available in stores, online and at www.cherryred.co.uk

Here at Cherry Red Books we're always interested
to hear of interesting titles looking for a publisher.
Whether it's a new manuscript or an out of print or
deleted title, please feel free to get in touch if you have
something you think we should know about.

books@cherryred.co.uk

www.cherryredbooks.co.uk
www.cherryred.co.uk

CHERRY RED BOOKS
A division of Cherry Red Records Ltd,
Power Road Studios
114 Power Road
London
W4 5PY